Withdrawn

Vietnamerica

Vietnamerica

THE WAR COMES HOME

Thomas A. Bass

SOHO

Copyright © 1996 by Thomas A. Bass.
All rights reserved under International and
Pan-American Copyright Conventions. Published in the
United States of America by

Soho Press Inc.
853 Broadway
New York, NY 10003

Library of Congress Cataloging-in-Publication Data

Bass, Thomas A.
  Vietnamerica / Thomas A. Bass
      p.   cm.
  ISBN 1-56947-050-2 (alk. paper)
  1. Amerasians—Vietnam.   2. Children of military
personnel—Vietnam.   3. Abandoned children—Vietnam.
4. Amerasians—United States.   5. Vietnamese Americans. I. Title.
DS556.45.A43B38   1996
959.7'00413—dc20   95-49994
                                                                    CIP

For my parents

Contents

Vietnam Vietnam Vietnam,
we've all been there.

Michael Herr

Preface

I am picked up early in the morning by a government car, which can barely wedge itself down the alley in front of my hotel. "Are you sure these accommodations are comfortable?" asks Mr. Chinh, the Ministry of Foreign Affairs official who is my guide in Saigon. Comrade Chinh has the worried look of a man headed for stomach trouble. I assure him the hotel is fine, but it will take another couple of days before I can convince him to skip the car and let me get downtown on my own.

We drive through the Ministry gates at one minute to eight. Mr. Chinh hustles me inside for the day's first official meeting. I find the reception room, a large chamber on the ground floor, outfitted with the usual instruments of protocol: tea, coffee, plates of oranges and bananas. These are served by a woman dressed in a white *ao dai*. The room is furnished with plastic sofas and chairs dating from the Nixon era, an ormolu clock, and an overworked air conditioner that barely stirs the dust balls in the corner. I will spend many hours here talking to a succession of lean cadres dressed in slacks and short-sleeved shirts. Mr. Chinh becomes so practiced at translating my questions that I barely have to ask them. I suspect the answers are similarly potted.

My first meeting is with Luu Van Tanh, the Vietnamese official in charge of the Orderly Departure Program. He begins with a minilecture on Vietnamese history, attributing the country's refugee flows to the American trade embargo. Left unmentioned are the Vietnamese gulag and other disastrous social policies, such as nationalizing the rice market.

Having circled around the subject for a decently long time,

1

I ask about fake families and other instances of fraud in the emigration program dealing with Amerasians.

"Both sides have their own skills in discovering fake families," he says. "The U.S. interviewers separate families and quiz them individually about the details of their lives. 'How many dogs in your family? How many chickens?' If the answers differ, they conclude the family has purchased the Amerasian. But maybe the answers differ because people feel afraid or intimidated. Many authentic families have been refused.

"We also notice a large difference between interviewers," he says. "One person accepts sixty-five percent of the cases that come before him. Another accepts only thirty-five percent. One man accepts fewer than ten percent. Everybody knows that if you are interviewed by Mr. Ten Percent, you will likely fail. People go to fortune-tellers to see if there is some way to avoid Mr. Ten Percent. Other people, who believe in Buddha, think that being interviewed by Mr. Ten Percent is a matter of fate. I must say that the government of Vietnam is not as interested as the Americans in a strict reading of the law, if this reading lacks compassion."

I ask Mr. Tanh if he knows of any Amerasians not yet registered with the Orderly Departure Program. "There may be Amerasians living in very remote parts of the country who have not yet decided to leave," he says. "But people go prospecting in these remote areas looking for Amerasians to buy. Amerasians are fetching very high prices now, and I even know of cases where people have sold themselves several times over. There is really no part of the country where the news has not yet traveled."

I produce a list of unregistered Amerasians I found yesterday in the park in front of Mr. Tanh's office. Without looking at the fifty names, Tanh waves away my list. "Tell these people to apply directly to me, and I will investigate their cases," he says.

Were we to pull back the curtains in the conference room and glance across the street, we would see these Amerasians sitting under a tamarind tree. But between us and them is a narrow gate through which none of them can pass.

.   .   .

"Bring the war home!" was the battle cry of the sixties. And for more than a decade, all across America, the Vietnam War did come home, in the form of body counts and body bags and protest marches in the streets. Later it returned as a V-shaped black memorial in Washington and innumerable handicap ramps sprouting on our public buildings.

Then in 1987, with passage of the Amerasian Homecoming Act, the war came home again. The act called for the natural children of American soldiers and civilians who served in Vietnam, and their close relatives, to be airlifted to the United States. This was conceived as a humanitarian gesture, a parting shot. The last casualties of the war were finally being evacuated, even if their faces by then were molded with the indelible imprint of Asia.

The war nominally ended with the fall of Saigon in 1975. But then came economic sanctions and waves of refugees launching themselves out to sea. Thousands died in the exodus, until forty countries, under United Nations auspices, created the Orderly Departure Program in 1980, an effort to turn Vietnamese boat people into airplane refugees. Small numbers of Amerasians managed to leave Vietnam via ODP, but for most of them, their ticket out of the country would come only after passage of the Amerasian Homecoming Act seven years later, which created a special ODP for Amerasians alone.

The act was a unique social experiment. Twenty thousand, thirty thousand Amerasians—no one knew the number for sure—would be transplanted across the Pacific. Teenagers at the bottom of Vietnamese society, many of them homeless and illiterate, would be flown straight to the land of the big PX. Overnight Amerasians in Vietnam went from being *bui doi*, "the dust of life," to "gold children" endowed with the power to fly themselves and their family members around the world.

To work this miracle they needed blood. They had to prove that flowing in their veins was the cellular legacy of an American posted to Vietnam during the war. Never before had a vanquished army been allowed to reclaim its offspring. About twenty-five thousand Vietnamese-Amerasians headed to the United States via their special ODP program, along with sixty thousand accompanying relatives. Several thousand more Amerasians remained behind, some by choice, others against their will.

Nothing about the Amerasian exodus has been easy. Their homecoming has been shabbier than that of their soldier-fathers, which itself was notably threadbare. Most veterans' groups originally opposed bringing Amerasians to the United States, and with rare exception, these men were absent when their children landed in America's inner cities. A pariah class on one side of the Pacific became a political embarrassment on the other. Amerasians remind us of the bad blood between their parents. They reopen wounds that have yet to heal, for either side. But Amerasians are also a bridge between cultures, a mirror held to our unsuspecting faces, and the first thing one might remark is that America's newest refugees are also its children.

Amerasia

Where do I get my ideas? Utica.

Stephen King

Looking for the Mohawk Valley Resource Center for Refugees, I drive into downtown Utica, New York, in the summer of 1990. I park my car and am standing in front of the Florentine Pastry Shop, when I stop someone to ask for directions.

He is a tall young man with red hair. He wears blue jeans and walks with a streetwise prowl. His exposed teeth are all I get by way of an answer. I look into his broad beaming face and realize the young man doesn't speak a word of English.

I meet a whole crowd of Amerasians across the street. They are milling beside a storefront window that bears a hand-lettered sign announcing the location of the refugee center. The former Brescia's Furniture Store is an eighteen-thousand-square-foot windowless cave that functions as Utica's Ellis Island. Played out here is what it means to migrate from the old world to the new. In some ways the passage is quicker than it used to be. In others, slower. Instead of sailing into New York Harbor, refugees now touch down at night into Oneida County Airport. As soon as they step off the plane they become supplicants placed in the hands of social workers who dress and feed them.

The famous "six-second medical" at Ellis Island lasted only long enough for doctors to chalk on one's sleeve an *E* for suspected eye diseases, *H* for heart problems, *Pg* for pregnancy, *X* for mental retardation, or *X* with a circle around it for insanity—all disqualifying conditions. The process today is longer, but no less intimidating. Arriving refugees submit to blood tests, TB tine tests, fecal exams, X-rays. They get three months of "services"—welfare, food stamps, clothing, counseling, a furnished apartment, "survival" English classes—and then they get a job.

About forty refugees a month arrive in Utica. These include Amerasians, their mothers and other family members, former Vietnamese reeducation camp prisoners, Byelorussian Pentecostals, and the odd Libyan, Eritrean, or Croatian Muslim. Founded by a Jew and staffed predominantly by Catholics, the Utica refugee center is affiliated with Lutheran Immigration and Refugee Services. LIRS is one of the dozen voluntary agencies, or "volags," that resettle displaced persons in the United States under State Department contracts.

The Mohawk Valley Resource Center for Refugees had twenty-one employees and a half-million-dollar budget when I first began visiting it. A special residential program for Amerasians called Welcome Home House, originally scheduled to open in the fall of 1990, would have a separate budget of $800,000 and a staff of twenty-five. Welcome Home House was the brainchild of Rose Marie Battisti, director of the MVRCR. It would take Amerasian kids fresh off the plane from Vietnam and house them in a building of their own. It would immerse them in American culture and offer a real welcome home. When hundreds of Amerasians started flying into Utica to join the two hundred already resettled there, this malled-over relic of an old mill town in upstate New York would suddenly become the Amerasian capital of the United States.

Into the refugee center walks a wobbly figure in a light blue polyester suit, white shirt, and striped tie. The suit is two sizes too big for him. His rubbery face is covered with sweat. His hands shake as he stubs out a cigarette. "The malaria is back," says Charlie.

Out of his suit pocket he pulls a brown paper bag. He empties the bag onto the picnic table in front of the snack machines. A sea of Amerasian faces stares up at us. Carefully pencilled on the back of each passport photo is the subject's name, age, and last-known address. "These are some of the kids I took care of in Amerasian Park," he says. "I made them get their pictures taken in triplicate. Two for ODP. One for the brown bag. I have two thousand of these pictures."

Charlie was born in Da Nang in 1959. His father was an American adviser to the Diem regime. "I never knew him or my mother," he says. "She threw me away." He lived in an orphan asylum until he was six. Then there was a big typhoon in Da Nang, and the dikes along the river broke. The First Marine Division, Seventeenth Corps of Engineers came to build a new bridge. "I ran away and started living in their camp," he says. "They gave me a Snoopy dog and called me Charlie Brown. Everybody loves Charlie Brown. I needed a name in this world, so I became Charlie Brown."

He takes a piece of paper out of his pocket and begins drawing a map of Da Nang, starting with Monkey Mountain to the north and Marble Mountain to the south. "Here's Red Beach Two where the Marines landed in 1965 to start the ground war. And here's Alpha Battery, 5/4 Artillery, Fifth Division, Fourth Battalion, where I lived next." Soon Charlie's map is a maze of airfields and military encampments lining the South China Sea.

Charlie moved to Chu Lai, where a captain in MAG 11 gave him helicopter rides and sent him to school. Then in 1971 he went to Laos. "I followed the Twenty-First Marine Battalion and a company of Vietnamese rangers through the mountains and jungles. I was the camp mascot. They dressed me in a cut-off GI uniform. When the men got drunk, they tossed me through the air like a football."

After his travels through Laos, Charlie joined Alpha Battery, 5/4 Artillery, 1/5 (Mechanized) at Ai Tu Fire Base in Quang Tri. "They taught me to shoot 155mm tank cannons. There were six guns in Alpha Battery. I lived with Gun Five. On this gun were Gary Sharp from Kentucky, Danny Lawson from Tennessee, William 'Tiny' Compton from Indiana, William Allred from North Carolina, and Smitty, our black soldier. At Khe Sanh we fired all day and night for twenty days. I saw a lot of GIs wounded and killed. We fired many, many rounds before falling back."

In December 1971 Charlie's battery got the order to stand down. William Allred cried and said he wanted to take Charlie home with him. "All I could do was write down their names and say I would remember them. They gave me money, cameras, electric guitars, radios. I couldn't take it all. I had no family to give these things to."

Charlie returned to Da Nang. It was 1972.

"I'm different from Vietnamese people," he says. "I can't eat rice, only bread or noodles. Because I grew up on American food, when I was twelve I looked like I was eighteen." He worked as a money changer on the black market. He sold newspapers and ice cream. He slept in the streets and markets. "I kept moving, so the military police, who threw kids like me in the army, wouldn't catch me. I was broke again, but I didn't want to live with Vietnamese. I have no relations with Vietnamese."

A half-dozen Amerasians have crowded around the table, listening to Charlie's story. "After 1975, when the Communists came in, I was afraid because of my past," he continues. "I changed my name and fled. All my life in Vietnam after that was just moving around the country, with worries and fear."

Charlie hid in the jungle with army veterans who foraged for food. Then he traveled to Cambodia and Laos, looking for ways to escape from Vietnam. "Amerasians are second-generation GIs," he says. "The first generation fought the Communists with guns. We fought them in our heads. The number of Amerasians equals the number of GIs killed in the war. We are their souls come back to carry on the battle."

Charlie was selling cigarettes aboard the Saigon-to-Hanoi train when he had the bad luck in 1982 to be caught by the police. Accusing him of being an American spy, they threw him in Hoa Lo Prison—the old Hanoi Hilton. Then they took him to Saigon and put him in a military prison called the Jack Tree Hotel.

"I was alone in a room like a coffin. There was no light. I

had one bowl of rice a day and spoke to no one for six months. Later I was moved to a room with two generals and other top leaders from the South Vietnamese government. I had no bed or blanket. I stayed one year in that room."

Charlie was transferred to a prison camp in the jungle. For three months he planned his escape. He gathered food. He dried rice in the sun. He hid a knife and cigarettes in a tree trunk. Finally he made his move. The guards followed him for three days, until they caught him in an open field and blew off the top of his head with an M79 grenade launcher. Charlie pulls back his hair to show us the long red scar on his forehead.

"They locked me in leg irons and tied me to a tree. There was no medicine for my head wound. The other prisoners dropped leaves at my feet. When night came, I wet the leaves and put them on my head. I ate another jungle leaf like a taro that is Asian medicine against infection."

After two months tied to a tree, Charlie was moved to a jail near the Laos border. Again he escaped, this time heading for the Mekong River crossing into Thailand. "I got lost in the jungle. Ten days later the Laotian army caught me. They beat me unconscious. They tied my leg to a wire and pulled me behind a horse to the Vietnam border. From there they walked me twenty days through the jungle to another prison. My hands were tied behind my back. I had no coat against the monsoon rains. I was ready to die. I don't know why I didn't die."

Charlie spent the next year in a prison camp near Pleiku. Many of his fellow inmates, former collaborators with the French, had been incarcerated since 1945. This time when he escaped, Charlie zigzagged for eight days through the jungle, before reaching Pleiku. "An old woman working in the fields hid me and fed me. If she hadn't helped me, I would have died in that hell. The woman had an Amerasian daughter. I loved her when I saw her. I asked her to marry me. 'Wait until she finishes school,' said her mother."

Charlie tells us that the girl and her family will be arriving in Utica next month. "I sponsored them," he says. "I am getting them a house, beds, TV, everything. They saved my life."

It was too dangerous for him to stay in Pleiku. Charlie hid under a lumber truck and rode to Saigon, where he lived in the train station with several hundred other homeless people, until he was arrested again and sent to another jungle prison. A failed escape attempt ended in Charlie's being shot down with a CKC, a Russian weapon. He rolls up his trousers to show us the scars on his legs.

"They gave me a stick and walked me for two days to another prison camp. I was there five months before I escaped again. My guard had been drinking. He fell asleep against a tree. I hit him on the head with a stick. I tried to kill him, but it's not easy to kill someone. I took his shoes and ID card. I sold his watch and necklace and used the money to buy a bus ticket to Saigon. I didn't want to be a robber, but that's life. The fish eats the ant; sometimes the ant eats the fish."

Back in Saigon Charlie added Phuong to his name. He grew a Fu Manchu mustache and a wispy beard and shaved his hair to look like a Buddhist. He kept moving around the city, before finally settling in Cholon. A million Chinese used to live here before many of them fled Vietnam as boat people. "I survived like a rat in those narrow streets," says Charlie. "I got fat from eating Chinese food." He smiles, remembering his foraged meals.

Eight months later Charlie was arrested again. The police were rounding up the homeless in Saigon and sending them to New Life camps. Inmates in these camps gave the government eighty percent of the food they grew and kept the rest for themselves. After toiling for a year they got a piece of paper saying, "So-and-so has been a good worker. Help this person have a new life." This is why they were called New Life camps.

Following his year working as a buffalo boy in the rice fields, Charlie was called to headquarters and asked where he wanted to go. "Saigon," he said. "When I get there, I will apply to the

Orderly Departure Program and go to America." They demanded money to write him a letter of introduction.

Charlie pulls out of his suit pocket a yellowed piece of paper, which he carefully unfolds to show us his New Life ID. It lists his birth date as 1964. "They didn't believe an Amerasian could be born before then," he says. The document describes how Charlie Brown Phuong, *con lai lang thang*, wandering homeless Amerasian, has proved himself ready for a new life. It also mentions that the government expects this person will leave Vietnam and go to the United States.

Back in Saigon, Charlie let his hair grow and got a new girlfriend. "I look like an old man, but I act young," he says. "I like to joke and have fun." He started sleeping in the park in front of the former Presidential Palace. It is called Thong Nhat—Reunification—Park, but after Charlie and other Amerasians began living there, everybody started calling it Amerasian Park. Two hundred people slept there at night, lined up side by side on mats.

"You have to realize this park is very important," says Charlie. "It faces the Ministry of Foreign Affairs and many big government buildings." The police wanted to throw the Amerasians out of the park, but Charlie paid money to have stories about them run in the Saigon newspapers. He buttonholed foreign journalists and tourists. He began filling out ODP emigration forms for everybody living in the park and started getting them interviews.

American war veterans were just starting to return to Vietnam in 1988. Their eyes flew open when they saw hundreds of Amerasians living on the streets of Saigon. "Some of them started crying," says Charlie. "They gave us fifty or a hundred dollars, which in Vietnam is a lot of money. I counted the money in the park, so everyone would see how much there was."

He removes from his pocket a notebook with a drawing of Charlie Brown and his dog, Snoopy, on the cover. The notebook is filled with the names and addresses of vets he met in Vietnam.

"They promised me apartments, jobs, everything when I got to America."

In March 1989, six months after applying to the Orderly Departure Program, Charlie was interviewed by Jonathan Cohen, a former officer in the First Marine Division. "I remember you," Cohen said. "You used to hang around our camp. Back then you were a little kid wearing an Army T-shirt down to your ankles. Now you look old."

Charlie was flown to a Philippines refugee camp in August 1989 and arrived in the United States the following March.

At noon the refugee center fills with the smell of steamed vegetables and fish sauce. Lunch is being served by the mothers who have accompanied their Amerasian children to Utica. These are work-hardened women, although, judging from the photos they carry, they were once slender girls in *ao dai*s, the traditional Vietnamese dress of flowing trousers covered by a tight-fitting tunic slit to the waist. The women all tell similar tales of betrayal. The war drove them out of the countryside to seek jobs at American military bases as cashiers, waitresses, maids. There they met the soldiers who fathered their children and then abandoned them, sometimes willingly, sometimes regretfully, as evidenced by money sent from America or letters signed "Love." What little the women remember from those days is scribbled on the backs of photographs showing Vietnamese girls wrapped in the big-shouldered embrace of GI John.

When the South Vietnamese government collapsed in 1975, these women feared their Amerasian children would be killed or taken away from them. Many families living in Saigon were expelled to labor camps in the countryside. Their property was seized by north Vietnamese carpetbaggers moving south. The next important date in these women's lives was their application to the Orderly Departure Program, which began airlifting refugees out of Vietnam in 1980. The women mailed their life stories and other scraps of evidence to ODP officials in Bangkok. They paid the required bribes to Vietnamese officials, passed interviews and health tests, and then waited years to leave the country. In the meantime, they were fired from their jobs. Their children were thrown out of school.

When their airplane finally took off for America, it followed a circuitous route that began with ten days' incarceration in a Bangkok prison. This stop was later replaced by six months' internment in a Philippine refugee camp. Then comes another date everyone remembers. They can tell you down to the minute when they first set foot on American soil. I initially thought they were describing a second birthday—the hopeful start to a new life. Then I learned Vietnamese do not celebrate birthdays. They celebrate death days. Souls in the afterlife apparently need all the help they can get.

The former leader of the Amerasians is now working for a small company in Utica that makes paper towel holders. His boss has bought him a bicycle to ride to work. Not trusting the neighborhood, Charlie locks his bicycle inside the refugee center before we head to lunch at a nearby Chinese restaurant.

Charlie is telling me about the kids who lived with him in Amerasian Park in Saigon and how he tried to keep them from joining a gang led by a rival Amerasian named Chau Van Raymond.

Charlie divided his encampment into work details. One group cleaned the park. Other groups took care of bedding and shopping for food. Twice a day they ate together, cooking over charcoal stoves. They got water from a government building and paid money to use the toilets in a nearby movie theater. Charlie forbade panhandling or stealing in the park, and he posted guards to beat up the Vietnamese who came to buy Amerasians, hoping to use them as tickets to America.

A black man at the neighboring table interrupts and asks if Charlie is from Vietnam.

"Yeah," he says. "I was there."

The man tells us he was drafted the day after he graduated from high school. He spent his eighteenth birthday leading a night patrol of green recruits into the jungle. "It never leaves me. I think about it every day," he says. Then he starts crying, tears streaming down his cheeks.

"It's tough, it's really tough," says Charlie, turning back to his lunch.

Saigon

To leave or stay—they all were wavering still.

Nguyen Du

Amerasian Park occupies a choice site in the center of Saigon. On the grassy knoll to the west stands the old presidential palace, which is now a pilgrimage site marking the end of the Ho Chi Minh Trail. To the north lie the Ministry of Foreign Affairs and ODP interview site. To the south rise two of the city's major landmarks: Notre Dame Cathedral and Gustave Eiffel's *belle époque* post office. Anchoring the lower end of the park is the French consulate, while just down the street sits the old American embassy, a bullet-pocked building turning green with mold.

Charlie Brown's strategy of camping on the most prestigious piece of turf in central Saigon worked brilliantly. It made him and his fellow Amerasians the country's most visible misfits. They parlayed their symbolic value into donated food and money and eventually into a piece of legislation—the Amerasian Homecoming Act—which gave every Amerasian in Vietnam, and every relative tacked onto their increasingly fanciful families, an airplane to the United States, along with job training, medical benefits, and welfare.

It was always a mystery to me why the Vietnamese government—which runs a police state capable of jailing its citizens without trial or trace—allowed a small army of Amerasians to squat in central Saigon. Then I realized the Amerasians garnered a lot of attention from foreign journalists, and these journalists tended to file similar stories. "We've just discovered live POWs trapped in Vietnam! Caught behind enemy lines is a battalion of twenty thousand Amerasians, hoping someday to get repatriated to their fatherland." And who was responsible for abandoning these children? The United States government, said the Vietnamese. "We want to let them go, but their way is barred."

And since all the obvious barriers were, indeed, on the American side, the Vietnamese thereby scored yet another media victory over their old aggressor.

On my second visit to Vietnam, in the spring of 1992, I find Amerasian Park, like everything else in Saigon, changed from the previous year. New stones are being laid in the walkways, the flower beds retrenched and planted. The tree trunks are getting a new coat of white paint, and the grass is being clipped by gardeners working with what look like scissors. Squatting on the park's shaded lawns are hundreds of men gathered into circles. "We sit here listening for news," says a former reeducation camp prisoner, who is waiting to be interviewed by the Orderly Departure Program. "Sometimes they ask strange questions so we have to be prepared."

Beyond the gallery of faces turned in my direction, I find what I am looking for—a cluster of Amerasians sitting under a tree. I walk over and say hello. They yell out questions. "Can you help me find my father?" "Will you take me to America?" Out the corner of my eye I see another dozen Amerasians scurrying across the street. From the sidewalk in front of the ODP interview site, out from alleyways and courtyards all around the park trots an army of homeless Amerasians. It is five years since passage of the Amerasian Homecoming Act, and still Saigon is crawling with half-American kids yelling, "Will you take me to America?" The numbers are down from a year ago and way down from the time when Charlie ran a soup kitchen in the park for two hundred Amerasians, but still there must be thirty people crowded around me clamoring for help.

On a neighboring bench sits a neatly dressed woman who offers me her services as a translator, a job she says she once performed for USAID. It is risky picking up a translator in the park. They present themselves too readily. They are too fluent, too solicitous. But there are good reasons for hiring a spy. The safest way to move around a police state is to let everyone know where you are going. This transparency will later work to my benefit, when the police become interested in my case.

A band of tattered, gap-toothed kids covered with burn marks and tattoos squats in front of me and Miss Hoa, my translator. They push letters, photos, and birth certificates into our hands. They barrage us with stories of abuse: official, personal, Vietnamese, American, accidental, ordained. It all adds up to the same thing: years of waiting as the clock frowns on their hopes of ever getting to America. They smell of sweat and dust. They have the hungry *voyou* look of veteran survivors. "I have no shoes. I have no money," they yell, and it is true. They have no shoes, no money.

Miss Hoa and I set about compiling a list of Amerasians. I announce that this list has nothing to do with botched interviews and other injustices of the refugee process. It is reserved for Amerasians not yet registered with the Orderly Departure Program. I start with the sorriest cases—women with children, barefoot boys, bewildered farmers from the provinces. Fending off the few well-dressed kids who have pushed their way to the front, I call on people at the edge of the crowd. Among the first to get recorded is an Afro-Amerasian with spatulate toes. Everyone laughs when he says his name is Ya Cob.

Jacob, son of Isaac, is a farm boy who is now sleeping on the streets of Saigon. He has never been to school. His daily wage for planting rice and herding geese is two bowls of food a day. Ya Cob has the startled look of a buffalo caught in city traffic. If he gets there, how will he survive in the United States? It is a mystery, but he is entitled to try.

We write down names, birthplaces, dates of birth, accompanying family members, knowledge of father, if any, and all the other minutiae required for establishing Amerasian identity, which is usually as plain as the nose on someone's face. For whatever reason, the genes tend to play themselves out three-quarters American, one-quarter Vietnamese. We register a tough guy in a shiny gold shirt, a farm boy with chipped fingernails, and an orphan who says her mother sold her to a family for 150,000 *dong*, about thirteen dollars, until she ran away to live on the streets.

Word is out by now all over the city that "Mr. Thomas" is registering Amerasians. Scribes at the post office begin drafting letters to Mr. Thomas. Documents addressed to Mr. Thomas are readied for shipment to Bangkok. Letters for Mr. Thomas are left at the desk of the Majestic Hotel, where the ODP interviewers stay when they are in Saigon. Documents for Mr. Thomas are shoved into *my* hands by people who think I might know the man or how to reach him. Mr. Thomas has become the Kurtz of Saigon, a new cargo cult, a rumor on the streets, a prayer for justice, an angle to play.

A seamless blue sky stretches over us like a wet blanket. With forty-five names on our list, we call it quits.

I walk out of the park and head toward the river. New paint and buildings are going up everywhere. Street vendors hawk no fewer than three English-language newspapers. Direct-dial telephones have sprouted on the street corners. Bicycles and motorcycles course down the boulevards. One of the few reminders that this was once Cochin China is the schoolgirls fluttering by in their white *ao dai*s.

The administrative entity called Ho Chi Minh City covers 2,390 square kilometers, a vast area stretching from the South China Sea almost to the Cambodian border. The city was called into being in 1975 to neutralize the population of Saigon—officially three million, actually closer to five—in a vast sea of peasants. Ho Chi Minh City (or Hoville, as the expatriates call it) is the name of the metropolis. The city's three central districts, however, are still called *Saigon*. This fact has allowed even the sternest cadre from the north to resume calling Saigon *Saigon*, which is what everyone else calls it anyway.

The city's streets and canals are lined with a hodgepodge of shops, cyclos, sampans, and ambulatory hawkers selling everything from lottery numbers and Honda generators to sugarcane juice and push brooms. Great rivers of commerce flow from the international traders into streams of market carts that wash into even the narrowest alleys of the city. Clearly the Vietnamese have nothing to learn from the West about marketing.

At the center of town stand the old colonial hotels—the Rex, the Continental, and the Caravelle. They face the opera house and Hôtel de Ville. Immediately after the Second World War, the Vietminh briefly ran a unified Vietnam from this white gingerbread building, until fourteen hundred French paratroopers, liberated from Japanese internment camps and rearmed by the British, were sent on a rampage through the city. The Vietminh fell back to the countryside, where they mounted a guerrilla war against the French and later against the Americans, before finally getting back to their desks at City Hall thirty years later.

I stroll down Dong Khoi Street, the old rue Catinat. This once fashionable promenade stretches from the red-brick Notre Dame Cathedral to the Saigon River. Only later when the Americans arrived did it fill up with strip joints. Past the curio dealers selling fake dog tags and other GI memorabilia lies Saigon's other landmark hotel, the Majestic. I turn left and walk along the river before mounting a flight of stairs into a small hotel facing the water. This is where I stayed when last in town. I am looking for Hanh, the young woman in the pink *ao dai* who worked the front desk.

"She has gone to America," the owner tells me. "Her father was ARVN."

If you can prove enough years of service in the Army of the Republic of Vietnam before 1975, and enough years of suffering afterwards, you and your family can get a ticket to Westminster,

California, or another of America's Little Saigons. Hanh is gone, but the hotel now has a white-uniformed doorman. Business must be good.

Business also looks good across the street at the Floating Hotel. This gleaming white barge was moored on Australia's Barrier Reef, until the hotel went bankrupt and got towed up the Saigon River in 1989. The Floater has nautical doormen guarding the gangplank and signs in the elevators warning that Vietnamese nationals are not allowed in the rooms. This is the place to stay in Vietnam if you don't want to be in Vietnam. In the traffic circle in front of the hotel stands a statue of Tran Hung Dao. Like most of the statues and street names and public spaces in Vietnam, this one commemorates a famous battle. Thanks to Dao, Vietnam is as far as Kublai Khan got before he was sent packing back to Mongolia.

I watch the ferryboats swing into the Saigon River and struggle across to the far shore. In that direction lie the mangrove swamps and aqueous no-man's-land of the Mekong Delta, which none of Vietnam's many invaders has ever pacified. Walking past the My Canh floating restaurant, rebuilt after it was blown up by Vietcong sappers in 1968, I arrive back at the street corner in front of the Majestic, where the cyclo men sit in their rickshaws waiting for business. I buttonhole the cyclo captain, a gray-haired gentleman who is more comfortable speaking French than English, and ask him where I can find Tran Van Hong, commonly known as Viet. Viet's Suzuki 100 is to Saigon what a gondola is to Venice. Piloted by a former opera singer turned cyclo man, this vehicle is the best way to get around town.

"*Il a des problèmes domestiques*," says the captain. "Maybe he can meet you here tomorrow." I know he will be there.

That night I meet Kyle Hörst for dinner at the Continental Hotel. Kyle is tall and gaunt from a bout with some unknown tropical disease. He wears wire-rimmed glasses, a full beard, and long brown hair. He is intensely focused, what the French call *maniaque*. "My bosses tell me my reports are too long," he says. "They have too much detail. But the truth is in the details."

An American married to a Vietnamese and fluent in the language, Kyle works for the United Nations as a repatriation officer. The British are emptying their Hong Kong refugee camps, by economic inducement, or, if need be, by force. The Vietnamese have signed off on the deal, in exchange for a lot of UN and European Union money, paid to both the returnees and their home communities. Key to the voluntary repatriation program's working are a handful of UN officials, like Kyle, who roam the Vietnamese countryside, visiting returnees and verifying that they are staying out of jail and getting the money they were promised.

We dine at Guido's, a restaurant occupying the hotel's old open-air terrace. The Continental was Graham Greene's address in Saigon. For all we know, we could be sitting exactly where Alden Pyle outlined his theory of the Third Force—the white knight who would rise up between Vietnam's warring factions and unite the country. But that game was up long ago. Now there is only one force in Vietnam, and a lot of would-be refugees.

Curious about his personal experience with Amerasians, including those in his own family, I tell Kyle about a dinner I had the previous year in Saigon with Robert McMahan, longtime State Department interviewer for the Orderly Departure Program and father of his own family of Amerasians. McMahan is an Air Force vet who married a Vietnamese woman and took a job during the war with RMK-BRJ, the consortium of companies that built South Vietnam's ship yards, airfields, and prisons.

A bear of a man, who rents a windowless room at the Majestic—"I like to take off my clothes and jump around a lot," he says—McMahan jogs twenty miles a week and ends his workdays eating double orders of vegetarian dinners. I joined him for one of these meals at the Rex Hotel.

McMahan and I began by talking about the number of Amerasians trapped in Saigon. "Denial of normal administrative procedures is a form of persecution in this culture," he says. "If you don't have a birth certificate or a ration card, they can pretend you don't exist. The Vietnamese are pissed at the Americans for screwing their women, and they take it out on the Amerasians."

Shocked by the number of kids living on the street, McMahan in 1989 convinced the Vietnamese to create something called the 37 AC list, a special fast track for registering Amerasian orphans without documents.

"The orphan list was created to mollify me," he says. "But I have to admit it's been abused. Amerasians run away from their families, thinking they can go faster. Then when you look at their cases, you discover they have families, and you have to do the paperwork all over again. The list proved enormously more complicated than anyone imagined."

After describing the bureaucratic thuggery of Vietnamese officials, McMahan surprises me by characterizing his fellow ODP interviewers as equally heartless, particularly those from the U.S. Immigration and Naturalization Service. This is the agency charged with deciding who qualifies to enter the United States as a refugee. "The INS interviewers don't give a damn about the welfare of the people they're interviewing," he says. "These guys are hard-nosed, legalistic types who hew close to the letter of the law."

McMahan admits that he himself was not always the most sympathetic interviewer. "I used to avoid contact with Amerasians," he says. "I thought their mothers were a bunch of whores. Now I see us fulfilling our obligation. I'd like to see the Amerasian Homecoming Act expanded, so we have consular officers doing this work, instead of INS guys." McMahan at the time was head of mission and senior American official in Vietnam, but the four other interviewers on his team were INS.

That day McMahan had rendered life and death decisions on two hundred cases, twenty per hour, three minutes per person. "I feel as if everyone interviewed got a fair hearing," he says, without a touch of irony. His acceptance rate was seventy percent.

"I've seen thousands, and I have two Amerasians of my own," he remarks over a dessert of flambéed bananas. "Amerasians are willful and stubborn. They have serious identity problems. They are unfocused. They have no discipline. They won't study. They're part of an unruly subset of society. Down the street at the Floating Hotel you'll find Amerasian prostitutes plying their mothers' trade. I think there's a racial thing here, something genetic."

Other fathers of Amerasians make similar statements, including Bill McCabe, who runs the Pearl Buck Foundation office in the Philippines. McCabe describes his own Amerasian children as "manipulative, complex, divided personalities. They can look me right in the eye and lie."

"You know what this sounds like to me?" says Kyle, ordering another round of beers. "This is a good description of the *Vietnamese* personality type. Amerasians spring from a race of survivors. They have the Vietnamese survival instinct cubed. They're thinking twenty moves ahead on the chess board, rather than two. Just because Amerasians have blond hair or afros, we expect them to act like Americans. But it's a myth that these are 'our' kids. They are Vietnamese. We're not bringing them home. We're taking them to a foreign country. Even Americans from Iowa who fought in Vietnam didn't come home 'our' kids. They were altered by Asia."

The restaurant is empty save for a party of Japanese businessmen. Guido comes out of the kitchen to chat with Kyle, a good customer. "How was the pizza?" he asks.

"It was fine," says Kyle. "But where was the oregano?"

Guido shrugs his shoulders and rolls his eyes upward toward the gods of state planning. "Nowhere in Vietnam can I find fresh oregano," he says.

After dinner, we retrieve Kyle's motorcycle from the hotel bike boy and begin rolling down the nighttime streets of Saigon.

We merge into a crush of kids on Dong Khoi Street. They are spinning their motorbikes around and around the block in a Vietnamese version of cruising Sunset Strip. We cycle through smaller streets and alleyways that even at midnight are still buzzing with commerce.

I stare into people's houses, which are lit with the yellow glow of oil lamps. At the end of the dry season, the hydro dams are so low that Saigon has run out of electricity. I see a woman nursing a baby. I watch men seated around a table dealing cards. I hear snatches of music and relish the breeze blowing over us. We are driving into the Binh Thanh district, which lies over a brackish stream that feeds into the Saigon River. As we cross the bridge at Da Kao—the bridge under which Alden Pyle's body washed up, dead, in *The Quiet American*—the ripe odor of sewage rises from the water below.

After months of living in a hotel, Kyle and his family have finally been allowed to rent a house in Binh Thanh. He has found a room for me nearby. We roll into an alleyway, where people stare after us slack-jawed with amazement. They have not seen Americans here since the seventies. We bang on the hotel's iron grate. A body rises from among the slumbering figures in the lobby and leads us upstairs to a large room complete with refrigerator and Russian air conditioner. These are powered by a generator thundering outside the window.

Kyle sits at the kitchen table as I unpack my bags, including a sack of money acquired downtown on the black market. One hundred dollars slipped across the counter of a jewelry store had come back as 1,130,000 *dong*, pressed into brick-sized bundles wrapped with rubber bands. This is socialist-realist money. On the face is a portrait of Ho Chi Minh. On the verso are steam shovels, steel mills, and freighters. The only natural scene depicts elephants hauling logs out of a clear-cut forest. "That's a new note," says Kyle. "It shows Vietnam gutting Cambodia's forests." I stash the money in the refrigerator.

Then I remember his presents. Knowing that Catholic mys-

ticism and rock and roll are the twin beacons by which Kyle
steers his life, I have brought him the collected works of Simone
Weil, the Gallimard edition, and a film canister of dirt from Jim
Morrison's tomb in Père-Lachaise cemetery.

"What was the scene like at Jim's grave?" he asks.

"It's a place where miracles are performed," I say. "You
should visit sometime."

Kyle flips through the uncut pages of Weil's books. He
opens the film canister and sniffs inside. Then he stacks Morrison's remains on top of the books. "You better get some sleep,"
he says. "You don't have a minute to waste."

That night, between listening to the prop wash out of my
Russian air conditioner and the clatter of high heels moving up
and down the stairs outside my door, I have a strange dream. Jim
Morrison and Simone Weil have changed places. *He* is the mystic
who starved himself to death protesting Nazi labor camps, and
she is the poet of rock and roll. They are buried beside each other
in Père-Lachaise, and staring down at the pilgrims surrounding
their graves is the grinning face of Uncle Ho.

Half Breeds

Whose fault is it that our child must lead a wanderer's life?

Nguyen Du

Women and children are the spoils of victory. Throughout history they have always been carried off by the winners. So how did eighty-five thousand Amerasians and their accompanying relatives get airlifted from Vietnam to the United States? Who thought up this idea, and why did it take twenty years to do it?

U.S. military involvement in Vietnam dates back to the Second World War, when Ho Chi Minh, our ally against the Japanese, was supplied by the Office of Strategic Services—precursor to the CIA—with small arms, Chesterfield cigarettes, and a copy of the Declaration of Independence, which Ho incorporated into Vietnam's own such declaration at the end of the war. Ally turned foe when the United States supported France's move to reimpose colonial rule. American advisers aided French troops in fighting the First Indochina War. America also paid for the war, to the tune of about two billion dollars a year. This venture collapsed in 1954 with the fall of the French garrison at Dien Bien Phu. After a 209-day siege, the Vietnamese captured ten thousand French prisoners, including a party of Algerian prostitutes flown in to boost morale.

The first American soldiers arrived in Vietnam in 1950, as part of the U.S. Military Assistance Advisory Group charged with training the South Vietnamese Army. By 1956, MAAG numbered several hundred men. The Marines hit the beach at Da Nang in 1965, and by the time the Second Indochina War ended a decade later, 3.4 million men and women were veterans of America's Asian error. This is nearly twice the number involved in World War I.

33

.   .   .

After a rash of embarrassing press reports about the number of Amerasians in Vietnam—over one hundred thousand, reported James Reston—the Department of Defense in 1970 issued the following statement: "The care and welfare of these unfortunate children . . . has never been and is not now considered an area of Government responsibility nor an appropriate mission for the Department of Defense to assume."

Other governmental organizations, such as the U.S. Agency for International Development, were not so cavalier. But no program for aiding Amerasians was implemented during the war, and every effort to do so was vetoed by the South Vietnamese government. They refused to distinguish between Amerasian and Vietnamese orphans. At the same time, they prevented Amerasians from leaving the country, holding them hostage for the billion-dollar handouts that kept the South going. They knew when the Amerasians went the game would be up.

The best the United States could muster was a general bailout of Vietnamese orphans called Operation Babylift. In the final, desperate days of the war, two thousand unaccompanied minors were flown out of Vietnam on C-140 cargo planes. The operation ended when a plane exploded on takeoff and scattered three hundred babies across the rice fields. A congressional investigation into the babylift later discovered that many of these children had not been orphans.

When one puts together all the government documents and congressional testimony about Amerasians, the issue shows a curious evolution. Immediately after the war, it was not an issue at all. Half-American children, or HACs, as the consular cable traffic referred to them, were presumed to be Vietnamese. The only exception to this rule were a few hundred American citizens—half-Asian children with American birth certificates or passports—who happened to be in Vietnam when the government collapsed. These children were called PAMs, presumed Americans, or AMCITs, American citizens. But no one argued that getting *these* children out of Vietnam was an Amerasian issue. It was a citizenship issue. They were like any other Americans caught behind enemy lines.

The parents of these children presumed the U.S. government would do everything in its power to get American citizens out of Vietnam. But the U.S. government maintained it had no power. It had no diplomatic relations with Vietnam, nor were any planned. It did not offer third-party help, back channel contacts, or solace. In fact, the government seemed *pleased* that American citizens were being held in Vietnam, since it offered yet more proof of Communist villainy.

While America obsessed about recovering the bones of its dead soldiers, the *living* American prisoners in Asia languished in bureaucratic limbo. The intransigence and callousness of the United States government toward its citizens in Vietnam would eventually backfire. The people originally concerned with a few hundred PAMs and AMCITs expanded into a lobby dedicated to getting *all* Amerasians out of Vietnam. No longer would an American passport be required for a ticket home. Now all you needed was an American face.

Virtually everything done to help Amerasians leave Vietnam has been accomplished in spite of State Department efforts to block these moves. This is surprising, considering the official platitudes delivered on the subject. The State Department did nothing to assist and often tried to hinder early contacts between Americans and the Vietnamese government. It placed legal barriers and quotas on the departure of Amerasians from Vietnam. It testified in Congress against two bills designed to help Amerasians, and, as I discovered on watching State Department interview teams at work in Saigon, U.S. officials habitually treat Amerasians with contempt and disdain.

Among the several hundred Americans held in Vietnam

after the war was the child of Michael and Ty Schado. They spent
fourteen years trying to get their son, Lance, back home. Mike
Schado was a twenty-one-year-old soldier in the Mekong Delta
when he met Thach Thi Ty, a shy young woman with a round face.
Her father worked as an interpreter in Schado's helicopter unit,
and one night he invited the young soldier home for a family dinner. Schado fell in love with Ty. He was transferred back to the
United States, waited four months, and then reenlisted for another tour of duty. He wanted to go back to Vietnam and propose
to Ty. "Everyone thought I was crazy," he says, "but I missed
her."

They were married in a Buddhist ceremony in 1970. Two
more years of red tape were required to secure a marriage certificate from the U.S. Embassy. In the meantime, Ty gave birth to a
son and Schado was shipped back to the United States. He was able
to get out his wife, but not his one-year-old child. The baby lacked
an exit visa from the Vietnamese government. This document was
another form of discouragement against local marriages.

Schado intended to leave the boy with Ty's parents only long
enough to get his papers in order. He went to work at the Pentagon as a clerk. He had no money for a trip to Vietnam, and his
parents, who had adamantly opposed his marrying a Vietnamese,
refused to help. To get his son an exit visa, Schado wrote letters
to the South Vietnamese government and to American officials in
Vietnam. He petitioned the State Department, the Department of
Defense, and the Immigration and Naturalization Service. Nothing happened.

Then in April 1975, when the South Vietnamese government fell, the Schados lost track of their son. At about the same
time, Ty had a hysterectomy and Schado was diagnosed as suffering from Delayed Stress Syndrome. "Our withdrawal from Vietnam devastated me," he says. "It would be a beautiful day and
Ty would say, 'Let's go for a ride,' but I couldn't do it. Nothing
was a good time anymore."

In 1980 a letter reached the United States from Ty's father.

It said the family was living in a Buddhist monastery. Schado launched another raft of petitions to get the boy out of Vietnam. "Jesus, now we have it made!" he thought, after passage of the Amerasian Immigration Act of 1982. But the State Department told him the legislation could not be applied to Vietnam, as the United States had no consular officials there.

Jan Olsen, a Minneapolis television reporter, picked up Lance Schado's story and went looking for the boy when she visited Vietnam in 1984. Her film footage gave the Schados the first glimpse of their son in thirteen years. Lance and his grandmother are wading in the muddy waters of the Mekong River. They are harvesting lotus stems, tossing the green shoots into a sampan, which is held steady against the current by the boy's grandfather. Later, the old man sculls the boat to a riverside hut made of palm fronds. The dwelling is nearly indistinguishable from the jungle around it.

Another year of paper shuffling and interviews—formalities required by the U.S. government—passed before American citizen Lance Schado was finally allowed to fly home to his parents.

After the mad scramble of Operation Babylift, the Amerasian issue does not resurface again until 1978, when "Rosie," the mother of an Amerasian, begins proposing to foreign journalists in Saigon that the United States, like France, should airlift its children "home." Nineteen seventy-eight is also the year that Vietnam begins hemorrhaging boat people. Amid accounts of rape and mayhem at sea, an international conference is called to stanch the flow of refugees.

In the 1979 protocols establishing the Orderly Departure Program, among the five pages of regulations outlining who would be admitted to the United States, there is no mention of Amerasians. Until the two countries later changed their minds, the United States and Vietnam were agreed: Amerasians are Vietnamese.

Rosie was undeterred. She and other mothers of Amerasians swamped the American ODP office in Bangkok with applications. "The letters sent in 1980 and early 1981 express great excitement over 'the new American policy,' " wrote Don Colin, head of the American office, to his superiors in Washington. "An activist mother [Rosie] has assembled a long list of Amerasian children, their mothers, and siblings. The ODP office sent them questionnaires."

By the end of 1981, Don Colin had 250,000 names on file, including three thousand Amerasians. Colin began pressing Washington to include Amerasians under ODP Category III, reserved for "people closely associated with the U.S. presence in Vietnam." In a cable to the State Department he speculated that "the large contractor community in Vietnam, sent there by the U.S. Government, is responsible for about half of our Amerasian cases." The average length of these Vietnamese relationships, he said, was four years.

Colin kept pestering his bosses for a policy statement on Amerasians. "We need authority to accept qualified Amerasian children and their immediate relatives as refugees," he cabled Washington in April 1982. "They are social outcasts who are not allowed to attend school and not allowed to work. Vietnam's mixed-race children suffer greater political and economic discrimination, being associated with the former enemy."

In the same cable Colin complained that a new piece of legislation then being considered by Congress, the Amerasian Immigration Act of 1982, would actually *hinder* Amerasians trying to get out of Vietnam. Among other strictures, the 1982 act demanded consular interviews, which were impossible in a country where the United States had no consular officials.

An episode of the television show *60 Minutes*, aired in September 1982, investigated why only a "dozen Amerasians," all of them documented American citizens, had managed to leave Vietnam since the end of the war. It quoted the Vietnamese prime minister as saying he was ready to release *all* Amerasians, not just the AMCIT cases. Meanwhile, ODP files in Bangkok had grown to include four thousand Amerasians, six hundred of whom were American citizens.

"The real tragedy is that we could have had these kids out in 1983," says Kyle Hörst. "That was the year David Guyer, head of Save the Children, pencilled an agreement with the Vietnamese government. But he was slapped down by the State Department, who vetoed any approach to the enemy.

"The guys at State were having wet dreams about killing VC through refugee policy," says Kyle. "They sent the message to Vietnam: 'If we have to talk to you directly about Amerasians, we don't want 'em.' In the meantime they did everything possible to prevent even legitimate American citizens from getting out of Vietnam. And tough luck for the rest of the Amerasians."

The first direct talks between the United States and Vietnam about Amerasians would not take place until September 1986, eleven years after the end of the war.

Besides Save the Children, the other philanthropic agency pursuing the Amerasian issue was the Pearl Buck Foundation. The American writer Pearl Buck, who described herself as "spiritually an Amerasian," had set up a foundation in 1967 to aid what she called a "new group of human beings, a group which Asians do not know how to deal with, illegitimate as well as mixed in race." Her goal was to keep these "piteous, miserable, hopeless" children from joining what she called the "criminal class."

According to Buck, who spent thirty-five years in Asia, Amerasians are caught between two conflicting ideas of citizenship: *jus sanguinis*—the rule of descent by blood—which bases citizenship on the nationality of the child's father at the time of birth, and *jus soli*—the right of the soil—which bases citizenship on the territory where the child is born, regardless of the parents' nationality. With the Vietnamese favoring *jus sanguinis* and the Americans insisting on *jus soli*, Amerasians fall into a double bind, whereby they inherit nothing from either side of their mixed lineage, neither a nation nor a recognized identity.

"This is the story of more than eighty years of American child abuse in Asia," wrote John Shade in a Pearl Buck Foundation monograph on Amerasians published in 1980. Then director of PBF, Shade estimated that two million Amerasians had been born since U.S. troops first landed in Asia during the Spanish-American War, and that 250,000 Amerasians in nine nations were currently alive. Amerasians in Japan are known as *hanyo*, half-people; in Korea they are *panjant*, half-breeds; in Thailand they are *farang*, foreigners; and in Vietnam they are *con lai*, mixed-blood. Everywhere in Asia, said Shade, Amerasians are "nonpersons" forbidden schooling, jobs, and other rights.

Hoping to get Vietnam to release its Amerasians to the Pearl Buck Foundation, Shade visited Hanoi in 1979. He traveled alone, "almost covertly," he said. "There was tremendous competition among the voluntary agencies. We all wanted to get back into Vietnam.

"The Vietnamese foreign minister told me, 'We don't want Amerasians in our country. They're yours for the asking.' I went back to Washington, and the State Department pooh-poohed me. They didn't want to hear what I had to say. The U.S. government was making bargaining chips out of these children. They didn't give a shit if they lived or died."

Shade dreamed of getting the Amerasians out of Vietnam by boat. "We would staff the ships with enough people to do all the paperwork and socialization by the time we reached New York Harbor. I estimated it would take about thirty or forty days. As we sailed past the Statue of Liberty in a huge flotilla, there was no way the U.S. government could turn us back."

By 1985, Shade had lined up a commitment for two luxury liners from Peter Grace, owner of the Grace Lines. The Vietnamese government had given him permission to transport eight thousand Amerasian children, and he had raised two million dollars for the program. "That's when the State Department spoke to a member of the PBF board, which nixed the project," says Shade. "The board took the money and built a fancy new building in Bucks County. I quit and was gone in thirty days. They swapped eight thousand human beings for a new building. It cut me like a knife when I didn't get their support."

In 1983 ODP director Don Colin finally got permission from the U.S. State Department to begin interviewing Amerasians and transporting small numbers of them out of Vietnam. The United Nations High Commissioner for Refugees, the original sponsor of the Orderly Departure Program, strenuously objected to the new policy. "Here for the first time the UNHCR is involved in creating refugees," complained a UN spokesman. "We are helping people leave their country." The Vietnamese government also complained. They argued that Amerasians were not refugees. They were immigrants or American citizens, depending on how one defined the issue, but in either case it should be settled by direct negotiations between Vietnam and the United States.

Of the forty signatories to the protocol establishing the Orderly Departure Program, only the United States had no diplomatic relations with Vietnam. A high-rise block in Bangkok, staffed by Thai employees working for the International Catholic Migration Commission, served as America's de facto Vietnamese Embassy. Delays in processing cases were chronic. ODP had already been operating for five years before jet refugees began to outnumber boat people. Don Colin, in the meantime, reported "signs of protein deficiency among many of the Amerasians and their families."

"Because of their undisputed ties to our country, these children and their family members are of special interest [to the United States]," declared Secretary of State George Shultz in September 1984. He was speaking at a ceremony announcing the creation of a special ODP subprogram for Amerasians. Its stated purpose was to airlift all Amerasians out of Vietnam within three years.

"There was nothing new in Shultz's initiative," says Kyle Hörst, "except for the fact that Shultz was saying it. He was getting outflanked by the volags and had to do *something*."

In January 1986 the Vietnamese government closed down the U.S. Orderly Departure Program. They were angry over a backlog of twenty thousand people who had been interviewed, but whose cases had yet to be acted on. Since the United States had capped total departures from Vietnam at one thousand per month, the Vietnamese saw no reason to keep the process going.

When ODP reopened a year and a half later, the revived program excluded Amerasians. The Vietnamese were making another point. They wanted a bilateral dialogue with the United States. Amerasians were not a refugee issue, but a war-legacy issue, like recovering prisoners of war or the bones of men missing in action. If the United States cared to retrieve these items— living or dead—it would have to deal directly with its former enemy. The children were literally pawns now.

At secret meetings in New York and Hanoi in the fall of 1986, the United States finally began face-to-face discussions concerning Amerasians and other war-related issues. A year later, in September 1987, a new Amerasian Program—working alongside the Orderly Departure Program (and in many ways indistinguishable from it)—went into operation. But by then the State Department had lost control of the issue, which had moved into the court of public opinion and produced legislative action. Congress was getting ready to adopt its own Amerasian program, which was more urgent and inclusive than anything the State Department wanted.

While Washington spent eleven years avoiding face-to-face discussions with the Vietnamese, various private citizens—dismissed by the State Department as "Lone Rangers"—began their own discussions. One was Judith Ladinsky, who became director of the U.S. Committee for Scientific Cooperation With Vietnam when her predecessor, a California physics professor named Edward Cooperman, was shot dead in his office by a disgruntled Vietnamese refugee.

"The old Republican forces run an incredible extortion racket," says Ladinsky. "They'll do anything to intimidate people and keep them from having normal relations with Vietnam."

Far from being intimidated, this portly, chain-smoking professor of public health at the University of Wisconsin began making regular trips to Vietnam, where she functioned as the surrogate American consul in Ho Chi Minh City. Using the doormen for crowd control, she registered Amerasians in the lobby of the Majestic Hotel, compiling lists of names that were later turned over to the Vietnamese government along with requests for exit visas. To this day, Amerasians still think there are two ways to leave Vietnam, via ODP or the Judy Ladinsky Program, and the latter is more effective.

Another Lone Ranger, a Jesuit-trained lawyer and Vietnam vet named Bruce Burns, began attracting publicity with something called the Amerasian Registry. This was a group of Vietnam veteran fathers who were trying to get their children out of Vietnam. Burns's most famous client was Barry Huntoon, a former Army medic, who worked for a water purification company in Paradise, California. Huntoon was lying in bed with his wife one afternoon when he picked up the August 1985 issue of *Life* magazine and found himself staring into the eyes of an Amerasian girl in Vietnam.

Staring back at him was the picture of Tran Thi Tuyet Mai, a thirteen-year-old Amerasian who lived by selling peanuts on the beach at Vung Tau. She had the same square jaw and pudgy, round face as Huntoon. "That's my daughter," he said to his wife. Huntoon would spend the next two years trying to get the girl and her mother, Tuyet Nhung, out of Vietnam. Nhung had been nine months pregnant when Huntoon was forced to leave her at the end of his tour of duty in 1972.

The case garnered a lot of publicity, including an ABC television special with Barbara Walters. She described how the U.S. government was blocking Huntoon at every turn. The State Department refused to let Tuyet Mai leave Vietnam while ODP interviews were suspended. They denied permission for her relatives to accompany her. They said she had emotional problems. They claimed she had flunked her psychological exam. In the meantime, Huntoon himself had a nervous breakdown.

Bruce Burns kept shuttling into Bangkok with TV crews and journalists, who had an easy time making ODP look callous. The final hurdle was overcome when Judith Ladinsky arranged another psychiatric exam for Tuyet Mai, which she passed. Incarcerated for ten days in a Thai jail and then separated from her mother and half sister, who were sent to a refugee camp in the Philippines, Tuyet Mai finally reached Paradise, California, in 1987.

The ironic part of the story is that the State Department, in some ways, may have been right. In a windowless restaurant deep in the bowels of the Rayburn Building, a former ODP interviewer gives me her side of the story: "While Bruce Burns was making us look like a lot of paper-pushing airheads, we were dealing with several veterans trying to get custody of young Amerasian girls who were not their daughters. Huntoon felt guilty about abandoning the girl, but we thought he had the wrong family."

As Huntoon himself later admitted in a 1989 article in *Redbook* magazine, entitled "I'll Always Believe She's My Daughter," the woman who accompanied Tuyet Mai to the United States and who claimed to be her mother was not the woman he had impregnated in Vietnam. Tuyet Mai, therefore, might not be his daughter. Huntoon promised at the end of the article to settle the paternity question by submitting to a blood test. He never did. Instead, he had another nervous breakdown.

.   .   .

Students at Huntington High School on Long Island were dismayed one day in 1987 to find in their *Newsday* newspaper a photo of Le Van Minh, a crippled Amerasian boy who survived by begging on the streets of Ho Chi Minh City. The students wrote to their congressman, Robert Mrazek, Democrat from Centerport, asking him to help the boy. A Vietnam veteran and member of the House appropriations subcommittee that financed the Orderly Departure Program, Mrazek flew to Vietnam, scooped up Le Van Minh, and deposited him in a foster home on Long Island. He then drafted the Amerasian Homecoming Act, which was signed into law by the end of 1987. The act set a two-year time limit on getting all Amerasians and their accompanying relatives out of Vietnam.

"We pulled this off by finessing the refugee issue," a Mrazek staff member explains. "We made Amerasians a special class of immigrants, with refugee benefits. This allowed them to escape the State Department's numerical limitations on refugees. We also demanded that the interview process and paperwork be greatly relaxed. We thought it better to have a few people cheat the system than drag out the process for ten years."

The most strenuous opposition to the Amerasian Homecoming Act came from the U.S. State Department. It lobbied against the bill, calling it an unnecessary duplication of existing programs, a bad piece of legislation, and a "budget buster," because of its twenty-million-dollar price tag. "Any demand by Hanoi that the United States tailor its refugee laws to suit Vietnam's preferences would be grossly inappropriate," it reiterated.

While the Amerasian Homecoming Act, part of an omnibus spending measure called Public Law 100-202, was being penned into existence, the new bilateral Amerasian Program, negotiated in face-to-face meetings between General John Vessey and Vietnamese foreign minister Nguyen Co Thach, was delivering its first planeload of sixty-five Amerasians to Bangkok. Even in the absence of Mrazek's legislation, the new agreement promised to speed up the departure of Amerasians from Vietnam. Its key improvement was a provision calling for U.S. interviewers to work in Ho Chi Minh City. For the first time since the Paris Peace Conference, the old enemies would no longer be slipping messages to each other through intermediaries.

Vietnam began registering its Amerasian population in 1988, but foot-dragging on both sides jeopardized the Amerasian Homecoming Act's two-year timetable. Set to expire in March 1990, the program was extended, first for one year, and then indefinitely. Amerasian departures, which had been proceeding at the rate of four hundred a year, skyrocketed to ten thousand. Another major change came in 1991 when Amerasian kids, instead of being forced to choose between mothers and spouses, were allowed to bring both to the United States.

In January 1988, immediately after the act was signed into law, Mrazek flew to Hanoi. He was nervous about Vietnam carrying through on its promise to release its Amerasians. Kyle Hörst, then working as a policy analyst in Washington, briefed Mrazek before his trip. "I told him to lay it on the line," says Kyle. "Tell the Vietnamese, 'I delivered this bill against written opposition by the State Department. If you don't turn over the Amerasians, we'll all look like fools.' "

Kyle foresaw another potential problem with the Amerasian Homecoming Act: "I told Mrazek to warn the Vietnamese against using the act as a license for rounding up Amerasians and throwing them out of the country. But in hindsight that's what happened."

Nyetnik

A prison, even though entirely surrounded by walls,
is a splendidly illuminated theater of history.

Milan Kundera

At noon, when I walk out of the Ministry of Foreign Affairs, dozens of kids rush over to greet me. They begin pushing into my hands the usual collection of letters, affidavits, birth certificates, snapshots, and other proof of their existence. I realize the list of names I collected yesterday in Amerasian Park is insufficient, and unless I open a one-man office, complete with photocopier, the only way I can hope to gather all the required documents is to have the Amerasians collect them themselves. I choose a likely scribe, a neatly dressed young man with wire-rimmed spectacles, and hand him a notebook and pen. Through Miss Hoa, who has reattached herself to my side, I deliver a stern lecture to the assembled Amerasians: "If I discover anything fraudulent in your files, I'll throw the whole lot of them in the river."

Although Mr. Tanh, the Vietnamese ODP director, is the official with ultimate authority over their fate, these kids have never heard of him. For them, the highest official they can ever hope to reach is a man in the immigration department called Mr. Khe. Mr. Khe presides over an office at 258 Nguyen Trai Street. Here on Tuesdays and Thursdays, between the hours of seventhirty and four-thirty, with a two-hour break for lunch, Mr. Khe and his colleagues are charged with registering homeless Amerasians and putting their names on the ODP interview lists.

On my first visit to Saigon in 1991 I had heard so many horror stories about Mr. Khe that one day I scooped up a dozen street kids and marched on his office. We entered a dirty, windowless cave filled with supplicants lined up on wooden benches. Among them was an Amerasian girl in tears. She had been coming to Mr.

Khe, presenting her papers and her wide black American face, for over a year. Also in the office were an Amerasian couple from the Delta, three boys who had escaped from a so called New Economic Zone, and a half-Montagnard girl from the highlands. All had the same story. For lack of some piece of paper—an original birth certificate, a ration card, or whatever—their applications had been denied. One girl told me she had been haunting Mr. Khe's office for five years.

Seated at wooden tables on a dais at the front of room are Mr. Khe and another officer. They wear tattered uniforms and bark their commands with the hard-edged accent of the north. I watch Mr. Khe brush off petitioners like mosquitos. In case after case he orders Amerasians back to the countryside for missing pieces of paper. He wants them to start the process all over again, working their way up the bureaucratic chain from township to district to province, before getting back to the very Mr. Khe in front of whom they now stand. Protocol demands it. So, too, do the outstretched palms of his subordinates.

Mr. Khe brushes me off as readily as the other supplicants. He tells me to go talk to the Americans, who must have their own chain of command for dealing with people like me. Our march on Nguyen Trai Street has fizzled into nothing more than the usual sit-in.

By the time I finish the day's meetings at the Ministry of Foreign Affairs, Saigon has baked itself into a steaming casserole of dust and diesel. I cross the park and head downtown to the Majestic, where I hope to invite myself to dinner with the American ODP interview team. On the way I stop at the post office, my favorite building in Saigon, built in 1891 by Gustave Eiffel. It has the same soaring ironwork as his other famous monuments. Etched in gold around the outside of the edifice are the names of Laplace, Ben Franklin, Ohm, Joule, Davy, and other great men presumed to support France's colonial empire in Indochina. Indochina got its name because it was neither India nor China—the two great trophies of the Far East (both already snatched by Britain)—but the territory in between, some tropical mountains and swampy lowlands that France had to settle for if it wanted any Asian empire at all.

Inside the post office, under a cathedral ceiling supported by wrought iron pillars, is a collection of wooden tables holding glue pots and brushes. Seated at these tables are a host of Vietnamese scribes, who labor under an enormous portrait of Ho Chi Minh. The scribes and their illiterate clients are piecing together the formulaic prose needed to find a job, woo a lover. The scribes are diligent men in black-framed glasses. I feel comfortable sitting among them, writing up my daily notes. We are in the same line of work.

Strolling toward the river, I find the magnolias and bougainvillea in bloom. The mango trees are laden with fruit, and even the stalls of the soup vendors are decorated with fresh flowers. The sweet odor of the tropics mingles with the smell of open sewers. Approaching the Majestic, I notice squatting on the curb my old friend Viet. He greets me with a big grin.

"No problem," he says, when I tell him I want to hire him on permanent retainer, twenty-four hours a day.

I had met Viet the previous year. It was 1991 and still difficult then for an American to get a visa to Vietnam, especially a writer interested in meeting Amerasians. So I traveled to Vietnam as part of a group of doctors studying the country's medical system, and thereby visited more hospital operating rooms than I ever hope to see again. In Saigon we paid special attention to skull fractures, which occur at the rate of two hundred a month and are the city's leading cause of accidental death.

Saigon is a mad scatter of bicycles and motorcycles zooming through a confined space without traffic lights, and the only way to survive this experience is to have a master at the wheel. Viet for many years was an opera singer with the Minh To opera troupe, one of the most famous in Vietnam. He played two roles—

the satyr and the noble king. It was the latter role he adapted to being a motorcycle driver in Saigon. He guaranteed our safe passage through the city by staring down other drivers with the deadly look of a warrior ready to disembowel.

Inside the Majestic, another of Eiffel's colonial buildings, I find a member of the ODP interview team, whom I shall call John Smith, seated at the downstairs bar. Smith and I know each other through mutual friends. He tells me the big news of the day. The Vietnamese government has submitted a "final" list of Amerasians to be interviewed by the Orderly Departure Program. The list has twenty thousand names on it.

"The fraud is out of hand," he says. "The new list is garbage. It's full of rejected families who have suddenly turned up with Amerasian 'children.' These are cases where the Amerasian can't tell the truth even if he wants to. He has saved his real family's life by getting them money, and now everyone is in danger if he can't pull off the deal. The kid is with the interviewer for three minutes. He's with his family for the rest of his life."

Section 212(a) of the Immigration and Nationality Act lists forty reasons for excluding people from entering the United States. Forbidden entry are Nazis, prostitutes, homosexuals, Communists, and polygamists. Also banned are smugglers of aliens, which is the term applied to Amerasians who lie at their ODP interview. They are given three chances to confess to being part of a fraudulent family, and if they do not confess and are unmasked, they are permanently barred from entering the United States. "You used to be able to buy an Amerasian for anywhere from one hundred to a thousand dollars," says Smith. "But as the program winds down, even the top price is getting doubled or tripled." This is only part of the story, though.

"Do you know how much money the Americans pay the Vietnamese to run this operation?" he asks. "It's *millions* of dollars a year, and this is money paid to a country we don't even recognize."

The United States pays the Vietnamese government eighty dollars per head for every Amerasian and accompanying family member who leave the country. Twenty dollars per head is paid for their medical exams. And fifty-seven dollars per head goes to the Ministry of Foreign Affairs for "administrative support."

"Every time the ODP interview team flies into the country, we bring a large box of cash," says Smith. Out of this box ODP pays the rent on its offices and the salaries of all the Vietnamese officials who work with it—about fifty people altogether, including six interviewers, eighteen form-fillers, six interpreters, and two drivers. ODP also supplies five motorcycles and six cars to the Vietnamese government to facilitate their searching the countryside for Amerasians.

Added to this is the half-million dollars the United States paid in 1989 to build the Amerasian Transit Center at Dam Sen. Dam Sen is an amusement park on the outskirts of Saigon, and when the Amerasian program eventually closes down, Dam Sen's list of attractions will include a handsome lakeside motel. "The Transit Center is run like a shell game," says Smith. "The airport departure payments are supposed to go toward supporting Amerasians at the ATC. But the Vietnamese turn a neat profit by keeping the place half empty. This is why so many Amerasians are sleeping on the streets."

ODP computers in Bangkok now hold more than a million Vietnamese and Amerasian names. The program is so huge, and there is so much paperwork being shuffled back and forth, that interviewers are just beginning to deal with cases filed thirteen years ago. "For whatever reason," says Smith, staring at the last light coming off the river, "a lot of Vietnamese want to change their address."

The restaurant is steamy, the walls yellow with age and diminished candle-power. This month's ODP interview team, consisting of four INS officials, a couple of State Department officers, and a handful of ICMC paper pushers, decide to move some tables and sit out on the sidewalk.

Seated next to me is the brassy blonde who is head of mission. The Vietnamese, with their wicked sense of humor, call her *Nyetnik*, because they think her manners boorish, like the Russians, and because she gives nothing away. At my other elbow is a thick-waisted giant, a former State Department consul in Thailand who is being rotated back to a desk job in Washington. He knows a lot about Amerasians in Thailand, having married a Thai and produced some of his own. He tells me that much of his work there consisted of dealing with children left behind by the forty thousand American troops who were stationed in Thailand during the war. "If your birth certificate lists your father as American, you can't go to school or become a Thai citizen," he says. "The law is supposed to be changed, but it hasn't gone into effect yet."

We agree to share our dishes around the table, Chinese-restaurant style. I order a plate of Szechuan chicken. "Road kill," exclaims the ICMC man across from me. "We never touch the stuff."

Another problem arises when the ODP program officer from Washington, who is visiting Asia for the first time, insists on eating bread with his meal. "I hate rice," he says. A waiter is sent scurrying down the street looking for a loaf of bread.

Nyetnik launches into a tirade against the Amerasian program. "The return we're getting on our investment is totally scandalous," she says. "It costs the U.S. government six million dollars a year to run the ODP office in Thailand, not counting all the money we shell out over here. And what are we buying? We're financing the Vietnamese version of the Mariel boatlift. The government scrapes up its social riffraff, its schizophrenics and criminals, and sends them to America. We're watering down our gene pool with Amerasian mental cases. We're flooding the social welfare system with fake families. We can't afford it. ODP has the lowest return on investment of any government program."

A loaf of bread arrives at the table. I alone am eating the chicken.

"I assume fraud in every case I see," says Nyetnik, who goes on to describe herself and her fellow interviewers as "trained interrogators. All we lack is the electricity. Sure it's fun playing God, but we sometimes get it wrong. So I long ago decided it's better to refuse a real case than let a fake Amerasian into the United States."

The next morning I take advantage of Nyetnik's invitation to visit the ODP interview site, which consists of a two-story office block built in the courtyard behind the Ministry of Foreign Affairs. The building has two entrances—a private one, communicating with the Ministry, and a public one off the street. Today I use the public entrance. I walk into a big room with a noodle shop canteen and loudspeakers calling out people's names. The room is filled with wooden benches on which sit hundreds of applicants dressed in their Sunday best. They stare at me as I walk through the room, no doubt wondering if I am the person who will decide their fate.

In an office behind the waiting area I find four International Catholic Migration Commission staffers shuffling paperwork. A plump blonde is eating jam spooned onto pieces of white bread. Next to her sit two young men swapping sports scores from stateside and an older man with close-cropped gray hair. Seven Vietnamese secretaries help the Americans sort through the paperwork, which is piled around them on tables and stored along the walls in plastic laundry bins. The remaining wall space is covered with charts tracking numbers of applicants and departures.

"All the files that would normally be kept in-country have to be carried back and forth monthly between Bangkok and Saigon," says the gray-haired clerk. He roots through a couple of bins, pulling out examples of what the files contain: birth certificates, love letters, family photos, GI dog tags, police records, X-rays.

"Here's another orphan who's just discovered his long-lost parents," he jokes. "And this guy wants us to put a Zippo lighter into his file. He says he's been saving it for us since '75."

The clerk flips me an envelope addressed to *Mr. Thomas, ODP Interviewer*. It is stuffed with photos of a GI, his Vietnamese girlfriend, and two Amerasian babies. "My guess is this woman is dead," he says, glancing at the photos. The package also contains a letter saying, *My mommy begs pardon for being in confused state of mind during interview with American team. No fraud being intended.* It goes on to apologize for the miscalculation that resulted in the two babies' being born within seven months of each other.

Another letter addressed to Mr. Thomas reads, *In the interview my husband declares to the U.S. official that my wedding party had no assistant bridegroom and siblings to participate. Meanwhile I confirm the fact to the official. In fact my husband's mind was not stable and embarrassed in the interview. No fraud was willingly falsified.*

Enclosed with the letter are two photos showing a burly GI and his slender Vietnamese girlfriend. Also enclosed is an "Agreement to Live Together" issued in 1969 by the Bien Hoa Police Department. Duly signed by the soldier and his girlfriend, the document asserts, *Both make the present agreement to live together while we are in the process of getting legally married. We guarantee that we will not make complains if something happens Later On.*

Nyetnik breezes into the room to pick up a stack of files. She motions for me to follow her. Walking upstairs and through another waiting area lined with benches, we enter an office holding a gun-metal gray desk and chairs. An air conditioner thunders in the window. Conducting a conversation in this room is like trying to talk to someone on the bottom of a swimming pool.

I sit at the desk, beside the Vietnamese interpreter. Everyone entering the room is asked to raise his or her right hand and swear to tell the truth. The first interviewee is a nineteen-year-old boy dressed in a long-sleeved white shirt, neat chinos, and flip-flops. He is applying to ODP with his natural mother, step-father, half-brother, and two half-sisters. He is questioned by Nyetnik about his birth certificate, which bears his mother's, but not his father's, name.

"What was your father's name?"

"Raymond Sambuno."

"How did your mother meet him?"

"He was a civilian radar technician in Pleiku."

The boy's family is summoned into the room. The mother wears a white blouse and slacks. The girls wear white dresses; the boys, freshly laundered jeans. The stepfather says he was a soldier from 1968 to 1975. The mother is questioned about her relationship to Sambuno.

"Where was Raymond Sambuno from?"

"Hawaii."

"Did you have other boyfriends?"

"No."

"Where did you work?"

"In a bar."

"How long did you live together?"

"From 1972 to 1973. He left when I was three months pregnant. I have not heard from him since."

"You didn't apply to leave the country until 1990. Why did you wait so long?"

"A friend told me if the father of your child was from Hawaii you could not apply to ODP."

The interviewer from the neighboring office is summoned into the room. The two officials stand in the corner staring at the boy and his family.

"What do you think?" asks Nyetnik, holding up a picture of the alleged dad.

"Sambuno looks just like the little boy there. He's got the same jaw line. The key here is the appearance issue."

The two interviewers squint at the family, trying to pick out resemblances and disparities. Their future hangs on whether an olive-skinned kid with black hair and eyes is going to pass for being half-Hawaiian.

Nyetnik motions to the boy. She leads him down the corridor, taking him from office to office, where he gets a thumbs-up or thumbs-down signal from the five other interviewers. "He's probably a Filipino," she says. Young Sambuno and his family are rejected. The interview, including what is called "walking the line," lasts seven minutes. And so it goes all day long. Thumbs up. Thumbs down.

I am strolling through Amerasian Park that afternoon when I see Huynh Thi Huong, her husband, and two children sitting on a bench. I had met Huong the year before, after she and her family had been living in the park for two months. They shared twenty thousand *dong*, about two dollars, between them. The little boy and girl were covered with sores. They looked hungry and frightened. I wrote a letter of introduction to the Amerasian Transit Center and pressed some money into her hand.

A handsome woman with large brown eyes, Huong wears her reddish hair in a ponytail. She has high cheekbones, a fine, wide mouth, and white teeth that one rarely sees because she seldom smiles. As attested by a photo of a GI standing in a radar shack during the war, Huong's little boy is the spitting image of his grandfather.

Huong thinks she was born in the Year of the Horse, which would be 1966. She lived in an orphanage until the end of the war. One day the staff disappeared. Then soldiers from the north arrived. They opened the gates and all the children walked out. She was nine.

She went to work for a woman selling tea in the market. The

woman died when Huong was fourteen. "I lived in the woman's cottage after she died, but soon it fell down in the rains," she says. "I went to the railroad station to sell tea on the trains. I lived in the streets. During the monsoons, I asked people if I could stay for a night under their roofs. I begged for food, because often I was hungry."

Huong went to work as a day laborer on the farms around Hue that grow sweet potatoes and beans. She was given a place to live and food to eat as she moved from family to family. Here she met the Vietnamese boy who became her husband. He too was an orphan, his parents having been killed in the Tet Offensive of 1968. They built a cottage out of rice stalks and farmed an abandoned plot in the village of Thuy An. After their son was born and their house fell down in the monsoons, they went back to living on the streets of Hue. "It would be impolite to tell you what tricks we used to survive," he says.

Market vendors who had read about the Orderly Departure Program in the newspaper told them to apply. Early in 1991 Huong and her family caught the train to Saigon, where Mr. Khe informed them their documents were not in order. They would have to return home. Since they had no money for this trip halfway across Vietnam, Huong and her children stayed in Amerasian Park, while her husband jumped the train back to Hue. "The Amerasians in the park helped me look after the children," she says. "But by the time you found us here, we were very hungry."

Huong and her family flourished during their year in the Amerasian Transit Center. They learned how to read and write Vietnamese and English. Their complexions cleared up. Their clothing got patched and cleaned. Huong had been worried but hopeful about starting a new life in America. "Americans are polite," she says. "It is a civilized society, and no one tells you a lie."

Today when I meet Huynh Thi Huong in the park, her face is a mask of despair. Tears roll down her cheeks, and the news hits me like a blow in the chest when she tells me they have failed their ODP interview. They had the bad luck to fall on Mr. Ten Percent, who rejected them for not being able to produce original birth certificates.

"What are you going to do now?" I ask.

"We will go back to living on the street," she says. "We will resume our wandering life."

"Can't you stay in the Transit Center while you appeal your case?"

"There are no appeals," she says.

We walk to a photocopy shop across from the post office, where I duplicate her file. In place of a birth certificate and government ID card, she possesses a letter from the Hue authorities certifying that these original documents are lost. There is the picture of her father, her marriage certificate, and three affidavits testifying that she is a "homeless wandering Amerasian with no fixed address." This is all the paperwork one can expect to retrieve from a war zone. It is not much. But according to the law, Huynh Thi Huong's face alone is all she needs to get to America.

I send these documents, along with photographs of the family and an official request for a rehearing, to the Orderly Departure Program, the State Department, various congressmen, senators and other government officials. Over the next three years the rejections accumulate into a thick manila folder. I am afraid Huynh Thi Huong is right. There is no appeal.

Apocalypse Now

Y'wanna join in a chorus
Of the Amerasian blues . . .
Let me tell y'bout your blood, Bamboo Kid
It ain't Coca-Cola, it's rice

Clash

Lyrics by Joe Strummer from "Straight to Hell," by the Clash, are used by permission of Mr. Strummer.

Opened in January 1990, the Amerasian Transit Center is a collection of neatly landscaped, two-story dormitories that already looks like the conference center it is intended to become. The food is plentiful. The violence, minimal. English classes and crafts keep fifteen hundred residents occupied while they wait to be interviewed. Accompanied by Mrs. Tam, the soft-spoken, Australian-trained chemist who is director of education and psychological counseling, I walk through the dormitory blocks looking for some of the Amerasians I had met the previous year.

We peer through louvered windows into rooms with green tile floors and wood-frame beds. In 1991, when the center was full, ten people lived in each room. Now, a year later, we see only a handful of Amerasians swinging in hammocks suspended from the ceiling or napping on the floors, which are cooler than the beds. We run into Le Minh Phi, whom I had found living in Amerasian Park and helped place in the center. He is an earnest young man with pale skin. I joke about returning to Vietnam to collect the money I loaned him.

Phi invites me into the room he shares with his half-brother and another family. A clothesline hung with T-shirts and trousers separates their living areas. The room measures forty feet by fifteen. It has a high ceiling, pale blue walls, and iron grilles covering the glassless windows. Mrs. Tam and I kick off our shoes and sit on one of the two wooden beds. At our feet gather a circle of Amerasians crouched on their haunches. The Amerasians are old enough now to have children of their own, who sit on their parents' laps or get passed from hand to hand.

Phi tells me when he comes to America he will work for me for free. I reassure him I was only joking about the money. He was a farm boy until he ran away to Saigon. "Life is much better here in camp," he says. He goes to school two hours a day and plays a lot of table tennis. The worried look on his face is owing to the fact that he and his brother are being interviewed tomorrow. They are praying to be spared from Mr. Ten Percent.

Other people I helped last year come to see me, including an Amerasian named Kim and her sister Anh, a gentle Vietnamese girl with a lustrous smile. They, too, are worried about their upcoming interview. The sisters are inseparable. They are all that remains of their family, but because Anh is over the age of twenty-one, she is technically not allowed to accompany her sister to America. Wearing a pretty blue headband and matching blouse, Kim looks thin, and she tells me she is ill. "When we lived in the country, I had to work so hard to make a living I had no time to be sick," she says. "But now I have time to be sick."

Mrs. Tam says Kim was sent to the hospital for X-rays. They found no cause for the pain under her ribs or the fact that she no longer eats. "We wonder if it is a psychological problem, but if it is, everyone thinks this is minor compared to all the other problems we see."

A little girl with fluffy brown hair comes up to pinch my arm and then scurries back to her father, a strapping young man who looks like an Amerasian Chuck Norris. He has been living at the transit center for a year and a half. Another Amerasian couple have been here two years. "Our son was born in the transit center, and if we stay here much longer, they'll have another mouth to feed," the woman says. Everyone laughs.

I ask the people sitting at my feet if they can think of any Amerasians who have decided *not* to leave Vietnam. They name an Amerasian girl in the Mekong Delta who is happily married to a bicycle mechanic and another girl, a black Amerasian, who failed her interview and decided to stay in Vietnam with her family. All over the country, they assure me, one can find Amerasian

rice farmers and tea sellers. Amerasian actors specialize in playing GIs in Vietnamese films, and this year's hot young rock star
and movie actress is an Amerasian. "Her name is Phuong Thao,
and you can hear her sing tonight at the opera house."

They mention another curious case: an Amerasian who owns
a silk store in Cholon called Tay Thi, which is the name of a tragic
heroine in Vietnamese opera. They are not sure why this Amerasian, whom I shall also call Tay Thi, decided to stay in Vietnam.
Was it for money or love? But everyone agrees she had a ticket
to America and chose not to use it.

"When I first took this job I had sleepless nights," says Mrs. Tam.
"But now I am growing hardened to it. If you listen to their stories,
especially the orphans, you burst into tears. Then they do something bad, and you realize it is not so simple. They are unsteady
psychologically, often violent and aggressive. Compared to Vietnamese orphans, they have an inferiority complex and don't be-
have themselves well. They are not the children of love, but the
children of violence."

She tells me it is not uncommon for legitimate Amerasians,
like my friend Huynh Thi Huong, to be rejected at their ODP
interviews. "The interview team says it is better to refuse a real
case than to accept a false one." Mrs. Tam also confirms that the
appeals process has been eliminated, which means that Huynh
Thi Huong and her family will be sent back to live on the streets.

Mrs. Tam invites me to lunch. "We are having a special
party today for Mrs. Rose Marie Battisti and her husband," she
says. I smile at the thought of having traveled halfway around the
world to dine with the director of the Mohawk Valley Resource
Center for Refugees and her boyfriend, Bob Capriles, a Syracuse lawyer.

The previous year I had shared many meals with Mrs. Tam
and her two senior colleagues, Mr. Tung, vice director of the center, and Mr. Thien, the director. Mr. Tung is a tall, thin man of

sallow complexion. He looks at his watch a lot and carries a walkie-talkie. Charlie Brown had told me Tung had recruited him into spying for the Vietnamese government. Whether or not this story is true, Mr. Tung strikes me as the power behind the throne.

The director of the Amerasian Transit Center, Le Van Thien, is a continually smiling, round-faced man who looks like the Cheshire cat. He is a graduate of Poulo Condor, the infamous island prison for political cases, where he spent eight years locked in a tiger cage. This was an open-air pit into which lime and feces were thrown on his head. He had no clothes. He lost his hair to scurvy. He wore leg irons and manacles and was gagged with a stick in his mouth. On his release in 1967, until the end of the Vietnam War, he lived underground in the Cu Chi tunnels, where he led a group of Vietcong sappers burrowing under the Michelin rubber plantation northwest of Saigon.

One day at lunch, over a meal of sea horse wine and fish soup, I screwed up the nerve to ask Mr. Thien how he felt about nurturing the bastard offspring of his former enemy.

"The Amerasian children are also Vietnamese children, and it is our responsibility to take care of them," he said. "They are the victims of war. They are the most unfortunate people in Vietnam." He refilled our wineglasses and asked me a question in turn. "As a writer, can you tell me why the Americans lost the war? They had so much more equipment, airplanes, guns, everything." All I could think to tell him was that America lost the war because of people like him.

Compared to the simple meals I shared with Mr. Thien the year before, the lunch for Rose Marie Battisti is a grand affair. A table has been laid in the reception room at headquarters. The sea horse wine has been replaced by cognac. The fish soup has given way to *steak frites*. We arrive just as everyone is being seated. Mr. Thien pours out large tumblers of cognac and proposes a toast to Rose Marie and her "husband" on their new marriage. She gives him a tight-lipped smile and looks at me out the corner of her eye. I don't let on that she and her boyfriend are actually in the middle of two tricky divorce cases. Instead, I quickly second her in proposing another toast to Mr. Thien, our host.

I am seated next to Battisti's boyfriend, a beefy vet who was stationed on a ship off Da Nang in 1964. "Even out at sea, the smell of *nuoc mam* coming off the coast made us want to puke," he says. Then he tells us how he used to lob "toe poppers"—antipersonnel devices and land mines—onto the coast.

Capriles announces he is going to Hanoi to be "briefed on the POW problem. I'm head of my veterans' group in Syracuse, and the boys want to get to the bottom of this business. We intend to straighten it out once and for all."

Mr. Thien gives him a Cheshire grin and cuts into his second piece of steak. Later in the afternoon, Mr. Thien will lead his American guests on a tour of the Cu Chi tunnels—at least those sections that have been enlarged for Western tourists.

Unlike their Chinese neighbors, the Vietnamese never migrated overseas in large numbers. They were too busy marching to the south, conquering Montagnards, Chams, and Khmers, or too happy at home in their emerald garden. But all this changed with the final defeat of the American invaders in 1975. At the most decisive moment in Vietnam's history, one it had been struggling to attain for four thousand years—a Vietnam unified from China to the Gulf of Siam—the country began disgorging refugees.

"In 1888 the king Ham Nghi was forced into exile in Algeria by the French colonialists. We consider him the first Viet Kieu," says the director of the government office charged with monitoring Viet Kieu, or overseas Vietnamese. Former refugees returning to visit Vietnam give chilling accounts of being summoned to this office for shakedowns. They are reminded that their leaving the country was a criminal act and then asked to make humanitarian "donations" to the socialist cause. As I sit across from him at his conference table, I wonder if the director of the agency, a humorless man whose Vietnamese sounds akin to German, is responsible for these sessions.

The initial major exodus of Vietnamese occurred during the First World War, when fifty thousand men were sent to Europe as forced laborers in French munitions plants. These Viet Kieu later proved crucial to Vietnam's anticolonial aspirations. They saw Europeans killing each other and the French losing battles— a lesson they carried back to Vietnam. The lesson was reconfirmed in the Second World War, when one hundred thousand Vietnamese were press-ganged into European service.

These are small numbers, though, compared to the Vietnamese diaspora of today, which includes eight hundred thousand Vietnamese in the United States, two hundred thousand in France, slightly fewer in Canada, one hundred thousand in Australia and Thailand, and smaller numbers scattered throughout eighty countries around the world. Left out of this head count are the Hoa, the ethnic Chinese who have fled across the border into China, and who number about three hundred thousand. One might also mention the one hundred thousand Vietnamese sent to the former Soviet Union to work off Vietnam's hard-currency debt.

Vietnam's greatest Viet Kieu, Ho Chi Minh, wandered in exile for thirty years before returning to found modern-day Vietnam. Ho was the son of a minor official in the French colonial administration who was cashiered for being a patriot opposed to French rule. Or so went the official story, until French historian Daniel Hémery dug up the original police records on the case. They reveal that Ho's father was removed from office for flogging a prisoner to death, which was a grievous abuse of power. Stripped of his rank, Ho's father abandoned his family and became a wandering practitioner of herbal medicine. He died a broken alcoholic in the Mekong Delta town of Sadec.

Stymied by his father's loss of face and his own repeated failures to secure government scholarships, Ho fled overseas. He worked as a cabin boy and pastry chef. He sponged up the world's cultures, learning to speak French, English, Russian and Chinese. He was a great synthesizer of ideas, a traveler turned patriot. Like George Orwell, Ho was down and out in Paris and London and then went home to make a work of art out of his experience—not a book, but a country. The first constitution he wrote for Vietnam was cribbed from the U.S. Declaration of Independence. The second was lifted from Marx, with a leavening of Mao. The virtuous man forced into exile, who dreams of returning to save his homeland, Ho might be called Vietnam's first boat person.

The director's eyes fly open at my suggestion that Ho Chi Minh in any way resembles the raft of misfits launching themselves from Vietnam's shores. "We do not talk about Ho as a Viet Kieu," he says emphatically. "Ho left the country to search for a way to salvation. This is entirely different from the motives of today's Viet Kieu."

"Is it?" I ask myself.

Kyle is at the door staring at his watch as I pull up to the Continental on the back of Viet's motorcycle. Standing next to him are the two Vietnamese officials whom he thinks best qualified to present *their* side of the Amerasian story. The younger man is dressed in blue jeans, the older man in slacks. Both wear short-sleeved white shirts with pens in the front pocket. Kyle introduces me to Nguyen The Dang, a high official in the Americas Section at the Ministry of Foreign Affairs in Hanoi, and Nguyen Quang Phong, who, from 1980 to 1989, was the Saigon official in charge of the ODP-Amerasian Program.

I have seen Phong before, in a television documentary on Amerasians. A film crew following Judith Ladinsky cornered Phong as he walked out the gates of the Ministry. Ladinsky confronted him with a handful of Amerasians whom Mr. Khe had refused to register at Nguyen Trai Street. Phong promised to look into the situation, but the aggressive questioning and camera angles made him look like a villainous bureaucrat.

As we seat ourselves in the restaurant, Guido rushes over to tell us we are in luck. He has just scored some fresh oregano. Kyle convinces our guests to try pizzas, which they have never eaten before. Mr. Dang reports he has just returned from Bangkok, where he was summoned by U.S. officials worried about fraud in the Amerasian Program.

"They said very tough things to me and put all the blame on the Vietnamese," he says. "They insist we get the fraud issue under control, so I traveled today to discuss policy with the People's Committee in Bien Hoa. They agree that all cases in the area should be reexamined."

Mr. Dang himself is ramrod straight in bearing and conduct, and he is too polite to mention it, but everyone at the table knows that what is going to be reexamined are a lot of bribes.

Guido presents our dinners with a Neapolitan flourish. Finding the taste peculiar, our guests spoon large servings of fish sauce onto their pizzas. We order Mr. Dang another beer and begin talking to his former colleague, a handsome man whose black spectacles give him the look of a perpetual student. Phong currently runs the Vietnam Airlines office in Singapore, where he is in training to take over the American office, when it opens. He describes how he tried for many years to get transferred to a new job at the Foreign Ministry, until he finally left. "I was under tremendous pressure, not only from my own government, but also from the United States and all the people like Judith Ladinsky, who flew into town demanding that the Amerasian problem be settled immediately. I had to play the bad guy in all the movies."

As an example of how perverse the Amerasian Program looked from *his* perspective, Phong tells us the story of Le Van Minh. Minh, his legs withered from polio, was a crippled Amerasian who crawled around town on his hands and knees and survived by begging from tourists at the downtown hotels. He was a cute kid with blue eyes and sandy blond hair. It was Minh's picture in *Newsday* that spurred Congressman Robert Mrazek into drafting the Amerasian Homecoming Act. Before it was passed,

Mrazek flew to Vietnam to pick up the fourteen-year-old Minh and carry him back to Long Island.

"I had to take Minh up to Hanoi and deliver him to Mrazek," says Phong. "It was a horrible media show. The boy was crying about leaving behind his mother, his stepfather, and four half-brothers and sisters. They lost his income from begging and almost starved to death. I kept telling the Americans, 'You can't do this. It's incredibly heartless.' But no one listened to me. Separating Minh from his family was the cruelest thing." Not until a year later was Minh's family allowed to join him in the United States.

I hand Phong the list of unregistered Amerasians I have been compiling. He looks annoyed. Obviously, too many people have waved similar lists in his face. He is tired of our gullibility, our self-assurance that after a couple of days in town we can straighten out the problem. "All the Amerasians have been registered," he says. "These people on your list have been rejected for fraud or because of their criminal records."

He is wrong, I think to myself, but even if he is right, what does this mean? It means, for one thing, that there will be thousands of Amerasians left in Vietnam when the airlift is supposedly finished.

"It was tough," says Phong of his ten years working with Amerasians. "I hated dealing, year after year, with these people and their stories. I tried to leave but the government wouldn't let me. I saw the program toying with people's lives. It was making Amerasians pawns in a high-level political game being played between the United States and Vietnam."

"There is a Vietnamese saying," says Mr. Dang, nodding toward my list of homeless Amerasians. " 'No matter how carefully you sweep the floor, there will always be some dust left in the corner.' "

After dinner, Kyle and I tour through nighttime Saigon. We head to the river and walk the gangplank into the Floating Hotel. Swabbies in tam-o'-shanters snap out a salute. They pull open the front door onto an air-conditioned lobby filled with businessmen and the sounds of a pianist playing "Moon River." We descend a spiral staircase to the Downunder, the hotel's floating disco, which is packed with gray-bearded oilmen dancing to the Beach Boys. The *ao dai*ed hostesses are Vietnamese, except for one girl who is Amerasian. Her wide hips look out of place in the tight-fitting tunic, but like other Amerasian prostitutes in Saigon, she is a sought-after exotic whose very existence portends broken taboos. The Amerasian hostess gets passed among three Taiwanese businessmen before being picked up by a table of Australians.

The Aussies are getting sloppy drunk, and the woman looks relieved when I invite her to join us, but a veil of suspicion drops over her face when she hears Kyle addressing her in Vietnamese. She says her name is Mai Lai, a pseudonym, no doubt. We ask her to accompany us to the opera, where we are going to hear Phuong Thao sing. She agrees to meet us at a nearby café and then excuses herself to the ladies' room. We never see her again. I send Viet back to the Floater to get Mai Lai's story from the cyclo drivers. She is one of thirty women who pay bribes to work at the Downunder. A date with her costs fifty dollars, plus another fifteen dollars for a room in the hotel across the street. She works in tandem with her husband, who is good at rolling drunks and other acts of petty thievery. Mai Lai can make in four tricks what the average Vietnamese earns in a year. Other prostitutes in town, Viet tells me, go for as little as five thousand *dong*, about fifty cents.

"Why the price difference?" I ask.

"She is export quality," he explains.

The Saigon opera house is a turn-of-the-century, buff-colored building that would look at home in Biarritz or any other French provincial town. In this former seat of the South Vietnamese legislature, we sit through two hours of pop hits from the fifties and sixties sung by an all-star revue of lounge lizards, faded opera stars, Yves Montand impersonators, and Vietnamese youths not yet schooled in the ways of MTV. This music was banned until recently, and the government still publishes a list of proscribed tunes. On tonight's menu of socialist-approved songs is Chubby Checker's version of "Let's Twist Again," Doris Day's "Que Sera Sera," and Ritchie Valens's "La Bamba." Then comes a bastard-ized version of the Chinese opera *Tay Du Ky*. A warlord, flanked by his pig-faced seneschal, gets into an altercation with a schem-ing woman—she wears a skintight pants suit—before being beaten to his knees by what look like two cowgirls from Buffalo Bill's Wild West Show. "This is what Communist realism does to the classics," says Kyle. "It turns the hero into a landlord and makes him eat shit."

Then comes a *Cage aux Folles* drag number in which not an inch of bare skin is shown, and a ballerina who wears tennis shoes and brown long johns under her tutu. Finally, Phuong Thao comes on stage, a tall young woman with a shag haircut.

"Look at those big hips and shoulders," says Kyle, peering at her white gown and the brown hair cascading over her arms. "Look at the round eyes, thick eyebrows, detached earlobes, hair on the arms, and white skin. Look at her nose. There's no doubt about it," he says with the authority of a trained investigator. "She's Amerasian."

The old songs are back in the socialist republic, and on this big night in Vietnam's cultural thaw, the star of the evening is a *con lai*, a half-breed, the loathed offspring of the colonial oppres-sor, who happens to be a sweet-faced kid with a good voice for belting out the American numbers.

After the show, Kyle and I trawl through a few more bars, begin-ning with the Queen Bee and ending at Apocalypse Now. The Queen Bee—not the original, but a copy built across from the Rex Hotel—is a fifties-style dance hall with the lights turned out.

It costs three dollars to enter and a few more dollars to rent a taxi girl for several hours of dancing. As you and your date sink into the black embrace of the Queen Bee's couches, other arrangements can be made on the side.

The band switches among three lead singers, one performing Vietnamese popular music, one doing Sade knockoffs, and a third fellow who can't decide whether he is James Brown or Bruce Springsteen. The *mama-san* comes over and sits on our couch. "How can I make you happy?" she asks. We tell her we want to dance with an Amerasian. She has heard stranger requests. "Difficult tonight," she says. "Only one girl, and she busy with regular customer."

A few minutes later an Amerasian wearing an *ao dai* comes over to talk to us. Like Mai Lai, she looks out of place in the Vietnamese native dress; her shoulders are too broad for the tailored tunic. But she moves her hands well, and she has a sweet air that must be attractive to regular customers. She says she will be free tomorrow, when her Taiwanese boyfriend is gone. All we learn about her tonight is that she has passed her ODP interview and will be leaving soon for America.

Down the street, there is no shortage of Amerasians working the crowd at Apocalypse Now. This street-front bar is the hot new address in town for intergalactic hitchhikers and Australian surfer boys. We sit in the back, with Jimi Hendrix blasting out of the speakers, and watch a blond man in a muscle T-shirt feeling up his Afro-Amerasian date.

"She's working her mother's trade," says Kyle. "What's the world coming to?"

"Quadroons," I say, referring to the global *métissage*, the mixing of races and categories, that is the wave of the future and will end only when the human race is slightly paler than Coca-Cola.

Going Native

It is part of morality not to be at home in one's home.

Theodor Adorno

"It is absolutely impossible," Mr. Chinh declares after my night at the Saigon opera. "Phuong Thao cannot be Amerasian." He excuses himself from the Ministry reception room and returns a few minutes later carrying a stack of magazines. Flipping through the Vietnamese equivalent of *True Romance*, he shows me a dozen articles on Phuong Thao and her new movie, *Ngoi Sao Co Don (Lonely Star)*. Opening next week at the Communist Youth Theater, it promises to be the big hit of the season.

"In none of these articles does it say that Phuong Thao is Amerasian," he assures me.

Mr. Chinh has arranged for me to visit Giai Phong film studios for a private screening of *Xuong Rong Den (Black Cactus)*. This was the most successful Vietnamese film of 1992, and it actually *is* about Amerasians. Tran Thanh Hung, the French-speaking director of Giai Phong, meets us at the front door of the studio and apologizes that his only tape of the film is missing the last two minutes, which were accidentally erased. The film stars a popular Vietnamese actor named The Vy, who plays the role of a black Amerasian. Filmed on a forty-thousand-dollar budget, *Xuong Rong Den* ran for a week in Ho Chi Minh City's eight biggest theaters, where it drew a crowd of forty thousand people a day.

The movie is a tale of star-crossed lovers. Lai, an orphaned Amerasian, falls in love with Ma, a Cham girl whom he rescues from a group of Vietnamese thugs. Originally settled by Malay seafaring traders, the Indianized kingdom of Champa once stretched across what is now central Vietnam. The Chams, who began losing ground to the southward-marching Viets in the fourteenth century, are now marginalized, along with Vietnam's sixty other "minority peoples."

The pregnant Ma is disowned by her parents, but not before her mother tries to give her a forced herbal abortion. Lai, who has been living by stealing grain off passing freight trains, cuts loose from his band of *bui doi* buddies and tries to go straight. He borrows money from his former girlfriend (she demands sex in exchange), builds a house for his new wife, Ma, and plants a corn crop that fails. On the edge of starvation, he jumps the train to Saigon and starts hanging out in Amerasian Park. A rich market woman hires him as a laborer, lures him into her bed, and then files an application with the Orderly Departure Program, claiming to be his mother.

"When you get to America, you just send for your wife, and you'll all be rich," she tells Lai.

In the meantime, after giving birth to a son, Ma goes to work as a scrap iron picker on an old American Army base, where she is injured by an exploding land mine. A friend of Lai's carries news of his wife's troubles to Amerasian Park. Lai flees Saigon the day before his ODP interview and rushes home for a touching sickbed reunion with his wife—the last two minutes of which are left to my imagination.

Xuong Rong Den is a better film, but perhaps not as politically important as the first movie made in Vietnam about Amerasians. Called *Tinh Khong Bien Gioi* (*Love Without Borders*), it was the big hit of 1991. The film was written and directed by the late Huynh Ba Thanh, a former political cartoonist and vice mayor of Saigon, who later served as editor-in-chief of *Cong An* (*Police*) newspaper, the official organ of the security forces in Ho Chi Minh City. *Cong An* sells six hundred thousand copies a week and is the most widely read newspaper in South Vietnam. This is owing to the fact that in a police state there is no more reliable source of information than the police.

When I met him the year his film came out, Mr. Thanh, a plump, middle-aged man with an impressive wristwatch, arrived for our meeting at the Amerasian Transit Center in a chauffeur-driven car. He wore a white shirt with a gold decal on the breast pocket and chain-smoked 555-brand cigarettes throughout our discussion. *Love Without Borders*, his third feature film, was privately financed for thirty thousand dollars. His two earlier movies, one about "state security" and another about international prostitution, were produced by the government.

"It was a departure for the Vietnamese film industry and a big risk," Thanh said of *Love Without Borders*, which he claimed was the first Vietnamese movie depicting a cross-cultural love affair. "This has always been a difficult subject," he said. "Only recently has it become accepted if the story involves 'true love.' We are against this type of relationship when it is exploitation, but the trouble the hero goes through in this movie to prove his love shows that it is 'true.' "

Love Without Borders is the story of Snyder, an American vet who sails a small boat to China Beach in 1986. He is trying to find the Vietnamese girlfriend he left behind fifteen years earlier. Snyder is played by Dao Ba Son, a well-known Vietnamese actor who is half-French. After walking into his old barracks and digging up a lucky-charm necklace given to him by his girlfriend, Snyder is arrested by patrolling soldiers. "I am here on my own. I came back to look for my wife and child," he says.

In a series of flashbacks to romantic love scenes intercut with one-camera action shots, the movie shows Snyder meeting a Vietnamese girl, Ngoc, who works at Marble Mountain as a stone-cutter. She is bitten by a snake. He rescues her. "Americans are not animals. We are people, too," he says. She gets pregnant. He is wounded and discharged back to the States. Ngoc becomes a fishmonger, then a prostitute. The screen fills with lots of rain and weeping.

The soldiers who have captured Snyder are so moved by his story that they release him, and he sets out wandering through

Vietnam, looking for his wife and son. He finds the boy digging for gold in the mountains.

"Please forgive me," says Snyder at their reunion.

"Let's go look for mom," says the boy.

They travel to Ho Chi Minh City, where Ngoc has become a torch singer at the Rex Hotel. She sings "To Love You Is To Love You All My Life," before being reunited with her husband and son. The film ends with the family standing on the steps of a Philippine Airlines Boeing 747 waving goodbye to Vietnam. "The Vietnamese have helped me greatly and everyone has been wonderful to me," says Snyder, before he and his family fly off to America.

Amerasians made another major incursion into Vietnamese culture in 1991, this time pushing all the way to Hanoi. In a novel by Pham Thi Hoai, published in France as *La Messagère de Cristal* (*The Crystal Messenger*), one striking passage describes a "dancer-singer-professional lover" with "fifty-percent Texan blood" who arrives in "medieval" Hanoi and takes the city by storm.

"To have the money to amuse herself, and to amuse herself as long as she has money, this is her entire philosophy of life. Lovers follow one after another; money flows from her fingers. Today's pleasures are replaced by others, it hardly matters which, since they all pass so quickly. She never dreams of earning a living. Let others worry about that. She never thinks about anybody or anything for more than five minutes. In the noisy streets of Saigon, her foreign beauty would pass unnoticed. The city is swarming with these last vestiges of American soldiers. But in the flat silence of Hanoi, she was a *sensation*."

In Hoai's novel, the Texas Amerasian represents all the corrupting influences that have begun to work their way from south to north Vietnam. I am reminded of Phuong Thao, who, according to one of Mr. Chinh's fan magazines, is being readied for a concert tour in Hanoi. But the managing director of Giai Phong studios seconds Mr. Chinh's denials. "We have worked with her on many projects," he says, "and I can assure you, Phuong Thao is not Amerasian."

Mr. Chinh looks even more nervous than usual as our driver lays on the horn and cuts a swath through the midday crush of bicycles. Jumping out of the car at Tan Son Nhat airport, Chinh flashes his credentials and pushes me through the mob of people pressed against the airport gates. In the international arrivals lounge we join a handful of Vietnamese and UN officials awaiting a Dragon Air charter flight from Hong Kong with 144 passengers on board. These are would-be boat people who have languished for years in Hong Kong prison camps, before being lured back to Vietnam with fifty dollars in pocket money and a monthly payment of thirty dollars per person for a year.

Out of the Dragon Air flight file 126 grim-faced returnees, eighteen people having changed their minds and withdrawn at the last minute. The voluntary repatriates, or volreps as they are called, carry blue-and-white shopping bags with their names and numbers written on them. The returnees are herded into a corner of the lounge near the toilets and asked to surrender their UN passports. A woman throws up on the floor. A Chilean film crew works the crowd for closeups.

The Vietnamese, with black humor, have begun calling volreps "failed" Viet Kieu, or Viet Kieu hoi hop, which means "befuddled" Viet Kieu. The other acerbic name for them is Viet Kieu *dom*. *Dom*, pronounced "zom," is a Viet Kieu Hoi Hop Vietnamese word for "fake." Most of the goods for sale and much of everyday life in Vietnam are now described as *dom*.

"These people have the hangdog look of failures," says Mr. Chinh. "They are afraid of what will become of them. Their neighbors might resent what they tried to do." He also explains that this group of volreps comes from the Sek Kong camp, where a riot earlier in the year between north and south Vietnamese resulted in twenty-seven northerners being burned to death.

The volreps, fishermen from the central coast, all have stories resembling that of Dang Van Thanh and his wife, Pham Thi Kim Hoa. They are a young couple from Da Nang whose bodies have plumped out from the forced indolence of camp life in Hong Kong. In July 1991, too late to escape being labeled "economic migrants" instead of refugees, they and ninety-six other people sailed to Hong Kong on Thanh's father's twenty-meter boat. Four days later they found themselves detained in Sek Kong Area F, where the riot later broke out. "Life was not normal there" is all they will say about their stay in Hong Kong.

The couple show me a propaganda pamphlet produced by the advertising firm of Saatchi and Saatchi. It is full of stories about volreps who have been happily reintegrated into village life. I ask Thanh and Hoa what they plan to do with the money paid to them for coming back to Vietnam. "We will buy a bigger boat and expand our business," says Thanh.

Among the officials performing the international alchemy required to turn volreps back into Vietnamese citizens is Philippe Chau, regional director of the European Union's $130 million Vietnamese program. This program is the carrot being used to lure would-be refugees back to Vietnam. Chau is Eurasian. The son of a Vietnamese pharmacist and a French mother, he grew up in Marseille and Vietnam, until his parents left Asia for good after the Tet Offensive in 1968. Chau is a French-trained specialist in aquaculture. He thought he was coming back to Vietnam for a monthlong consultancy, until scandals in the EU program catapulted him into running it. An urbane young man in yellow socks and a sports shirt, Chau looks fresh off the tennis courts.

"Population movements are like hydrodynamics," he says. "The flow follows the path of least resistance. As things get worse in the camps and better in Vietnam, we'll see more people returning." Chau is launching credit schemes and job-training centers throughout Vietnam, nine in Ho Chi Minh City alone. "This program is designed to give people an escape from the half-life in the camps, which is really prison," he says.

Chau tells me he is the only Eurasian he knows who has come back to work in Vietnam, although a lot of Viet Kieu from the United States have returned to do business. I ask him to describe the difference between these two communities.

"The French got the Vietnamese elite: the doctors and educated people," he says. "The Americans got the soldiers and con artists."

Following an official transfer of documents from the United Nations to Vietnam, the repatriates are ordered to retrieve their luggage and line up for immigration officials. Vietnam is one of the few nations in the world that X-rays luggage coming *into* the country. In a parody of real Viet Kieu arriving from the West on scheduled flights, the Viet Kieu *dom* push a flotilla of luggage carts piled high with motorcycle tires, bolts of fabric, VCRs, camcorders, and other goods acquired during their days in camp. I stand behind an immigration officer and watch his X-ray machine while mountains of trade goods pass across the screen.

"What are you looking for?" I ask the policeman.

"Gold," he says.

The bags and boxes pass in front of him without stopping. There is no gold in them.

Pham Xuan An, a small man with bushy eyebrows, lives in an airy villa with two dogs and numerous birds in wicker cages. These include laughing thrushes, golden-throated leaf birds, magpies, and canaries, one of whom knows how to sing "The Bridge On the River Kwai." Another bird has been taught to wolf-whistle at girls. "We have a Vietnamese saying," says An. "Birds are active. Dogs are loyal. Fish teach you to keep your mouth shut. . . . My fish died."

An is the former chief Vietnamese correspondent for *Time* magazine. While ably filling this post, he had a second career as regional commander for the Communists' National Liberation Front. "I had to make my living somehow," he says with a smile on his face. "I wanted to be a medical doctor. Instead I had to be a fighter."

An joined the Communist party during the Japanese occupation of Vietnam and then fought against the French. During the American war, he specialized in providing the Vietcong with intelligence on economic and political matters, while simultaneously analyzing the war for *Time*. After 1975, when the Vietcong lost control of the south to their northern compatriots, he spent a year in a prison camp outside Hanoi. An is barefoot, dressed simply in a blue shirt and white trousers, as we sit drinking tea in his book-lined living room. Overflowing with stacks of paper and old magazines, the room fills with smoke as the afternoon wears on. "I burn incense to calm my mind," he says.

The first subject we broach is the difference between Vietnamese Eurasians and Amerasians. "The French intermarried. They went native and took care of their offspring like the Americans never did," he says. "The Eurasians were of great social utility to the French, as soldiers and administrators. This is why they suffered reprisals after the French defeat at Dien Bien Phu in 1954, and it helps explain why Amerasians, although in a very different position, suffered similar consequences after 1975."

The French in Indochina, the Dutch in Indonesia, the Portuguese in Goa and Macao, and even the British when they first arrived in India encouraged intermarriage with the natives and used their offspring as allies in the colonial cause. Dutch support for *métissage* was so fervent that by 1940 eight to nine million Indonesians were of mixed blood. The French were no less diligent. Taking a *vo le*, or second wife, was standard practice. But the French also displayed a certain ambivalence toward their *métis*.

By 1900, Eurasians formed a recognizable subclass of petty criminals and prostitutes in Saigon, and soon a spate of articles was appearing in the French press about Indochina's "Eurasian problem." Mixed-blood Vietnamese were suspected of being "irreconcilable enemies" of French colonialism. Seeking revenge for being abandoned by their fathers, they easily became "agents of disorder and revolutionary leaders."

The history of all colonial nations shows that it is above all from the half-breeds that one recruits the malcontents and rabble-rousers who give the most trouble to the local authorities, said a 1929 government report on Eurasians. *The* métis *is all the more dangerous for having a foot in each camp and for possessing natural qualities of intelligence and flexibility that he can be tempted to put to bad use.*

Most supposed authorities on the subject declared Eurasians genetically defective. They were capable of inheriting the vices but not the virtues of their parents' mixed genes—a complaint one still hears today about Amerasians. *Because of their genetic irregularity, the* métis *are incapable of understanding ideas such as family, country, honor, work, frugality, regularity, and foresight, ideas that constitute the foundations of the normal social order*, wrote Dr. Barillon in the *Revue de Psychologie Appliquée* (1924–1926). "Missing the superior faculties of judgment and social control, the *métis* is the plaything of his passions and the tool of his appetites. In the midst of social crises, it is the *métis* who gives the signal to revolt and who throws himself headlong into the worst manifestations of violence and anarchy."

To head off a disaster of its own making, France decided to legitimate unrecognized Eurasians. The government also decided to elevate them high enough in the colonial hierarchy to give Eurasians a stake in preserving the status quo. "We must respect the blood of France," wrote one colonial administrator. "Be it no more than a drop that flows in all the veins in which it runs, this sole drop should suffice to ennoble all the rest." A legal decree in 1928 stated that any child born of a French father, even if not legally claimed by this father, was "presumed to be of the French race." French nationality—or *race*, since the two were now confounded—could be decided by a doctor's certificate, the testimony of two witnesses, or visual inspection by a French official.

With French nationality came a rise in social status for Eurasians. Subaltern posts in the colonial bureaucracy were reserved for them. They sorted the mail, ran the trains, and manned the police force. But the position of many Eurasians in Vietnam remained precarious. As R. Bonniot wrote in *L'enfance métisse malheureuse*, published in 1940, "How is it that so many mixed-blood children are living on the street, without education, training, or a job? Having allowed us to become French citizens has solved nothing."

The status of Eurasians really only improved after the Second World War, when France, trying to reestablish its Asian empire, needed all the help it could get. In its last official census, in 1946, French Indochina counted no more than forty-five thousand "Europeans" in Vietnam, Laos, and Cambodia. One-fifth of this number was Eurasian. But the French presence increased in 1947 with the arrival of the Expeditionary Corps—and so, too, did the number of Eurasians. By the end of the First Indochina War in 1954, between twenty and thirty thousand Eurasians were living in Vietnam.

Their position in the French bureaucracy earned *métis* the special hatred of their compatriots. In the last months of 1954 and throughout 1955 Ngo Dinh Diem launched a pogrom against Eurasians. Those too highly placed to be killed outright were told to opt for Vietnamese citizenship or lose their jobs. Only a handful of the seven thousand Eurasians remaining in Vietnam took him up on the offer. Diem was thereby able to replace many functionaries with his own Catholic clientele.

Using alcohol taxes and proceeds from off-track betting, the French in 1939 had established the Fédération des Oeuvres de l'Enfance Française d'Indochine, the Federation for French Children in Indochina, which was charged with caring for Eurasians, securing their education, and ultimately evacuating them to

France. Over the course of its active existence, the Fédération financed the education of twenty thousand Eurasians. Among these were three thousand orphans dispersed to boarding schools throughout France. Between thirty and forty thousand Eurasians and their family members were evacuated to France in the 1950s. More were airlifted out of Vietnam in 1975, and again in the late 1970s and early 1980s. These latter evacuations, employing the only Western airline still flying into Vietnam, came to be known as the Air France Program.

In the summer of 1992 I drove into the rolling French countryside southeast of Paris to visit Noyant, one of the "reception centers" for Eurasians "repatriated" to France in the 1950s. Noyant lies in France *profonde*, the deep countryside of peasant farms and village curates that has remained relatively unchanged since the French Revolution. Part of Noyant was an abandoned coal-mining town before the first contingent of Eurasians arrived at midnight on October 28, 1955. It was an exceptionally cold winter. The old miners' houses, with pit latrines and water pumps in the yard, had no heat. "We thought we were going to the Devil," said one of the three thousand Eurasians resettled there. Most of them had never seen their "native" country. Included among the repatriates were the children of Senegalese soldiers demobilized in Indochina, Pondicherrians from the former French colonies in India, Franco-Khmers, and other hyphenated products of French colonialism.

"Almost all the Vietnamese women here are old taxi girls and prostitutes from Saigon," reported one Noyant resident. "Already having mixed-blood offspring, they wanted to come to France for their children's sake. So they purchased relationships to French-citizen-Eurasians for a thousand piasters."

To avoid the envy of their neighbors, the repatriated Eurasians were forbidden all outward signs of wealth. This included automobiles, washing machines, refrigerators, and TV antennas.

So they watched TV without antennas. They were given enough coal and food to see them through the winter, as well as free housing, medical care, and social security. They were provided with a yearly Christmas tree, but the New Year's celebration, Tet, was forbidden.

Noyant today is a well-scrubbed little village with TV antennas sprouting from the roofs and a new Buddhist temple. Many of the old row houses have been turned into summer homes for Eurasians working in Paris. I was invited to attend a ceremony at the·temple, the one hundred–day memorial service and commemorative feast for a deceased Eurasian. Across from me at the meal were a monk in saffron robes and a nun in gray, neither of whom spoke French. But next to me sat a young Eurasienne, a graduate student in chemistry at Montpellier, who was back in town to visit her grandmother. Her mediation allowed me to chat with the *bonze* and nun, as we worked our way through a feast of potato and carrot *beignets*, fried tofu, bean sprouts, fish soup, sesame balls, and almond-milk pastry.

After lunch I struck up a conversation with a retired army officer, a Eurasian, who invited me to pick plums off the trees in his front yard. As we strolled the streets of Noyant, he pointed to the old coal miners' houses, with their steeply pitched roofs and tiny dormer windows. "You can see how people over the years have changed the houses," he said. "They've raised the roof line, enlarged the windows, put up brick facades. Here's someone who bought the house next door and knocked down the common wall." He gestured toward the yard of some Parisians who had fallen behind in mowing their grass. "Noyant is not as lively as it used to be," he said. "We have more money now, but not as much fun."

In the languor of a Saigon afternoon, Pham Xuan An, my *Time* magazine mole, tells me what he remembers about the privileged position of Eurasians in colonial Vietnam. "When I was growing up, only the Eurasian children were allowed to have shotguns or

BB guns for shooting birds. They also had the right to go to French schools."

Then the tables turned and Eurasians were lumped with the losing French. "Edward Lansdale and the Americans were behind Diem's anti-French demonstrations," he says. "Extremists in this campaign killed the Eurasian children of prostitutes in Vung Tau and elsewhere in the country. This was part of the psychological warfare Lansdale introduced into Vietnam."

An walks over to the bookshelves that line the walls of his living room. The books are dusty, their pages disappearing under leprous spots of mold. He pulls down a volume called *Jungle Mission*, by René Riesen, and flips to a photo of Monsieur Riesen standing beside his bare-breasted Montagnard wife.

"The Vietnamese, unlike the French, are racist," says An. "No Vietnamese would marry a Montagnard, or even a Laotian or a Cambodian. But the French had many amorous relations with the hill tribes." When I later have the chance to read Riesen's book, I discover that Ilouhe the Montagnard is one of his *two* native wives, and he also has a slave girl "in heat." At least one Franco-Montagnard *métis* has entered the story when Monsieur Riesen's narrative breaks off with the "regrettable events" of 1954.

While An sips his green tea and alternately pets his German shepherd and his chihuahua, I broach another sensitive subject. A lot of American soldiers in Vietnam jumped the fence. More than a million incidents of GIs absent without leave were recorded during the war. By the time one of the least disciplined military forces on earth had skedaddled out of Vietnam, hundreds, if not thousands, of former soldiers had acquired Asian wives and gone native. What became of these rogue GIs? What became of their Amerasian children?

"The Vietnamese women married to these deserters were all working for the NLF," says An. "The GIs existed thanks to their Vietnamese wives, and we kept a very close eye on them." He mentions a large community of deserters living on the road to

Bien Hoa. "They survived by buying ice cream and cigarettes in the PX, which their wives then sold on the black market."

An maintains that only a few hundred deserters remained in Vietnam after 1975, all of them in Saigon. "The animosity of people in the countryside was too high for Americans to continue living there. The Americans were not Tarzan. They couldn't survive by themselves in the jungle."

"So what happened to them?" I ask.

"They were taken to the Soviet Union or Cuba and made into new people with plastic surgery," he says.

An's answer is not entirely convincing. Throughout their bellicose history, the Vietnamese have been known to hold prisoners of war for decades. Captives from the French war were still being released in the late 1960s, and An himself tells me about an aide to commanding General Tassigny who escaped only in the 1980s. Robert Garwood, the sole American prisoner of war to emerge from Vietnam after 1975, reported that Frenchmen were still living in the Vietnamese highlands.

"The Vietnamese are paranoid," says An. "We need a good psychiatrist, or Dale Carnegie. Somebody has to help us forget the war and learn to make friends again in the world." As for his own postwar rehabilitation, "I talk to my dogs and my birds, and this is my freedom," he says.

Soon after nightfall, Viet drives me over the bridge to Binh Thanh and drops me at Kyle Hörst's house. Kyle's wife, Khanh, who has the round face and high cheekbones of a northerner, is in the middle of telling him that "the local police chief stopped by the house this afternoon and asked a lot of questions. Then he invited you out to eat dog meat."

"That's all right," says Kyle. "I don't mind eating dog meat."

"You don't understand," she says. "It will be a big feast. You'll have to pay for it, and then every week you'll have to feed the police their dog meat."

"Now I understand," he says. "This is a shakedown. It sounds like something I should mention to my friends in the Ministry of Interior."

Kyle is wearing a T-shirt that says,

> Ronald Wilson Reagan
> Official Anagram
> Insane Anglo Warlord

He is surrounded by a jumble of unopened packing boxes and teak furniture. This newly rented house, with a couple of bedrooms upstairs and a large room downstairs, comes complete with a landlady-spy who lives behind a chicken-wire mesh partition in the kitchen.

I ask Khanh—a boat refugee who fled by sea in 1981—how she feels about being back in Vietnam.

"People in the market call me a prostitute," she says. "Even after one hundred years of living with the French, twenty years with the Americans, and ten years with the Russians, it is still a shameful thing for a Vietnamese to go with a foreigner."

"The Vietnamese call themselves *chinh goc*," says Kyle. *Chinh* means 'true.' *Goc* means 'origin.' Put them together and you have the 'true race.' A Vietnamese betrays her *goc* when she marries an American. Basically, we're polluting God's chosen people with monkey genes."

Khanh has to go visit the children, who, Vietnamese fashion, have been sent to live with relatives. Kyle and I walk through the steamy night to a nearby restaurant. We take a table on the second floor and open the doors onto the veranda, which holds a pine tree decorated with blinking Christmas lights. We order beef seven-ways. We are the only customers. The waitress, a friend of Kyle's, comes to sit at our table. She has a problem. An American veteran has proposed to marry her. He is forty. She is twenty. What bothers her is not the age difference, but another question. "Should a good Vietnamese girl marry an American?"

Kyle advises more reflection on the subject.

Kyle first got involved with Asia in 1981, when he took a break from managing rock-and-roll bands in Los Angeles to teach English at a Laotian refugee camp in Thailand. "The people in this camp had a more meaningful existence than I did," he says. "Even as refugees, they were whole human beings. They had a keen sense of family and the natural environment. Their lives had a vibrancy we don't have in the industrialized West."

Hörst comes from a family of Old Order Mennonites in Lancaster, Pennsylvania—people who don't wear buttons, look in mirrors, or perform other diabolical acts. His father had broken away from the community to become an electrical engineer, and Kyle, after getting a degree in geology from Penn State, was supposed to follow in his father's scientific footsteps. But first came the L.A. music scene, and then in 1981, at the age of twenty-three, he went to work for the U.S. Catholic Conference running a refugee agency in the Midwest.

"It was me and a couple of half-time interpreters resettling three hundred people a year, mainly North Vietnamese Army regulars and government cadre getting out through Hong Kong. I picked them up at the airport, got them TB shots, apartments, jobs. I was their godfather. I viewed these people as innocent victims of Communism," he says. "Only later did I realize they were economic migrants more savvy about the world than I was."

He was not only working with refugees, but also beginning to live like one. He underwent a religious conversion after reading the *Little Flowers of St. Francis* and the works of the French-Jew-turned-Catholic-radical Simone Weil. Kyle converted to Catholicism. He named his first child Simone.

In 1984 he headed back to Southeast Asia as an interviewer for the Orderly Departure Program. He was one of the first Americans allowed to live in postwar Saigon. "It was like Casablanca," he says, "a city full of intrigue, rumor, scandal. It was pitch black at night save for little oil lamps placed along the roads. The only foreigners in town were five Americans, a few Frenchmen, and a handful of Russians."

He worked fourteen hours a day, six days a week, interviewing ODP cases, including hundreds of Amerasians. "We busted our butts, and then cases would sit on a desk in Bangkok for six months. The operation was grossly understaffed." He also realized that ODP was "a poor counterfeit to diplomatic relations. It was a weapon the Americans and Vietnamese were using to continue the war.

"It was criminal and immoral to have the policy guys in Washington playing with Amerasians as political pawns," he says. "They had no conscience. If they had wanted, they could have had a deal five years earlier. We could have got these kids out when they were twelve, instead of twenty. I came to the conclusion that the State Department people making this policy were depraved."

When Kyle quit in October 1985, ODP had twenty-seven thousand interviewed cases stacked up in Bangkok. On January 2, 1986 the Vietnamese expelled all ODP interviewers from the country and closed down the program, claiming bad faith on the part of the Americans. It would be nearly two years before interviewers returned to Saigon.

"No matter how hard you work in the field, there's always some jerk in Washington who is calling the shots," Kyle says. "So I thought I'd go be the jerk in Washington."

Working as a consultant to the U.S. Catholic Conference, he spent six months writing a white paper on the Orderly Departure Program. The State Department asked USCC to kill the document, but they published it. When Congressman Robert Mrazek later drafted the Amerasian Homecoming Act, he called Kyle's white paper his "bible."

Kyle had another reason for returning to Washington. He

was in love. Before going to Vietnam, he had moved into a refugee ghetto in Falls Church, Virginia, complete with cockroaches and rats. Here at the neighborhood church he had met Khanh. "I was already impressed by the beauty of the Vietnamese," he says. "Only later did I discover how tough they could be." He flew back twice from Vietnam to visit Khanh, spending two days on the airplane for a week in Washington. They had to wait for Khanh's mother to get out of Vietnam in 1986 before they could marry the following year and start a family that now includes four Amerasians.

"It sounds like the old days," says Kyle, when I tell him the story of Huynh Thi Huong and her family, who are being expelled from the Amerasian Transit Center after failing their interview with Mr. Ten Percent. "The interview team wants people's life stories papered over. They think they're examining kids from Boston who summered on the Cape. But unless you spend two hours asking arcane questions, you can't get an Amerasian's life story to hang together. That's why Congress mandated that Amerasians be accepted on appearance alone."

I ask him if he can intercede. "I've already been scolded by ODP for describing an Amerasian's appearance as 'convincing,' " he says. "The State Department doesn't like that kind of language coming from the UN. But let me think about it."

He goes on to explain that the recent flood of refugees out of Vietnam is not a radical break in the country's history. It is a *fulfillment* of this history. Nor is this mass migration an accident. It is the calculated outcome of government policy. Vietnam rids itself of malcontents and a fifth column that might side with China during one of their all-too-frequent wars. At the same time, Vietnam populates the world with loyal settlers dedicated to sending remittances back home to their families. Throughout its four thousand years of recorded history, the Viet tribe of the Red River Valley has been engaged in the *nam tien*, the southward march. They inched down the Annamese Cordillera, conquering Chams and Khmers on the way, until they reached the Gulf of Thailand and ran out of room. "That's when they started colonizing Orange County and Paris's 13th *arrondissement*," he says. "They ate Champa. They ate Funan. They ate Lower Cambodia, and now they're eating Silicon Valley."

To position two million refugees overseas, Vietnam played every angle it could find, and the Amerasian angle was one of the best. The government pleaded dumb to accusations of political repression. Nowhere in the country's laws was it written that Amerasians should be thrown out of school and spat upon. These excesses were due to popular sentiment. According to the Vietnamese—and the record supports them on this charge—they wanted Amerasians out of the country long before the United States agreed to accept them.

The United States, in turn, tried to milk all the propaganda it could out of the suffering Amerasians. They were further proof of Vietnamese villainy. Once again, these dirty fighters were attacking women and children. While the Vietnamese called for negotiations—and more tickets to the West—the Americans dreamed of Rambo busting these kids out of Saigon. "What the Vietnamese pulled off with the Amerasians is only slightly less brilliant than outsmarting Henry Kissinger at the Paris Peace Conference." says Kyle. "These guys are good."

The electricity cuts out. The night turns deathly quiet. Then comes the rain, in driving sheets of water that turn the street below us into a river full of pushcarts and cyclos. It is April 13th. The monsoons have arrived. The breeze is sweet after the dog days of winter. Everything turns moist and soft. We finish our meal by candlelight and stare over the veranda at bolts of lightning flashing across the sky. On the walk home, we get blessedly drenched to the bone.

Tay Thi

Exile given to me I have taken as honor.

Dante

"I have a big surprise for you," says Mr. Chinh, greeting me on the steps of the Ministry of Foreign Affairs. "Phuong Thao is coming to see you in half an hour."

Chinh and I repair to the reception room, which has been laid with a particularly nice spread of tea, coffee, oranges, and other tropical fruit. Every few minutes he runs outside to see if Phuong Thao has arrived. Eventually, I join him on the front steps, where we stare across the street at a group of Amerasians sitting on the grass.

A motorcycle, driven by a handsome young man with a Clark Gable mustache, pulls through the gates. Seated behind the man, with her arms wrapped around his waist, is a young woman in a white miniskirt. Mr. Chinh bows to Phuong Thao and her husband, Le Tuan Anh, who is also a well-known actor, and ushers them into the building. Phuong Thao has an almond-shaped face surrounded by a fringe of brown hair. She wears white pumps with leopard-skin spike heels, a red silk blouse, a gold watch, and pink lipstick. Obviously nervous about being summoned to the Ministry of Foreign Affairs, she sits with her black purse clutched between her legs. After some pleasantries, tea, coffee, peeled fruit, and more pleasantries, I ask Phuong Thao about her parents. Mr. Chinh refuses to translate my question. He tells me it would be rude so early in the conversation to mention this subject. So I lean back in my chair and let him lead us through a two-hour examination of Phuong Thao's "artistic soul" and her "struggles as an artist to fulfill herself."

"I play the part of a girl who through talent escapes her humble beginnings," she says of her role in *Ngoi Sao Co Don* (*Lonely Star*), which is scheduled to open next week and promises to be Vietnam's hit movie of the year. The girl is a singer in the countryside. She falls in love with a boy (the role is played by Phuong Thao's husband) who is drafted into the army to fight in Cambodia. "The girl lives around bad people, like her stepfather and the vice director of her provincial artistic group, who try to abuse her."

Her boyfriend loses his legs in the war. The girl doesn't know it, but her father, a rich man who fled the country in 1975, is still alive. She falls in love with the spy her father sends to find her and eventually becomes a big star in Ho Chi Minh City. "When she learns the spy does not love her for love's own merits, and the true story of her father, she dies of the psychological shock," says Phuong Thao.

Except for the Cambodian land mines and Viet Kieu boyfriend, I could be listening to one of Vietnam's sentimental tales from a thousand years ago. The meeting is nearly over when Mr. Chinh thinks it appropriate to pose the delicate question of Phuong Thao's family background. She tells us she was born in 1968 in Sadec, the Mekong Delta region south of Saigon where Ho Chi Minh's father died. Not being able to contain myself any longer, I ask her if she is Amerasian.

"Yes, I am *lai My*, half-American," she says, nervously twirling the straps of her purse. "I know nothing about my father, except that he was in the U.S. Army. My mother kept this information secret. She came from a family of officials who worked for the government. She herself was a state worker. Then after 1975 the family situation changed."

"Do people know you are Amerasian?"

"Yes," she says. "Children in Sadec taunted me in the streets and called me *con lai*. Still, I finished high school, and now these people who used to call me names respect me. A magazine article about me said I 'carried two strains of blood in my veins,' but this is the only public mention of my being Amerasian."

I ask if she is thinking of moving to America. "My case is different from other Amerasians," she says. "My husband and I are developing our careers. I am like any other Vietnamese girl dreaming of becoming a star through hard work and talent."

We are shaking hands goodbye when Phuong Thao surprises me. "Will you help me find my father?" she asks. "There is a wound in the heart of my mother that I want to help her heal. We argued about this," she admits. "My mother wanted to go to America to find her husband. For my part, I preferred to lead my life in Vietnam. She finally came to respect my wishes. But if my father is still alive, perhaps we should rethink our possibilities. Even if he is dead, I would someday like to see my father's land."

Outside the gates of the Ministry, Viet rushes over to tell me he has found Tay Thi, the Amerasian silk merchant. We buzz toward Cholon on his motorcycle. The midday traffic is a wild dance of particles in Brownian motion. The confusion is enhanced by street-side vendors hawking their wares: glasses of sugarcane juice filled from hand-cranked presses, soup stirred over charcoal braziers, live chickens pulled from under bell-shaped wicker cages, and huge piles of coconuts and durians—green, spiky fruits that look like sea urchins crossed with hand grenades.

The clouds are piling up for the rains that every afternoon ply across the sky in glorious bursts of thunder and lightning. We cycle past the Arc-en-Ciel, the big hotel in Cholon, and stop at a roadside café for bowls of oxtail soup. The day is so hot, I am melting into my chair. Fortunately, this is a real chair, not the usual three-legged stool. I stare stupidly at the traffic rolling by as Viet reads a copy of *Ngoi Sao Co Don*, the novel from which Phuong Thao's movie was adapted.

"There is one thing I don't understand about her version of the story," I say. "Is the singer's father Vietnamese or American?"

"He is Vietnamese," says Viet. "But he went to America in 1975, so maybe he's not a real Vietnamese."

After lunch we drive through Cholon's jumble of Buddhist temples and street stalls, before coming to the city's best address for commerce, the great hall of the new two-story An Dong market. Getting nowhere by himself, Viet had enlisted his wife to help search for Tay Thi, and today he has thoughtfully arranged for my assistant from Amerasian Park, Miss Hoa, to join us. Viet had located Tay Thi's store several days ago, but it never seemed to be open, and no one in the market would tell him where she lived. Viet's wife, for some reason, had more success.

We ride the escalator upstairs to the silk merchants, who are located between the tailors and hat makers. Here we find a stall with the name Tay Thi written over it. Stocked to the rafters with bolts of American and Chinese cloth, it is the biggest fabric store in the market. Standing inside is a beautiful young woman in a blue and gray shot-silk dress. Her long brown hair is pulled to the side of her head in a ponytail. She is statuesque, with sweeping eyebrows, large brown eyes, and a high, straight nose. I introduce myself to Tay Thi, who gives me an unflinching look and suggests we go to her house to talk.

Back on our motorcycles, we turn off the main thoroughfare into a maze of alleyways so narrow that one can almost reach out and touch the houses on either side. Even in this dense quarter the streets are filled with women selling produce from panniers draped over their shoulders and men pushing carts full of fruit and vegetables. I peer through open doors at family shrines covered with joss sticks and women sewing dresses. We pass children rolling a hoop down the street, turn left, right, and left again before dismounting in front of Tay Thi's two-story wooden house. She rolls her motorcycle inside and offers Miss Hoa and me glasses of seaweed juice.

Along with the Honda motorcycle, which is parked next to

a Vespa scooter, the ground floor holds a Sony stereo, television, and mahogany sideboard where rows of empty Martell cognac boxes prop up the family altar. The electricity and ceiling fan die with the afternoon storm. Tay Thi lights an oil lamp and sits cross-legged on a grass mat. Her fingernails are polished bright red. Among the rings and bracelets on her hands is a gold wedding band. In a soft voice she begins telling her story.

She was born in 1967 in Vinh Long, a provincial capital in the Mekong Delta. Her mother was a market seller and bar girl who worked her way up to a secretarial job with the Army.

"When my mother first met my father she did not love him. He was a security officer in the Army. She got pregnant the month he left Vietnam. She hid from her family the fact she was pregnant. She was ashamed. When I was born she wanted to give me to an orphanage, but then she changed her mind. Her sister worked in the PX. Together they raised me. My mother wrote to my father telling him about me, and he wrote back saying he didn't believe I was his child. He accused her of sleeping with other men. My mother got angry and never wrote to him again."

What does she know about her father? His name is Ray Williams. He has a wife and three children in the United States. "Here are their pictures," she says, showing me an album of Kodak snapshots from the sixties. The book is full of middle-American scenes posed in front of houses newly built in subdivisions. The Williams kids in short-sleeved white shirts and neckties stand with Dad next to their Ford Fairlane station wagon. Here are shots of men in sweater vests and women wearing gull wing eyeglasses, shots of the kids in their pajamas hanging up their Christmas stockings, shots of Ray's grandparents, stern midwestern stock. The one person absent from these photos is the wife—"soon to be divorced," said Williams, until he mailed a final letter to Vietnam announcing their reconciliation.

Williams himself is a middle-aged man with a crew cut. Like his kids, he wears creased trousers and short-sleeved white shirts with neckties. He looks the same in America and Vietnam, with two exceptions. In Vietnam, he adds a pair of sunglasses and a beautiful long-haired mistress. The girl sitting in front of me has the same square-jawed face as her father, but she is by far the most handsome of Williams's four children.

After 1975, the eight-year-old Tay Thi and her mother sold cigarettes from a street-side stall in front of their house in Vinh Long. "I was the only Amerasian in my school," she says. "They cursed me, even my teachers, and kids fought me in the street. Except when I was walking back and forth to school, I didn't dare go outside my house. I hated my father whenever I thought of him. He ruined my mother's life. She never remarried. She thought only about him, but he never thought about her."

Tay Thi finished high school in 1986. She had good grades and dreamed of becoming a doctor, but was too poor to pay for medical school. That year someone approached her mother about escaping from Vietnam by boat. "I thought it was too dangerous," she says. "My mother scolded me and struck me with a chair. She beat me until I bled. I had saved a little money from selling cigarettes. I bought a bus ticket and ran away to Saigon.

"When I reached the city, I went to a friend's house, where I stayed for ten days. Then my money ran out. A neighbor approached me and said she could help me get money. She sold me to a Chinaman for $250. She gave me twenty dollars and kept the rest. It brings luck to a Chinaman when they sleep with a virgin. Before they negotiate a business deal they try to buy a girl. Her blood will bring them much money. The Chinaman locked me in a hotel room for three days, until I was able to break out and run away."

We listen to the rain falling in the street outside. Tay Thi pours me another glass of juice and continues her story. "I became a taxi girl at the Queen Bee. I worked there for a year. I usually went with foreigners. After a fire closed the Queen Bee, I moved to the Arc-en-Ciel. I had been there four months when I saved enough money to buy this house. It cost six thousand dollars. A year later I had saved enough money to buy my silk store in the market. It cost twenty thousand dollars.

"I had no pimp," she says. "I took care of myself. I paid all the bribes that had to be paid to the owners and doormen and fixers at the clubs. I am not married. I have no boyfriend. I would like to have a child, a daughter, but I am afraid of men. There are many men who would like to marry me, but I have refused them all. I think about what my father did to my mother, and I tell myself I will never marry.

"My mother is ashamed of me. Every time I see her, she reminds me of my father and our history and scolds me. I don't want her to live with me, so I send her money in the countryside. We registered with ODP. We passed the interview and were going to go to America. But then I thought, 'My father is not responsible for me.' I got mad and changed my mind. I hid from my mother. She searched for me all over the city, but couldn't find me. I still get letters from ODP asking, 'Why haven't you picked up your ticket?' I tear up the letters, because whenever my mother finds them, they provoke a fight.

"Everywhere in the world is the same," she says, describing why she decided to stay in Vietnam. "I would have to do the same work in the United States. People tell me Amerasians are despised in America. I don't like the Vietnamese authorities or this country's politics, but the land is beautiful and this is my home. I worship Buddha. I pray at my family altar. Some days I dream of becoming an actress. I will play passionate roles, because my life is so sad. Other days I dream of buying a house in the countryside and retiring to a quiet life."

After hesitating, Tay Thi shows me a second photo album. It documents a trip she and a Vietnamese boyfriend took around the highlands near Dalat. They are feeding deer in the forests, rowing on the lake, posing in front of a Montagnard ox cart. They look like newlyweds on a honeymoon. Maybe the young man paid for her time. Maybe he only paid for her trip. But he is gone from her life, and the honeymoon album is a bad joke—like the photos of Tay Thi's mother in Williams's embrace.

"In Vinh Long, when I was a student, I had a boyfriend whom I loved very much," she says. "His family despised me because I was a poor Amerasian. I never heard from him again after I came to Saigon. People tell me he remains unmarried and that he still thinks of me. But I don't love him anymore. He was too cowardly to disobey his family and marry me. Vietnamese men are weak and ignoble. They are not worthy of me."

I ask why she chose to call her silk store Tay Thi. She tells me this is the name of one of the many heroines in Vietnamese literature who loses her virginity to a Chinese man. "Tay Thi was a poor Vietnamese girl caught in the middle of a war," she says. "The Vietnamese were forced to send their one most beautiful woman to China. They wanted her to be a spy and kill the Chinese king, but instead she fell in love with him. He was killed in battle by the Vietnamese general Pham Lai, who was Tay Thi's former boyfriend.

"Pham Lai asked her to go with him, but she refused. She had lost her honor. Instead, she asked Pham Lai to grant her one wish, that she be allowed to go live alone in the forest.

"My life is sad, like Tay Thi's. I have spent my soul to get these possessions," she says, gesturing around the room at the television set and motorcycles. "I can never marry, because any man who knew my history would mistreat me. In my shame, I often cry myself to sleep at night."

I am telling Kyle Hörst about the day's remarkable encounters, first Phuong Thao and then Tay Thi, when Viet interrupts. "I know the history of Tay Thi," he says. "That's one of the operas I used to sing. I was the Chinese king. But the story doesn't end the way she tells it."

Viet was apprenticed as a *cai luong* opera singer at the age of nine. He used to travel Vietnam with the Minh To troupe, the best-known opera company in Saigon. "I played the king and the goat," he says. "I was the cruelest person and the most promiscuous." He sang for twenty years until his wife made him quit. "We starved in the rainy season, when there were no performances. Then in the dry season, when we toured the provinces, we were treated like princes." He mimes how women used to rest their heads in his lap and gaze up at his face. "My wife got jealous. She made me choose between my family and opera."

Kyle and I ask him to sing the role of the Chinese king in *Tay Thi*, the part he used to perform. My noble cyclo driver, dressed in flip-flops and a tattered red shirt, stands to deliver the king's final aria. His voice is packed with tritones and half-tones foreign to Western music. At once nasal and sweet, it quavers in strange keys. The Chinese king is refusing to be saved by Tay Thi, who has asked the Vietnamese general to spare her lover. Instead, the king is carving out his guts in an act of noble disembowelment. He glowers at the Vietnamese general. He gazes fondly on his lover. He staggers to the floor. He dies.

"You never should have retired," says Kyle. "You're not the first Vietnamese man whose career was ruined by a jealous wife, but she made a mistake."

"What happens to Tay Thi?" I ask.

"After winning the war, the Vietnamese general is in danger of being killed by the Vietnamese king," says Viet. "We have a saying, 'You no longer need your bow after the bird has been killed.' He and Tay Thi decide to run away together. They get in a boat and sail around the world."

The story of Tay Thi, like most Vietnamese narratives, comes in different versions. Viet thinks of Tay Thi as a precursor to the boat people. My Amerasian friend imagines her going off to live alone in the forest. I later read another account in which Tay Thi moves back home to die a stranger in her own land. All three versions agree, though, that her life is tragic.

.   .   .

Mr. Chinh informs me that the most important cultural event in postwar Vietnam is about to take place. The French filmmaker Jean-Jacques Annaud is coming to town to show his new movie, *The Lover*, which was shot on location in Vietnam. Realizing that his Vietnamese colleagues would never see the film intact once the censors got to it, Annaud is hand-delivering a copy for a private screening at the Rex Theater. *L'Amant* is Marguerite Duras's autobiographical story of a love affair in colonial Saigon between a European teenager and a wealthy Chinese man twice her age. After thirty years of war and fifteen years of socialist realism, Vietnam is about to get bedroom scenes reintroduced into its culture.

The Rex is packed for the three o'clock showing. Annaud says a few words of thanks to the Vietnamese crew who helped him make the country's first big-budget Western film. Then two translators take the stage, a man and a woman, to do simultaneous Vietnamese voice-overs on top of the narrative. Following the movie there is a reception at the French consulate, where someone has developed the mistaken idea that an American writer has come to Saigon to cover the opening of *The Lover*. So on arriving at the consulate, I am rushed into the library for a private interview with Annaud.

"You have to remember that for the French the Orient is 'feminine,' sensual, the perfect place to make a film about sexual awakening," he says. Annaud tells me all the non-Asian extras in the movie were played by Russian oil rig workers bussed in from Vung Tau. "They were the only Europeans willing to work for ten dollars a day. But they were perfect. They look exactly like French colonialists in the 1920s."

I ask Annaud about the sudden spate of French movies featuring Vietnam, three of them coming out almost simultaneously: *Dien Bien Phu*, *Indochine*, and *The Lover*. "France, like America, has never come to terms with the war it lost in Vietnam," he says. "We are dealing with the trauma still unspoken."

I tell Annaud about my ambivalent feelings toward his film.

It is a love story, a brilliant vignette about the sexual awakening of one of France's most celebrated authors. But it is also the story of a mercenary mother who concurs in her daughter's prostituting herself to a Chinese man. She swaps her daughter's virtue for a large diamond ring, which allows this family of failed colonialists to retreat back to France.

"You're right," says Annaud, waving his hands and getting visibly excited. "This is why the Vietnamese helped me so much to make this movie. This is exactly how they saw the French colonialists—as mercenaries. And the noble man in this film is Asian!"

The wife of the French cultural attaché tells me later that she and her husband thought the film was "almost pornographic. We didn't find the movie's depiction of colonial life at all convincing." The Vietnamese at the reception, on the other hand, all agree that the film is "a very touching love story, very true to life."

Sick of the heat and dust in Saigon, Kyle, Khanh, their daughter Simone, and I rent a car and head to the coast. Our destination is Long Hai, a fishing village north of Vung Tau. We drive out of Saigon on the Bien Hoa road and then take a sharp turn to the south at the old American military base. Empty for twenty years, this huge expanse of land is finally getting its first tentative settlers. Kyle plays Jane's Addiction full blast on the car stereo. "They're the only group in the last twenty years that comes close to writing music like Jim," he says, meaning Morrison.

Past Bien Hoa we turn off the main road onto a secondary route. We roll through little hamlets with houses built in the French colonial style. They have colonnaded porches and red-tile roofs. We pass Buddhist temples and Cao Dai churches adorned with Buddhist swastikas. We overtake ox carts trundling pigs to market and look out on fields being burned off after the recent harvest. Other fields are shining emerald green with new shoots of rice. Beside the road are fruit-laden mango trees and

Chinese pines that look like brush strokes out of the Edo period. Hummingbirds feast on the tamarinds and plantains, and everywhere the landscape is splashed with the color of blooming magnolias.

We reach the coast at sunset and rent two shacks on the beach for three dollars apiece. Then we walk through the dune grass to put our toes in the South China Sea. We stare at a fishing boat with the all-seeing eye painted on its bow. Khanh sits on the beach and thinks back to the days when she rode a boat like this to the Galang refugee camp in Indonesia. "We were lost for three days at sea in a typhoon, before we reached an oil rig off the coast," she says. "This was our twelfth escape attempt. The other times we got caught and put in jail."

I ask what she did during her year in a refugee camp. "I typed letters for the priest," she says. "I studied English and taught school to the younger children. It was the happiest time of my life."

"Why did you leave Vietnam?"

"My mother had worked for the Americans during the war. She wasn't allowed to get a job after 1975. When all the furniture and savings were gone, we had no choice but to go."

I leave her to her reverie, staring out over the water. She must be thinking about the peculiar twist of fate that brought her back to Vietnam ten years to the day after she risked her life escaping. Later we walk down the coast to a beachside restaurant and eat all the food in the kitchen: a dozen small lobsters still wriggling as they go in the pot.

Khanh and Simone retire for the night, while Kyle and I walk up a bluff overlooking the ocean to a little bar, which is really nothing more than a patio holding a few plastic chairs and tables. We stare at a full moon rising over the sea and order a couple of beers. The beers come with a half dozen female companions. "These are *bia om*, 'hugging beers,'" they say. We tell them we want the *bia* without the *om*, but in the course of talking to the women, Kyle asks if any Amerasians work at the bar. "Yes," they say, "would you like to meet one?"

A few minutes later a sleepy-headed woman appears at our table and sits down for what she expects will be a night of work. She is startled on hearing Kyle address her in Vietnamese. This brown-haired woman with Irish freckles was born in Saigon in 1970. Her mother died when she was ten. After that she lived on the streets, working as a dishwasher in a noodle shop, a ball chaser at the tennis club, and finally as a prostitute. She has a four-year-old child whose father is unknown. She was part of Charlie Brown's gang in Amerasian Park. He helped her fill out the forms and pass her ODP interview. "Now I'm waiting for my airplane ticket," she says.

Kyle and I order another round of beer—regular beer—and look at the disconsolate women sitting at the table next to us. "You know what happened to America in the Vietnam War?" he asks. "It started with 'hugging beer' and got stuck for life. The Amerasian Homecoming Act is the biggest paternity settlement in history."

The next day, Easter Sunday, Kyle and I decide to hike into the mountains. Long Hai marks the southern end of the Annamite Cordillera, the granite backbone of Vietnam that stretches all the way from China down to the rocky beach on which we are sleeping. We borrow a motorcycle and drive toward a mountain that is said to hold a Buddhist shrine. It is also an old Communist hideout. The mountain is named for two Vietminh soldiers who died there fighting the French in the 1940s.

At the base of the peak, we discover a temple occupied by a nun with a shaved head. Her rose-colored smock is covered with patches. The nun offers to lead us up the mountain to the shrine, which is hidden in a series of caves that used to double as a Vietcong outpost. After strolling through the temple's cashew grove, we come on a strange sight. A military camp has been built across the path leading up the mountain. A dozen soldiers come out to stare at us. Finally the captain barks out the command allowing us to pass.

Cut in the face of the mountain is a series of steps. The ascent is easy until the steps give out onto a root-gnarled path. The nun tells us a story about the monk who built these steps. He was too diligent in his work, so the government sent him away and stationed soldiers at the base of the mountain. They were afraid that this newly accessible shrine would become a pilgrimage site, not one controlled by the government-run Buddhist church, but a site spontaneously chosen by the people. I wake up on hearing the nun's story, realizing that I have been lulled, like a lot of casual visitors, into confusing hugging beer—sexual freedom—with the real freedom still not found in Vietnam.

We rise out of the jungle onto a rocky ledge, where we discover three grottoes lit by oil lamps. Each grotto holds an altar bearing fresh fruit and incense. In front of us, along an obscure network of trails stretching deep into the mountains, lie more shrines, each faithfully maintained with burning lamps and incense. Behind us is a breathtaking view of Cap-Saint-Jacques and the nine mouths of the Mekong River. The only discordant note in the vista is the antenna of a police listening post.

Back in Saigon, at my second meeting with Phuong Thao, she hands me a letter written by her mother, Nguyen Thi Hoa. The letter details everything she can remember about the man who fathered her "half-American child." His name is James Brown Yoder. He was a sergeant first class in the Ninth Infantry Division and worked, from 1964 to 1967, for Civil Operations and Revolutionary Development Support Advisory Team #60 in Hau Nghia Province. Phuong Thao's mother also worked for CORDS from 1966 to 1972 as a clerk typist and interpreter. "James Brown Yoder is from Virginia, USA," says the letter.

"During the period Mr. Yoder had been in Vietnam, he and I we loved together," she writes. "When I was working in Hau Nghia Province, I received a letter from Mr. Yoder in Sadec that he was going to leave Vietnam in the middle of June 1967.

"Because of the reason my family didn't agree I get married with an American, I couldn't live with Mr. Yoder as a couple. But I loved him. Therefore, before he left me, I couldn't keep my love for him in my heart.

"Before we said 'good bye,' Mr. Yoder gave me his address and told me to write him when he was in the U.S.A. When I had gotten pregnant, I didn't write any letter to him, because I didn't want him back in the battlefield of Vietnam again.

"From the date Mr. Yoder returned to the U.S.A. until now, he doesn't know anything about me or my half-American child whose father is Mr. Yoder. However, I believe he has never forgotten me. He was a good man."

The letter goes on to explain that in Vietnam when "a celibate girl gets a baby without a father, it is not good for the family's honor." This is why Phuong Thao's birth certificate lists the girl's uncle as her father. It also describes how "Mr. Yoder's address, photographs, and all papers concerning my HAC [half-American child] were lost after the event of the year 1975."

That night, at the gala opening of Phuong Thao's movie at the Communist Youth Theater, several hundred people are gathered in front of the building when an official from the Interior Ministry comes out to announce that the film will not be shown. He offers no explanation.

The next day I receive a warning from Mr. Chinh. The Interior Ministry has been making inquiries about me. He lowers his voice. "It would be advisable for you to stop visiting Amerasian Park," he says. A rush of paranoia comes over me. By drawing attention to her being Amerasian, was I responsible for getting Phuong Thao in trouble?

I walk out the Ministry gates for my last visit to the park. From the crowd of Amerasians that rushes around me, I collect the notebook in which they have recorded Mr. Thomas's final list of unregistered souls. I promise Ya Cob and the other orphans that I will do my best to get them ODP interviews. Then I remember the Vietnamese aphorism, "No matter how hard you sweep the floor, there will always be some dust left in the corners."

I photocopy the information collected in the notebook, write a cover letter, and drop this material at the Majestic Hotel and other ministries and offices in the city. Then Viet and I motorcycle out to the Amerasian Transit Center. We are met at the gate by Mr. Tung, the tall man with the walkie-talkie. He gives my notebook a cursory glance.

"This boy I registered three years ago," he says. "He took drugs. He had to have a psychological test. He was caught fighting and sent to a labor camp. He must have escaped."

"How about Ya Cob?" I ask. "He's a country boy who really does need help."

"Last year when we tried to interfere, some cases were reversed, but not this year," says Tung. "The people last year were more understanding. Now all they think about is fake cases, not helping the real cases."

"What about the other people?" I ask, holding my notebook in front of his face.

Tung laughs and points to one of the names. "This boy we call the Gray Tiger, because he has a tiger tattooed on his back. He climbs our fence at night and rapes girls. He'll never get to America," says Tung, shaking his head. "It is too late now for any of them to get to America."

Viet and I stop for a last bowl of soup at the noodle shop across from the Institut Pasteur. I give him some money for Huynh Thi Huong and a message saying I will do whatever I can to get her case appealed. I write a note to Phuong Thao. I wish her well and tell her I will write again when I have found her father. We swing by the Majestic Hotel for a final nudge to the ODP interviewers and then cycle out to Cholon to say goodbye to Tay Thi.

Short of Vietnamese money, I try to settle my hotel bill in a stew of Japanese yen, French francs, and American dollars. The hotel owner is too suspicious to take anything but the dollars, so I send Viet out to the market to convert all my foreign currency into *dong*. I pay the bill and stuff the extra money in Viet's hands. I ask him to send me a tape recording. I want to hear him singing the opera *Tay Thi*.

Their credentials at the ready, Kyle and Chinh accompany me to the airport. We clear the police checkpoints with no problems. In the departure lounge, Kyle gives me a going-away present, a vintage Zippo lighter inscribed with a peace sign and the motto "When I die I know I'm going to heaven because I have spent my time in hell." We laugh at this GI memorabilia from the sixties. I apologize to Kyle for having monopolized his evenings. "It's my work," he says. But the next time you come back, I want you to bring James Brown Yoder with you."

The first leg of my flight out of Vietnam is doubling as a refugee run to the Philippines. The waiting room is filled with families headed to Bataan. Across from me sits a Khmer woman, her husband, her Amerasian son, and the Chinese woman who is passing as his wife. A peasant from deep in the countryside, the Amerasian boy is dressed in a new white shirt and necktie. His mother wears a floral *ao dai*, his stepfather a paisley Mao suit. Judging from the gnarled toes sticking out of their flip-flops, the family is not accustomed to wearing shoes.

Miss Wife, on the other hand, is dressed in spike heels and a purple miniskirt. She is dripping with gold jewelry. She keeps a permanent scowl fixed on her face and her back turned to her "husband." Her scowl looks particularly ferocious because of the bruises between her eyes where she has pinched her skin. This is a Chinese cure for stress. It seems not to have worked.

She is taking the expensive, slow route out of Vietnam, but

in six months she can dump her rube husband and hightail it to Orange County. Everybody is doing good business out of the arrangement. The Chinese woman who gets a ride to California. The officials who wink at her paperwork. The airline that fills its planes. The refugee camp that meets its payroll. The Khmer family with new clothes. The only people not making out on the deal are Ya Cob, Huynh Thi Huong, and the other Amerasians left behind on the streets of Saigon. God is quite a joker, I think to myself.

It is one hundred degrees Fahrenheit with matching humidity as we board an overstuffed Airbus and sit baking on the runway. Next to us are the concrete revetments and fighter bomber hangars left over from the American war, which is already three wars ago for the Vietnamese. It takes a long time to instruct all the passengers in how to buckle their seat belts. Four hours behind schedule, we take off over the Mekong River. Somewhere in the haze below is the provincial town of Sadec, which produced Tay Thi, Phuong Thao, and Marguerite Duras. But no landmarks are visible in the great green mass of silt scoured down from Tibet to the sea.

Confucian Cocktail

A fish does not campaign against fisheries—
it only tries to slip through the mesh.

Aleksandr Solzhenitsyn

On the four-hour bus ride from Manila to the big refugee camp in the mountains west of town, we crawl through a blue haze of traffic, break free of the city into low-lying rice paddies, and then start crawling again into the hills. All around us are oozing rivers of lahar, a mixture of mud and ash spat out by the 1991 eruption of Mount Pinatubo. Typhoons have washed the silt into the valleys, where it lies mounded into huge levees and dunes. The road itself is raised twenty feet over its old bed, so that now we look *down* into the swimming pools of the walled estates along the highway. To our left we catch a glimpse of the South China Sea. On a clear day one could have looked all the way back to Manila. But it will be years before there is another clear day in the Philippines. We drive past a naval magazine and nuclear power plant, now closed, before reaching the memorial marking Kilometer One of the Bataan Death March.

A few miles down the road the highway ends at the Philippine Refugee Processing Center. Guards in riot gear check our papers before flagging us into camp. All around us are rows of wooden billets laid over the hills. Most Amerasians spend six months at the PRPC as the first stop on their way to the United States. When I visited the camp in the spring of 1992, ten thousand of the PRPC's eighteen thousand refugees were Amerasian cases—mostly family members riding to America on the backs of their relatives. But the camp also held 1,669 Amerasians, which was probably the largest concentration of Vietnamese Amerasians outside of Ho Chi Minh City.

Stretching my legs after our bus ride, I go out for an evening stroll. I have strayed off the main road onto a dirt track when, suddenly, at nine o'clock, the electricity is killed for the night. Oil lamps begin to flicker in the narrow alleys, where refugees sit in front of their billets talking or singing under a moonless sky. Through open doors I see people playing chess or writing letters. I am invited into a roomful of young men gathered around a blackboard. Under the motto *To study hard is to succeed* appears a list of American idioms. "*Slacking off,*" someone asks me, "what this mean?"

Other refugees have turned their billets into little stores selling condensed milk, coffee, incense, and rice cakes. The walls are covered with advertising photos clipped from American magazines and yellow *mai* blossoms left over from Tet. I find more groups of students gathered around blackboards, and I begin to understand why some refugees have fond memories of their months in camp. They go to school, learn English, and get part-time jobs as secretaries and counselors in this alternate world out of time. But I am reminded where I am when the young refugee accompanying me suddenly jerks my arm and begs me to turn around. Standing at the guard post in front of us is a rank of blue-helmeted policemen. "All they think about is bribes and stealing food," says my guide, steering me back to the main road.

Rising above the billets at the Bataan refugee camp is a blue line of mountains, where the nara trees and mahoganies have been logged off for the Japanese lumber trade. A road winds over the hills to the naval base at Subic Bay, although no one is allowed to use this road except the Aeta, the curly-haired Negritos who originally lived on this land.

The U.S. Navy towed its dry docks out of Subic Bay in 1992, but back in the days when the big American ships used to land here, ten thousand sailors would swarm ashore. For their plea-sure, the Navy regulated a honky-tonk fairyland filled with "hos-pitality women." Registered prostitutes received regular medical checkups from Navy physicians. They also had access to the naval hospital, which included a maternity ward. As a result of this benign policy, the Philippine archipelago is estimated to hold fifty thousand Amerasians.

The appearance of Amerasians in Asia dates from nine months after Commodore Matthew Perry steamed into Tokyo Bay in 1853. The onshore revelry was repeated again in 1898, when George Dewey bombarded the Spanish fleet off Manila and captured the town. By 1905, the American presence in Asia merited the following description in Henry Parker Willis's *Our Philippine Problem*:

"The American volunteer regiments marched into Manila in good order like regular troops, but as soon as the novelty of their strange environment had worn off, they gave themselves up to all sorts of excesses, debauchery and vice. Drinking bars were opened up all over the city and suburbs. Drunken brawls, indiscriminate revolver firing, indecent assaults on women, kicks and cuffs to any Filipino, burglary in broad daylight, and thefts from shops and street vendors were of hourly occurrence. Towards evening intoxicated groups took possession of the highways, entered any Filipino's house, stole what they liked, maltreated the inmates, and attempted to ravage the women."

The Philippine census of 1920 counted eighteen thousand Amerasians in Manila alone.

Opened in 1980 on a site chosen by Imelda Marcos and blessed by the Pope, the Philippine Refugee Processing Center is run by the United Nations High Commissioner for Refugees as a front for the U.S. Department of State, which finances the operation to the tune of six million dollars a year for food and basic personnel.

Twice this amount is paid to the voluntary agencies (volags) who staff the camp's instructional programs. The largest of the volags is the International Catholic Migration Commission. With a yearly budget of eight to ten million dollars, ICMC employs over four hundred English teachers at the Bataan camp, making it the biggest English-as-a-second-language program in the world. The curriculum is divided into a bestiary of acronyms specifying programs and subprograms directed toward various clientele. But ICMC has *no* programs for Amerasians, and even the word *Amerasian* appears nowhere in the curriculum.

"Amerasians have no particular problems," I am told by the stylish Filipina who directs the YA, or Young Adult, unit. "They are serviced by our normal programs," she says. Her assertion that Amerasians are indistinguishable from other Vietnamese refugees flies in the face of every published study on Amerasians, including those financed by ICMC and the State Department. These studies all agree that Amerasians have less schooling, fewer skills, and lower opinions of themselves than other Vietnamese refugees. They lack the family support that would help them get settled in a new country. Their mothers are castigated as whores. Their fathers are long gone. They are unloved, unwanted, the rotten fruit of bad seed. *My den, My do, dem bo, chu-ong heo*, kids yell at them on the street. *Black American, red American, put them in the pig sty.*

The majority of Amerasians at the PRPC live in fake families or *ghep phom*, as they say in Vietnamese. The expression literally means "to put together forms" or paper over phony relationships. Staff members at the refugee camp, people who speak Vietnamese and know what they are talking about, estimate that ninety percent of the Amerasian families have a fake mother, husband, wife, or sibling attached to the case.

Even some of the Amerasians themselves are fake. With dyed hair and silicon injections around the eyes, these fake Amerasians are known in Vietnamese as *lui*, which means "crappy" or "defective." This refers not only to the Amerasian's status, but also to the fact that many of these attempts at plastic surgery have failed. One *lui* I meet has a nasty red ribbon of skin across his cheek where the silicon migrated down from his eyes.

The fake families are well organized. They know all the zip codes in California, I am told. The heads of fake families also manage to monopolize the peer counseling jobs at Community and Family Services International, the organization that mediates family disputes. "They arbitrate Amerasian cases to death," someone tells me. "In the name of protecting clients' confidentiality, rapes and other forms of abuse against Amerasians are never reported."

At one off-the-record meeting, an ESL teacher, a young man obviously nervous about talking to me, grabs my notebook and begins drawing a map of all the fake families in camp. "Here's the Amerasian who arrived looking like a wild animal. He had been put down a well for punishment. Here's the black Amerasian who was raped by her 'stepfather' and got pregnant. Here's where there was a riot and the Amerasians set the market on fire. Here is the Amerasian who was stabbed when he tried to report his fake family. Here in Neighborhood One is the Amerasian whose 'mother' was fingered as a big retailer of Amerasians. Here in the back of Neighborhood Four is an Amerasian who's gone crazy. Here's another Amerasian who wanders around camp naked except for a pair of shorts."

I arrange for two Amerasians who speak English to guide me through camp. Lien is an attractive twenty-three-year-old with a heart-shaped face and thick mane of brown hair. She wears a gold necklace and earrings and carries a pink parasol to shade herself from the sun. Minh is a twenty-five-year-old *ipanhon*, an "American who looks Vietnamese," which is the term used to describe Puerto Ricans and Chicanos. He has a dark, feral face with a pencil-thin mustache. His English is less accomplished than Lien's, but he carries a dictionary under his arm and cares about getting the words right.

Lien is in camp with her foster parents and their seven children. The family comes from Bien Hoa, a wealthy area north of Saigon that is known for producing *ghep phom*, fake families. She finished high school, the best student in her class, but was barred from going to university. "The government wouldn't accept a Catholic," she says. "I want to be a social worker. I hope to return to Vietnam and help my country." The only cloud on her horizon is a boyfriend left behind in Vietnam. "If I took my boyfriend to America my parents couldn't go. I sacrificed my boyfriend for them."

Lien introduces me to her foster mother, a plump woman with a nice gold necklace of her own. Inside their billet, Lien's half-brothers and sisters are excitedly trying on the new sneakers bought for the family's upcoming flight to Dallas. Lien notices me looking at the walls, which are covered with pictures of suburban mansions and big cars. "This is so we know what to expect when we get to America," she says.

My would-be social worker looks vaguely disgusted by the other Amerasians in camp. Soon she pleads a headache from the midday sun and returns home. Minh looks relieved. "Now we get to work," he says. Abandoned by an unknown mother, Minh was raised by a woman and her policeman husband in Vung Tau until 1975, when the policeman was sent to prison. Minh dropped out of school to hawk bread in the city and work as a porter in the market until his foster family was sent to a New Economic Zone in central Vietnam. Here he worked as a duck boy, herding fowl.

By 1987 he was back in Vung Tau earning five thousand *dong* a day parking bicycles at the cinema. He bought a tape recorder and started teaching himself English. That same year he learned about the Orderly Departure Program. He registered and waited two and a half years for an interview. His foster parents said they were too old to go to America. Nor did they want to leave behind their four older children. So a fake family was papered together.

The first substitution was a fake mother, who was actually Minh's foster father's niece. "At first I didn't want to take her," Minh says. "She had nothing to do with me. But my father threatened to disown me. He took care of me when I was a baby, so I agreed."

Then came an arranged marriage. "I didn't want to get married, but I thought I would be sad if I went alone," he says. "My wife loves me. She is not lazy. She is a tailor. She is a high school graduate and can get a better job than me."

Kim, the fake mother, came with two sons and a nephew of her own. Then Minh's wife tacked one of *her* nieces onto the family by claiming the girl as their child. When this twenty-five-year-old Amerasian with a forty-year-old "mother" and seven-year-old "child" presented himself at the Ministry of Foreign Affairs, he flunked his ODP interview. "Kim couldn't answer any of the questions," he says.

"My father was very angry and insisted I ask for a rehearing. I went back inside to talk to the interviewer. The translator wouldn't tell her what I was saying, so I had to speak English." The interviewer changed her mind—the first time this miracle had ever been known to happen—and the "family" walked away with seven airplane tickets to America.

How does an orphaned Amerasian end up transporting a fake family to the United States? His motives are a Confucian cocktail of family obligations, blackmail, money, guilt, and fear of crossing the ocean by himself. Should the Immigration and Naturalization Service catch wind of this scheme, the *Amerasian* will be charged with perjury and expelled from the country. "All the Amerasians are like mice in a trap," says Minh. "They have no money, no skills. Their level is low, and no one is going to help bring them up."

Minh's fake mother turned out to be as rotten as her papers. She gambled away the family's money and started telling people that *she* had paid the bribes to get them out of Vietnam, while the money had actually come from Minh. He reported her to the authorities. They moved her into a separate billet and began the usual mediations by which fake families are held together long enough to get them to America.

I ask Minh what he will do in the United States when the resettlement agency puts him in the same house with Kim. "I will move away," he says.

"But it will be *your* house."

"Who am I?" he asks.

Once he moves away, Minh will become a secondary migrant cut loose from refugee center benefits, housing allowances, schooling, and welfare. He will become a criminal liable to expulsion from the United States, and he will be disqualified from sponsoring for immigration any of his real family members. His fake mother will get the apartment, food stamps, cash assistance, Medicare, ESL, and sympathy for having raised a "no good" Amerasian.

Minh shows me the garden he planted in front of his billet, complete with bean trellises and a prized melon he keeps hidden under a pile of grass. Behind the house is a cabana he has built for cooking. It holds firewood gathered from the hills to supplement the kilo of charcoal that is their weekly ration. Inside his two-and-a-half-meter-wide house is a sleeping platform made of rattan. Another platform, built on a balcony under the roof, is too hot to use during the day. Big signs warn people not to collect rainwater off the roofs, which are made of asbestos. Everyone drinks the rainwater anyway.

On a table holding a vase full of flowers is a small library, including two Vietnamese-English dictionaries and a couple of well-thumbed textbooks covered with newspaper. I pick up a grammar book from Minh's ESL class, *Your New Life in the United States*, published in 1991 by the Center for Applied Linguistics in Washington, D.C. The book's concluding paragraph reads: "The police are your friends. Do not try to bribe them. Do not run away or they might shoot you."

Minh and I start jumping open sewers and threading our way down the narrow paths that lead deep into camp. The first Amerasian we visit is Tran Thi Hoa, a twenty-nine-year-old karate black belt and kung fu master. A compact woman with freckles and straight brown hair, Hoa is the scion of Ken O'Leary. "All I know about him is that he wore three stripes on his shoulder," she says. "I guess that made him a major in the Army." Even though her schooling was interrupted by three years of forced labor planting rice in the countryside, Hoa is a high school graduate. She registered to leave Vietnam in 1983, but it was not until 1990 that she could pay a large enough bribe to get an ODP interview for herself, her mother and her five half-brothers and half-sisters. This was the family with whom she had lived all her life. They failed the interview.

"They put me in a separate room and asked, 'Do you keep an animal in the house?' I thought they were asking if I fed the family dog, so I said, 'No.'

"My mother was brought into the room, and they asked her, 'Do you keep animals in the house?' She said, 'Yes, a dog and two cats.'

"Then the interviewer said my family was denied permission to come with me. I complained, but the case was not changed. At first I was so angry I wanted to stay in Vietnam. Then I decided to go alone."

The kung fu master's house is empty, save for a sleeping hammock and walls covered with the red ribbons and medals of her victories. In this bare room she spends her days fighting imaginary opponents, some of them very strong. Hoa spent the past week in the hospital after a failed suicide attempt.

"It's not fair," says Minh. "All around us are fake families, and this girl is not allowed to bring her mother." To drive home the point, he introduces me to a couple of *lai gia*—fake Amerasians living next door. The first is a twenty-six-year-old woman who, except for her bleached hair, looks entirely Vietnamese. Her husband's blond top knot is even less convincing. Their big fake family is jumping up and down with joy at leaving tomorrow for California.

The next Amerasian we meet is a sad-looking woman with a naked two-year-old baby on her lap. The woman is dressed in a thin cotton blouse and threadbare pants. She has never been to school and does not know how to write her name. Her neck is striated with welts. She was feeling faint from lack of food, so she coined herself, ardently rubbing her skin with a Philippine peso to raise the blood blisters Asians believe are therapeutic. She is pregnant.

She tells us she was married five years ago, at the age of fourteen. She shows us a picture of her husband, who is ten years older than she. He sits with his family at an outdoor café. Everyone in the picture is well dressed. "I am nervous about going to America," she says. "My husband is a playboy. He married me only to leave Vietnam."

I ask why she married him. "To escape from the family where I lived," she says. "They treated me worse than their animals. They said at least their animals could be eaten, but all I did was eat."

A girl with the freckled, all-American face of her father writes his name in my notebook as *Roblester*. Mr. Lester, a former Air Force mechanic at Chu Lai, hails from San Francisco, where the girl's mother lived with him for a while, before she got homesick and returned to Vietnam. It took her twenty years and a lot of money to get back out again. "We paid ten thousand *dong* per name to register and three hundred thousand *dong* to get a passport for the family," says the girl. "We applied to ODP in 1983. They 'lost' our names, and we had to pay more bribes in 1988. Then we had to pay more money to the translator at the interview site, the fat woman dripping with gold."

"We know her!" yell the half-dozen people who have crowded into the room to listen. "She's the woman with eye-glasses and a North Vietnamese accent." Then they start calling out the names of Amerasians turned away for lack of money. "Saigon is full of Amerasians who failed their interviews," they assure me. "Only the rich ones get out."

The next day from morning to night and then again the following day the faithful Minh and I comb the neighborhoods looking for the homeless Amerasians marked with Xs on my map. We jump sewer ditches, circle the barracks, scour the weed lots and bathhouses searching for people cut loose from their families. We stop only once, at midday, for a quick bowl of soup in the camp market, a huge bazaar teeming with everything from live ducks and pigs to photo booths and record stores. We buy a couple of sodas and walk back into the afternoon heat.

The second-to-last X on my map is Trinh, a strapping twenty-year-old Amerasian with curly brown hair. The soft-spoken Trinh wears a T-shirt saying, "The one with the most toys wins." He tells us how his mother sold him when he was nine to a family for whom he labored planting beans and tobacco, until he ran away after two years and returned to his mother. "Amerasians were like dogs in the street until ODP started," he says. "Then we began living like rich people." The fake mother with whom he came to the Philippines bought Trinh for ten rings, or one tael, of gold. This equals six million *dong*, or five hundred dollars. "People can pay three or four taels of gold, as much as two thousand dollars, to buy an Amerasian," he says. Trinh gave the money to his mother.

He describes how the woman who bought him and her daughter cribbed for their ODP interview. "They talked to people who had been interviewed and wrote down the questions and answers. They quizzed me, 'How many rooms are in your house? What pictures hang on the wall? How many cats and dogs do you have?' There was one trick question they asked me over and over, because they thought it was so important. 'If there is only one seat on the airplane, will you take it?' A proper son is supposed to say, 'No.' "

The last X on my map is the homeless Afro-Amerasian who was turned out of his house with nothing more to his name than a pair of shorts. We find him camped in an alleyway with a blanket and pot that someone has given him. He was born in Cambodia in 1970. He has never been to school. He cannot read or write. All he knows is that the name on his documents is fake. He stands over me, staring in my notebook, as he insists I write down his real name, Le Tien Dung.

He and his mother were farm laborers. A big family of North Vietnamese offered to buy him for three million *dong*, about $250, in cash. "It is not much money," says Dung, who realized after getting to the Philippines that he had sold himself cheap. "The man lied to me. He said he could get my family here right away." From a pouch around his neck Dung pulls out a piece of paper. It is a marriage certificate. He wants us to know that both his wife and mother have been left behind in Vietnam. Two weeks ago the family that bought him kicked him out of their house.

As Minh and I trudge through camp, my notebook fills with more tales of duplicity. By nightfall we are back at the market, where I buy a few dozen eggs, papayas, and melons. "These are a present for your wife," I tell him. Then I tear the map out of my notebook and ask him to give more food to the pregnant woman, to Dung in his alley, and the other hungry Amerasians. I know he will do it.

I run to catch the bus down the mountain to Manila. We churn through the dust and volcanic ash that have destroyed the roads around Mount Pinatubo and arrive in the city at midnight. I check into the old Hilton, where I have a sweeping moonlit view over the South China Sea. After a fitful night's sleep, I drive to the airport early the following morning, where I watch the dawn flight to Saigon—the one that will turn around at the end of the day and bring back another load of refugees.

Security Warrior

We're surrounded.

The Lone Ranger

Who's *we*, kimo sabe?

Tonto

It was once a thriving city of a hundred thousand people on the upper reaches of the Mohawk River. Utica is now a shell. The old red-brick buildings are tumbling into ruin. Entire neighborhoods are gutted by fire and arson. Still standing are the *belle époque* train station and Utica Club brewery, but gone are the factories that once made General Electric radios, Savage guns, and Univac computers. Beginning in the 1960s, people got in their cars and drove to the suburbs, never to return. The population plummeted forty percent. Uticans today walk around a city two sizes too big for them.

A million years from now, archaeologists excavating Utica will discover a city laid out on a vertical gradient. Starting at the railroad tracks in the valley and working up to the highlands overlooking the Mohawk River, Utica's cultural record passes, in ascending order, from welfare mothers in public housing projects, parolees, and deinstitutionalized lunatics through old-world Italians and Polish brewers up to Utica National Insurance agents and Rome Laboratory engineers. The only exception to this vertical segregation is the elevated slum called Cornhill, which is steadily filling with Vietnamese refugees. Much of Cornhill is dilapidated or torched, but what remains is still a decipherable simulacrum of the American Dream: two-family houses sitting on handkerchief lawns with room out back for a clothesline and a victory garden.

Behind one of these clapboard houses, with a FOR SALE sign permanently nailed to the front porch, is the cottage where Charlie Brown lives. Charlie's face is flushed and his hands are shaking again. Another bout of malaria, he says. Instead of a blue suit, today Charlie wears a T-shirt bearing a map of Vietnam and the old slogan about *The Land That God Forgot.*

Charlie squats Asian style among a mess of packing boxes, brown shopping bags, and plastic suitcases. Today is moving day. The refugee center has rented him a house large enough to be lived in by Charlie, his fiancée, and her Vietnamese family, who should be arriving soon from the Philippines. "It's like during the war," he says. "Everything is in bags, and I'm ready to run."

Among Charlie's belongings are a mattress and box spring, a manual typewriter, some old suit coats and shirts on hangers, four Western landscapes bought from Goodwill for ten dollars, a bouquet of plastic flowers, a box of paperback books by Dostoyevsky, Nietzsche, and Henry Miller, two large tins of USDA honey, and a collection of dark, hyperrealist oil paintings done by Charlie himself. One, called *The Lonely Bird,* shows an eagle soaring toward the sun. "I'm flying toward my dream," Charlie explains. His most recent painting shows the Statue of Liberty rising out of a pile of guns, grenades, dollar bills, and gangsters in pitched battle. "It's called *America Freedom Country?*" Charlie says. "They got really mad at me down at the refugee center for putting in the question mark."

Out of a knapsack stuffed with photographs and letters, Charlie pulls a sheaf of paper. "This is the first installment of my autobiography," he says, handing me thirteen handwritten pages entitled "Amerasian Children in Vietnam, the Cause of Past Distress and a Future Still Ahead."

Charlie's autobiography begins with a description of refugees fleeing the war-torn countryside. When Saigon fell in 1975:

> The rumor spread that the Communists would kill all the women who had had children by American soldiers. Anyone who had a secret in her past tried to throw it out or hide it. But in this case the evidence was made of flesh and bone and was all the more fright-

ening for having yellow hair or black skin. To the Communists, this was the picture of their mortal enemy! In these anxious days, many mothers abandoned their children and vanished in the chaotic stream of refugees. Other mothers tried to hide their little Uncle-Sam-secret in their houses. They shaved the heads of their Amerasians, cut off their eyelashes, poured ink on their hair.

Even those who protected their Amerasian children found the social pressures unendurable. Because of economic difficulties and discrimination, they moved their families to the New Economic Zones or to the jungles or mountains. They had hardship in their lives. They began to live like nomads, ravenous, wandering, hopeless.

Another group of Amerasians wandered into the cities of south Vietnam and found work picking up wastepaper on the streets, digging in rubbish heaps, or hawking ice cream, newspapers, or lottery tickets. Others traveled on the trains, begging, picking pockets. They needed to be quick-witted and nimble-footed if they didn't want to go hungry. . . .

In 1980 the ODP program began. This program was like a bomb with a long delay fuse. It smoldered in Vietnamese society, waiting to explode. People now sensed that here was a safe ticket to the holy land— USA. Wealthy people went around the countryside, convincing families to sell their Amerasians. They bustled down alleys and cul-de-sacs. They stood lookout at rubbish heaps, trying to get their hands on Amerasians at any cost. They argued, traded, bribed their way into obtaining falsified records and documents. During that time, only God knew what was real and what was fake.

Amerasians began to appear in wealthy families.

It was like being sprinkled with a wonderful magic powder. Yesterday you were living in hardship. Today you are a little prince or princess! The Amerasians were more coddled than the real children of these people. Then in 1986, when the ODP program was stopped, many people who had used Amerasians for this purpose were dazed. Suddenly the little princes and princesses were turned out of their houses to return to their wandering lives.

When the Orderly Departure Program resumed in 1988 it provoked another mad scramble to find Amerasian "family" members. "More gold, more money changed hands on both sides," writes Charlie.

He unfolds a map of Vietnam on which he has traced his wandering life among the Viets, the Khmer, Cham, Hmong, Lao, and besieged Americans. "Blood, blood, blood. I look at this map and all I see is blood," he says.

Charlie holds up a Coca-Cola T-shirt and begins telling me a long story involving a black American vet named John Rogers and his Amerasian buddy, Raymond, who is Charlie's archenemy. "John Rogers gave us these T-shirts and told us to wear them, because Coke was supporting his foundation to help Amerasian children. But John Rogers and Raymond never played straight with us. Raymond wasn't really Amerasian, anyway. He was the son of a Moroccan legionnaire in the French forces."

Charlie unfolds letters from another Army veteran who visited him in Amerasian Park, Al Webb. One of these letters, dated April 12, 1990, reads: "I came home from the war twenty-four years ago, and I have thought about Vietnam every single day for all that time. So in a way I am an Amerasian, too. I am an American, but part of me is Vietnamese, just like you." The letter ends with an invitation for Charlie to join Webb at his farm on the Hawaiian island of Maui.

Next Charlie shows me a letter from Herman T. Laurel, director of the Philippine Refugee Processing Center. The letter thanks Charlie for helping authorities quell a riot at the PRPC. "He didn't know I was the one who started the riot," says Charlie, grinning. "I sent the Amerasians to beat up the Filipinos. They broke a lot of glass and burned the market. Then when the army moved in with M16s, I jumped on top of a water cannon and grabbed a megaphone to call back my troops."

The Amerasians were protesting reductions in the food rations. The supply of fish had been cut in half, and meat and vegetables were eliminated entirely.

"The Filipinos stole most of the food anyway," Charlie says. "If you didn't have money, you didn't eat."

Charlie shoves another collection of papers into my hands. On top is an elaborate matrix of letters and numbers. "It's a key for sending secret correspondence," he says. "I've been recruited as a security warrior—a double agent and spy—for the Vietnamese police." So that I can understand why he would agree to do such a thing, Charlie describes his years in prison, beginning with the Jack Tree Hotel in Saigon.

"I couldn't stand in my cell. It was so small, I had to sleep curled in the fetal position. I pissed through a hole in the floor. There was no light. Twice a day they shoved rice through a window in the door. We were always hungry. The only salt we got came from licking the sweat off our skin. Sugar and cigarettes were nothing but a dream."

After six months in the hole, where he became so ill he stopped eating and fell unconscious, Charlie was released to the general prison population and then sent to the jungle. Twice he tried to kill himself. "I bit my vein and almost bled to death. Once

I drove a nail through a stick and used it to stab myself in the heart."

He tells me again about his attempted escapes and the guard he attacked. "I'm hurt when I think of that man. I saw him on the ground and couldn't hit him anymore. I needed freedom, but I was really sorry. When the guards beat me up in Pleiku, six or seven of them, I was like a small animal curled under their rifles. How did *they* feel doing that?" Charlie puts his head in his hands and breaks down crying. "Why did my mother and father bring me into this life and throw me away?" he asks.

Charlie had finally made his way to Amerasian Park, passed his ODP interview and medical exam, and was scheduled to fly out'of Vietnam in August 1989, when, a month before his departure, the police arrested him. "They interrogated me every day. They went back over my record, telling me they knew everything about who I was and where I was from. They told me they had enough evidence to convict me of assembling the homeless wandering Amerasians in Saigon for the purpose of making propaganda and subverting public opinion. They threatened to put me back in prison! They told me they would let me leave Vietnam only if I worked for them as an overseas spy. Confronted with this situation, I accepted."

Charlie was given a code name and list of contacts. These include two "security warriors," overseas Vietnamese, who are coming to Utica for his first debriefing. What is he going to do when the spies find him?

Charlie pulls out of his knapsack a photograph of Truong Thi Le Ha, his eighteen-year-old Amerasian fiancée. "My girlfriend is all my life to me," he says of this young woman with a sweet moon face. "Her family took care of me after I escaped from prison and spent eight days wandering in the jungle. They were living in a New Economic Zone outside Pleiku. I would have died without them."

Charlie met the family again in the Philippines and promised to sponsor them to Utica. Traveling with Thi Le Ha are her Amerasian brother and sister, four Vietnamese siblings, and her mother, a former washerwoman at the Air Force base in Pleiku. Charlie produces another photo of a bandy-legged little girl in a white dress and sandals. This is a picture of Thi Le Ha taken in 1975, when she was four years old.

The last item Charlie shows me is a photo of David M. Smith, a former Air Force radarman stationed in Pleiku. Half obscured by mold is the image of a bare-chested young man holding his ring finger to the camera. Is this meant to be a gesture of undying love? Pinned to the wall behind Smith is the picture of the bandy-legged girl he fathered in Vietnam.

The night his "family" is scheduled to fly into Utica I pick Charlie up at his new house on Blandina Street. Everything is in place: tables, chairs, TV, even the pictures on the walls. The closets have been stocked with clothing scavenged from the refugee center. Charlie tells me he hasn't slept for a week. His blue suit swims around his neck. He asks me to knot his tie. "Two years ago I looked like an animal. I weighed eighty pounds and was covered with dirt. Now look at me," he says, admiring himself in the mirror.

Charlie rolls down the car window and yells to the empty street, "God, if everything turns out all right, I'll return to the church! I'll get down on my knees and pray."

The eleven o'clock flight from New York is rescheduled for midnight. "I've already told my boss I'll be late for work tomorrow. American jobs are easy," he says. "My hands used to be like rock. Now look at how soft they are." Charlie is the only employee at his company who stays a few minutes after quitting time to clean his workbench. "Americans have no loyalty," he says. "They just look out for themselves."

The airport is empty, save for a handful of Amerasians and two translators from the refugee center. I buy everyone a round of sodas at Ferlo's Runway Cafe. Charlie plays "Hotel California" on the jukebox.

"The GIs in Vietnam used to give me money for the juke-box," he says. "They'd flip quarters across the room and watch me catch them. My two favorite songs were 'Jingle Bells' and 'Let It Be.' I learned to play the guitar. Once in the jungle I made a guitar out of an iron box and telephone wire strings."

Charlie and the other Amerasians sing along to the music. They know all the words by heart. "My dream, in ranked order," he says, "is to get a car, a guitar, and a Keystone organ. I also don't want to lose my job," he adds.

A voice over the loudspeaker announces another hour's delay. "One more hour, one more century," says Charlie. He gets up to drop another quarter in the machine, a big Rock-Ola with a glowing purple face. "I hate Michael Jackson and Madonna," he says, cuing up The Eagles' song about the new kid in town.

Charlie shows us his collection of military IDs. These used to belong to men who took an interest in him, before they died or got sent back to the States. Then Charlie starts doodling on a nap-kin, drawing pictures of tanks and guns, while explaining the dif-ference between M41s and M48s. The kids watch him sketch a 155mm cannon and listen to his stories about living in the field on C rations.

The plane finally lands; we rush out to stand by the door. Arriving with Charlie's girlfriend are her mother and six of her seven half-brothers and sisters. The eldest has been left behind in Vietnam. The reunion is done Vietnamese style. The mother is greeted first and everyone else in ranked order of age. There is no public display of affection, no tears, kisses, exclamations. There is nothing to read on people's faces except the gray pallor of exhaustion and a barely suppressed look of terror. They carry all their worldly belongings in one plastic bag apiece. We get in our cars and drive home.

The Sins
of the Fathers

There is no way for me to get home again.

Antigone

The leader in Utica of the Bleecker Street punks is Duc, a handsome young man with jet black hair. A sharp dresser and great dancer, Duc has already been to jail a couple of times, once for stealing a Honda, the second time for stealing a Pontiac Trans-Am. This shows his developing American tastes. Duc's sidekick is a black Amerasian named Quoc who sports a Bart Simpson flat top, which is dyed a different primary color every week. Quoc wears a lot of jewelry and has a buck-toothed stare. "We just eat, sleep, lounge around, and get in trouble," Duc confesses in his excellent streetwise English.

I enter the refugee center and thread my way upstairs to one of the half-dozen classrooms knocked together out of ready-made windows and wallboard. Sharon Eghigian, a young, dark-haired woman, obviously devoted to her students, has invited me to attend the English class she teaches for a young Amerasians and Russian Pentecostals—"the wild ones," she calls them.

Eghigian directs me to sit facing the dozen students who have shown up for class that day. She tells them to start asking me questions. The Vietnamese inquire about my family. "Are you married? Do you have children?" The Russians, stocky teenagers who tower over their Asian classmates, ask, "Where do you work?" "How much money do you make?"

Eghigian thanks me afterwards for talking to the Russians. "They get angry at visitors who come only to stare at the Amerasians," she says. But I understand why the Amerasians attract visitors. There is something uncanny about them, like an M.C. Escher painting that flips, as you watch it, from birds to fishes.

One minute these young people look like Western teenagers in T-shirts. Then their high cheekbones and the epicanthic folds over their eyes make them look Asian. They display a surprising number of scars—lumps of red flesh raised on their necks and arms. I learn later that some of these scars are signs of attempted suicides—the stigmata of Amerasian life.

To spark another round of discussion, Eghigian holds up a copy of the Utica newspaper. It contains an article on Welcome Home House, the Amerasian residential program slated to open in the fall of 1990 on the grounds of the old New York State Lunatic Asylum. The program will allow three hundred Amerasians a year to skip internment in the Bataan refugee camp and fly straight to the United States.

"They so lucky, they come direct to their fatherland," says a black Amerasian girl with a puffy face.

"Didn't you like the Philippines?" Eghigian asks.

"No," she says. "I was hungry all the time." I later learn she was also raped by a camp guard and is now pregnant.

After class, an Amerasian boy with a toothy smile comes up and asks me if I like to dance. Thang sports a diamond in his left ear, a bouffant hairdo, and lacquered nails. He was a taxi dancer at one of the big hotels in downtown Saigon. He sold makeup, he sold perfume, he sold himself, and now he lives the same life on this side of the Pacific. He works as a waiter at a bar on Genesee Street and then stays out dancing until three in the morning.

"Last night an old man offered to keep me," he says. "He wants to rent me an apartment and buy me clothes. I turned him down. I have too many boyfriends."

"Aren't you afraid of getting AIDS?"

"No," he says. "If you love boys, you're OK. Only boys who go with girls get AIDS."

"I know this isn't true," Thang later admits. "But I am more afraid of going hungry than getting AIDS."

Much of what Thang initially tells me is untrue. He gives me a false name. He tells me his mother is dead, when she actu-

ally lives in Dallas. And so on. I am being introduced to the circu-
larity of Vietnamese discourse, in which truth is neither singular
nor evident. In fact, many of the stories in this book may be untrue. The pain behind them, on the other hand, is real.

The following morning on Bleecker Street I witness a fight between some Amerasian boys and young Russians. The dustup begins with a visit by the Amerasians to the Saigon Club. Here the
boys indulge in red-eye specials and converse with Sanh Chi Do,
Utica's resident bad guy. He is instructing them in the basic curriculum—stealing cars and things like that—before they move
on to advanced work in home invasions. Home invasions are
Vietnam's greatest contribution to crime in America. Mobile
teams of hit-and-run robbers, aided by local informants, spend
weeks scouting out Asian targets with liquid assets and a cultural
reticence about reporting losses to the police. When they strike,
home invaders tie up their victims with duct tape, brutalize, rape,
and rob them, and then disappear back onto the interstate highways that are the gangs' transnational turf.

   After their tutorial with Sanh Chi Do, the Amerasians are
walking back to the refugee center when they meet a Russian girl
and make some remarks. To her defense come several compatriots. The Russians deliver a few roundhouse blows before being
lowered to the pavement by their more agile, and more numerous,
opponents. Beefy adolescents known for getting drunk before
lunch, the Russians are rolled down the street like beer kegs.

   The fight spills over into Sharon Eghigian's class. An Amer-
asian runs into the room yelling, "We're going to clean out the
Russians." Eghigian flees to Rose Marie Battisti's office, crying,
"I can't take it. I don't want to teach here anymore."

   At this point, Samedy Sok is called in to cool things down.
Job counselor and youth adviser at the center, Sam's specialty is
punks. He clears the Amerasians out of the building and arranges
a standoff on Bleecker Street. One of the Russians will later get

knocked on the head with a 38mm gun and sent to the hospital for six stitches. But for the moment, the action is limited to swearing at Sam, who stands between the combatants with upraised palms.

A slender man in his twenties with ropey earlobes, Sam, the good Buddhist, says, "I love you, and even if you don't like me, you are still my students." He says this in Russian, Vietnamese, Cambodian, and English, so everyone will understand.

I gain newfound respect for Sam as I watch him in action. Before today, I had been put off by his social-worker jargon, shiny suits, and red Fiero. But beyond the trappings—which are nothing more than a Cambodian refugee's idea of how to look successful in America—I realize Sam is the mainstay of the agency. He is the guy who handles the nighttime crises. He is job consulor, psychiatrist, banker, and confidant to a lot of teenagers who would be nowhere without him. When Sam utters the word *love*, it has authority, because everyone knows he has been on intimate terms with its opposite.

After their lecture, the Amerasians return to hanging in the 'hood. Their Bleecker Street view of the world differs substantially from that inside the refugee center. These two perspectives diverge most widely on the subject of Rose Marie Battisti, executive director of the Mohawk Valley Resource Center for Refugees.

While Battisti gains national attention for running what many people consider the country's most successful Amerasian resettlement project, the Bleecker Street crowd vilifies her as the bad mother who abandoned them to illiteracy and poverty. She does nothing to help them when they get thrown out of school or lose their jobs, they say, and when they try to enter the building, she calls the police to arrest them for criminal trespass.

From Battisti's perspective, these kids are off the books. They received four months of job consuling and remedial English. This is what the government owed them, and they got it. From the Amerasians' perspective, this is a betrayal of what their "homecoming" was supposed to be. Worst of all, they feel unloved. This is no light charge in Vietnamese culture, where people kill themselves for lack of love.

Vietnam's national epic, a poem many people know by heart, is Nguyen Du's *The Tale of Kieu*. It is the story of a young Vietnamese woman, Kieu, who sells herself into prostitution in order to save her father from debtors' prison. All Vietnamese refugees are called Viet Kieu, "overseas Vietnamese." The name Kieu and the word Kieu, meaning "overseas," are false cognates, derived from different roots. But it is not farfetched to say that one Kieu evokes the other. Life in exile for a Vietnamese is never far from feelings of compromise and betrayal.

The sense of loss felt by Utica's Amerasians is doubly compounded. Rejected by their Vietnamese motherland, they feel equally unwelcome in the land of their fathers. No more than a handful of veterans have stepped forward to claim their Amerasian children. The remaining Amerasians have had to settle for four months of "survival" English and a minimum-wage job. Refugee agencies call this "successful integration into American life." Amerasians call it "lack of love."

These kids have graduated to the street to do what? Rob people? Die? They vow to do both, and they insist on doing it in front of Rose Marie Battisti's large storefront window. The other value deeply ingrained in Vietnamese culture is shame. How can she watch her Amerasian "children" suffering without rushing out to help them? Battisti keeps her office blinds shut tight. But still, inside, the Amerasians are sure of it, she must be deeply ashamed.

At ten o'clock on Thursday Sam teaches "cultural orientation" to the Vietnamese. Thirty-five people are gathered in the big windowless room at the back of the refugee center. He removes his suit jacket and rolls up his sleeves. His remarks, made in English, are translated by a fellow staff member into Vietnamese.

Seated on battered couches and old office furniture, Sam's students are dressed in polyester trousers, eggplant-colored track suits, acrylic sweaters, fake fur overcoats, and bell-bottomed leisure suits. The lapels are too wide, the knees bagged out. These clothes have been worn five seasons past when they were no longer in style and then dumped in the basement at 666 Bleecker Street, where they were pawed over by successive waves of refugees, before emerging on what look like time-warp dioramas of the sixties.

"Asian culture is very tight," says Sam. "Children speak to parents. 'Mom, I made a mistake.' This is called *relationship*."

He draws a picture on the blackboard. "To make a house, you start with the foundation and add walls. The walls are mother and father." I look around the room at the Amerasian students and wonder how they feel about living in a house that is missing half its walls.

"Many of you look happy because you're here in America, but I know inside you're unhappy. In Vietnam you lived day to day, with no thought for the future. But in this country, we think all the time about the future. We live for the future."

Sam hands out a list of cultural differences between the United States and Vietnam. "This will be given to your boss or supervisor when you get a job," he says. Selected items on the list include:

American	*Vietnamese*
1. Touching between members of the *same* sex is not acceptable.	It is quite acceptable. One often sees men or women in the street holding hands.
5. Americans say "grace" before eating.	Vietnamese children ask parents to eat first and then they follow.
7. The smell of American food is weak.	The smell of Vietnamese food is strong.

11. Americans use waving motions to call people.	Waving motions are used only to call little children.
13. Americans can greet anyone in the family first.	A Vietnamese greets the head of the family or an older person first, then the younger ones.
24. Spouses are considered equal legally and mentally.	The husband is superior and the wife is subordinate.
25. Women are independent and have legal and marital rights.	Women, in general, must obey their fathers (when they are young and unmarried), then their husbands, and then their eldest sons (in the case of the death of the husband).
30. Talking directly about the main subject is preferable.	Vietnamese talk around and around a subject before coming to the point.
31. Looking straight into someone's eyes during a conversation shows honesty and frankness.	It is not respectful, especially to older people or superiors.
32. A smile means happiness.	A smile means everything: happiness or sorrow, agreement or disagreement, understanding or not.
39. Success is the key word. Always strive for one step higher.	Life is like the theater; everyone plays his or her role and then disappears.

Rose Marie Battisti sits in her office behind a desk overburdened with papers. A blonde in her midthirties with bobbed hair and pink cheeks, she spent the summer studying Vietnamese at Cornell University and then had her appendix removed. "I'm supposed to be home recuperating, but with eight kids in the house, I was going crazy." I look down to see her youngest child tumbling in the papers behind her mother's desk.

Battisti was nineteen years old and pregnant with her second child when she saw a TV show in 1974 that changed her life. Called *The Sins of the Fathers*, it was an exposé on Amerasian children abandoned in Vietnam. When her husband, Ed, came home from working the three-to-eleven shift at the dairy, she said, "We have to do this."

"We have to do what?" he asked.

"We have to adopt one of these Amerasian children."

"Rose Marie, you're nuts," he said. "We've got a child, and you're pregnant."

They worked out a deal. A year after the birth of their second child, if Rose Marie still wanted to adopt an Amerasian baby, they would do it. She started writing letters and filling out applications. She tried to get one of the children on Operation Babylift, but their airplane crashed, and they all died. Then she was told she was too young to adopt an Amerasian. You had to be twenty-one. By the time she was old enough, Saigon had fallen. She then learned that lots of Korean babies were available. Four of Battisti's eight children are adopted Koreans.

"Every night we watched the body count on TV," she says of the Vietnam War that dragged on through her teenage years growing up in Little Falls, a Mohawk River town southeast of Utica. "Vietnam must have affected me more than I realized at the time. I've always been fascinated by Asia. One of the earliest books I remember reading was Pearl Buck's *The Good Earth*. My father served in Korea. Then he ran a social club in Japan. We have pictures of him holding little babies in a Japanese orphanage."

The summer she graduated from high school Battisti married her hometown boyfriend. He had just received his orders to Vietnam; he wore his Army uniform to the wedding. "I thought it was really glamorous to be marrying a soldier about to go to war," she remembers. But by then—it was 1972—the war was winding down. So instead of going to Vietnam, Ed went to Arizona and was soon back in Little Falls.

Battisti was "Susie Homemaker for ten years," she says, "a regular Kool-Aid mom," before she enrolled in college part-time and finished a two-year degree in human services. In May 1983 she read in the newspaper that Utica was about to resettle its first group of Amerasian refugees. Thinking this was the perfect job for her, she made an appointment to speak to Roberta Douglas, director of the refugee center, which she had founded in a Utica storefront in 1979. Straight away Douglas put Battisti in charge of the Amerasian program. Her first day on the job she went to the airport to meet the plane.

"Three families got off," Battisti remembers. "Among them were a scrawny little black kid named Nguyen Anh Dung and his mother. She was crying so hard she filled a dish towel with tears. 'I'm happy my Amerasian child won't have to eat out of garbage cans,' she said. 'But I'm sad about leaving my other son behind in Vietnam.' I cried. Everyone cried. Then we took them to their apartment for a home-cooked meal.

"A lot of families are fragmented like this," she says. "The mothers get out with their Amerasian, but not their Vietnamese, children. I suppose you have to draw the line somewhere, but it's frequently done in an unfair manner. That's why we spend so much time appealing cases to the government. Sometimes we're successful. Often we're not."

Battisti admits to making some mistakes of her own. "For the first year and a half, we thought, 'Oh, wonderful, these kids can now go to school.' Then we discovered it wasn't so wonderful. We were throwing teenagers who had never been to school into tenth grade. They screamed about being there, and soon the teachers were ready to strangle us."

Battisti became resettlement director and then executive director of the refugee center in 1985, when Roberta Douglas left town. The agency soon tripled in size and was on the verge of doubling again when Welcome Home House opened in the fall of 1990.

"We do our best with all the refugees, but basically my heart is with the Amerasians," Battisti confesses. "I'm incredibly nervous and excited and happy about the new Amerasian project. I can't believe after two and a half years of planning that it's finally going to happen. It's my baby. It's a dream come true."

The first thing one notices about Nguyen Anh Dung, or Clarence Taylor III, is how fast he moves. He hustles into the refugee center, greeting everybody by name, and looks at his watch before sitting down at one of the picnic tables in front of the snack machines. The skinny little Afro-Amerasian child whose mother filled a dish towel full of tears when they landed in Utica has grown into a barrel-chested young man. Anh Dung was the first Amerasian in Utica to finish high school, the first to go to college. He works part-time for the phone company. He runs a video rental operation and auto driving school. He coaches the Amerasian soccer team. He tutors refugees in English and leads the volunteer work crew getting Welcome Home House ready for its first Amerasian occupants.

Graced with a marriage certificate issued by the local police station, Anh Dung's mother, Bang, and his father, "Bill," (which is the only name she remembers, or chooses to remember, for this black soldier from Oklahoma) lived together in Vung Tau for two years. He was an Air Force radar technician. Bang got pregnant. Bill reenlisted for a second tour of duty, but his son was stubborn. He stayed in the womb two months past his due date.

Anh Dung (the "D" in his name is pronounced like a "Y") was born on a Navy medical ship off Vung Tau in 1968. Forty-five days later his father was discharged back to the United States. Bill wrote letters to his Vietnamese family, begging them to join him in Oklahoma, but Bang refused to leave her parents.

"Before, I wanted nothing to do with him," Anh Dung says of his father. "Now I want to tell him he has a son in America. I want to meet him once to know this man is my father. I don't need anything from him, but if he doesn't accept me, I can only feel worse. I have this emotional wound, and it can't be healed.

"It's bad enough not to know your father," he adds, "but it's worse to know he doesn't want you. This is why many Amerasians don't look for their fathers. We came here searching for a home and don't want to be abandoned again."

With increasing urgency, from 1968, when he left Vietnam, until 1975, when it was too late, Bill wrote to Bang, begging her to join him in the United States, where he remained unmarried and childless. In 1973, when Anh Dung was five years old and the war was nearly over, his uncle, a staff sergeant in the Air Force, came to Vung Tau with airplane tickets for the boy and his mother. He gave them twenty-four hours to think about it. When he returned, Bang said, "I'm not leaving. I have a family to support, and Vietnam is my land."

"Then give me the baby," he said. "I'll take him to America." Again she refused.

Anh Dung and his mother moved to Saigon, where she worked as a housekeeper for an American Air Force colonel and former B-52 pilot nicknamed Ong Diec, "the Deaf Man." "He paid my school fees," says Anh Dung. "We'd go shopping and I'd point to things and he'd buy them for me. I even had my own cyclo driver who'd wait for me when I went to the movies. One day the Deaf Man took me to the officers' club and got me a membership card. But the Communists came too fast. I never got to use it."

Two days before the collapse of the South Vietnamese government, the colonel handed Anh Dung and his mother airplane tickets to the United States. They drove to Tan Son Nhut airport and boarded a helicopter evacuating military personnel to ships in the South China Sea. The rotors had begun to turn when Anh Dung's mother started yelling, "Let me out! I'm going home!"

Grabbing her son, she jumped out of the helicopter. The colonel yelled to her, "When the Communists take over, you won't even have shit to eat!" Then he threw his wallet after her.

Anh Dung's mother opened a food stall on the street and began hawking the family furniture. She used the money to educate her son. He was forced to stay after school to clean the classrooms and got in lots of fights. In seventh grade, when they ran out of furniture, he left school and went to work. He sold rice in the market. He sang Vietnamese opera. He painted houses. He worked as a handyman, plumber, electrician—anything to make money.

"You take the pain and forget it," Anh Dung says about the special burden of being a black Amerasian. "Life is meant to have problems. If you are a good human being, you try to solve these problems quietly," he says, restating the Four Noble Truths of Buddhism, which begin by asserting that "existence is suffering."

"We are the war kids," he says. "Our fathers destroyed Vietnam. The Vietnamese know enough about racism in America to know that my father was 'lower class.' But the Vietnamese are also racist. They don't like the Chinese, Cambodians, Japanese. The Vietnamese are even racist among themselves. They look down on farmers whose skin is dark from working in the rice paddies."

In 1978 Anh Dung's mother changed her mind about going to America. This was a year before the Orderly Departure Program officially came into existence, and two years before the first refugee flights left the country. There was a rumor on the streets that the United States was taking back its kids. She went to the Fifth District police station in Saigon and demanded that she and her son be registered for ODP. "We have never heard of this program," they said. She kept shoving documents at them. "Take these papers. Even if nothing happens, I want my son registered." Later she would pay bribes to get the paperwork advanced.

"She was taking a big risk," says Anh Dung. "She was fifty-four, no longer a young woman. The Communists punished people who tried to leave the country. They seized your house and belongings. By the time we were finally allowed to leave, my mother was sick. She couldn't take care of her business, and I thought I was going to be dumped in an asylum. We were saved in the nick of time."

In 1983, after a five-year wait, they were called for an ODP interview. Termites had eaten holes in their papers, which had to be retyped. After being accepted by ODP, Anh Dung and Bang faced another wait. People advised them not to go. "They will kill you in the middle of the ocean and dump your body out of the airplane," they said.

Anh Dung was one of the first Amerasians allowed to leave Vietnam with his family. The police at the airport seized everyone's money and jewelry. But when people saw they were flying Air France to Bangkok, they knew it was going to be OK. They don't kill people on Air France, they thought.

There were seventy-one Amerasians on board, 291 people altogether. "Look out the window," said the pilot when they took off. "This may be the last time you see your native land. I wish you a happy future."

They spent nine days in Thailand's Phanat Nhikom refugee camp filling out paperwork and getting shots. This was a closed camp for boat people.

"It was a dangerous place," Anh Dung says. "You had to depend on others to survive. There were no beds or water. We slept on a cement floor, a dozen people to a room. This is where a lot of young girls got pregnant."

They spent another night sleeping in the Bangkok airport. When their plane took off, Anh Dung watched *Fistful of Dollars* and *Superman* and filled himself with American food. They stayed two days in a motel in San Francisco and then flew to New York. This time he watched a John Wayne movie. After a night in New York they started flying again on a little twenty-seater airplane. They had been traveling so many days that Bang was afraid they were going to end up back in Vietnam.

Three Amerasian families, nine people in all, landed in Utica on May 10, 1983. Rose Marie Battisti met them at the airport. She was waving an American flag. The ground was covered with snow. The trees were dead. "Is this where we are going to live?" asked Anh Dung's mother. "Yes, Mom," he told her. "We are going to be cowboys." She broke down crying. She thought they were going to die here.

The three families lived in the same apartment for a month. Anh Dung rode in a car for the first time when Rose Marie took him to the hospital for a checkup. "She asked me, 'What do you eat?' and tried to serve me milk and hamburgers." He was sent to ninth grade on the school bus. He was fifteen years old.

The teachers couldn't pronounce his name. "They gave me a huge pile of schoolbooks. When I tried to read them, the letters looked like ants shaken up in a jar." The school had no course in English as a second language. It didn't even have a Vietnamese dictionary. "I learned my English from Lucille Ball and Fonzie on *Happy Days*," he says. "I speak English like the Smurfs, not Hamlet."

On finishing tenth grade, Anh Dung became a tutor at the refugee center. By then another fifty Amerasians had been resettled in Utica. They were becoming a common sight, but people still called them names in the street, and once Anh Dung got arrested for fighting in the mall.

He graduated from high school in 1987. Rose Marie came to the ceremony. She was so proud she cried. He began studying computer science at Mohawk Valley Community College, until he noticed he was the only boy in a class of forty-nine girls. He switched to electrical tech, graduated, and began studying for an electrical engineering degree at the SUNY College of Technology in Utica.

"I'm going to be an air traffic controller," he says. This is the first of many career paths Anh Dung will mention, including joining the Air Force and opening a restaurant. "If I had money, I'd have America in my hands," he says. Ambition aside, there is one constant in Anh Dung's life—his mother. "I'll always take care of her like she took care of me."

The second mother in his life is Rose Marie Battisti. Anh Dung describes himself as "Rose Marie's sidekick. I do the outside work. I keep an eye on problems in the community. Without me, Rose wouldn't know what was going on." He and Battisti have appeared together at numerous conferences and congressional hearings. "My second year here, she had me give a speech in New York City in front of four thousand people and three congressmen. She makes them cry. I make them laugh."

On June 29, 1989, Anh Dung became a naturalized American citizen and legally changed his name to Clarence Taylor III. Soon after arriving in Utica, at the refugee center's annual Thanksgiving dinner at St. John's Church, he had met Clarence Taylor, Jr., who would later adopt him as his godson. A retired Army officer and Korean war veteran, Taylor has a Korean wife named Star. "He is a black man," says Anh Dung. "His story is just like my mother and father's, only he doesn't have any children."

Anh Dung changed his name, he says, so he'd "have an easier time fitting into American society. There's discrimination here against foreigners. I didn't want to swim alone."

He describes how it feels to be a triple minority in America: black, Amerasian, and foreign-born. "I feel more accepted by the Vietnamese than the blacks. The blacks don't know who I am. First, they called me *wetback*. When they figured out that wasn't right, they started calling me *chink*. Anyone with 'flat' eyes, a flat nose, and yellow skin is called *chink*. Chinks eat dogs and worms. There are lots of fights in town between Asians and blacks. Blacks used to dominate, but now the chinks have formed their own gangs. We take advantage of the fact that the blacks can't tell one Asian from another. We single them out and beat them up one at a time, just like the Vietnamese used to do to the Americans in Vietnam.

"The grownups don't accept me either. The first few times I went to Thanksgiving dinner with Clarence Taylor's family, I could tell they didn't like having me there. When I'm with Vietnamese, I'm Vietnamese. When I'm with Americans, I'm American. I am more Vietnamese than black, but the longer I live in America, the less Vietnamese I become. Amerasians don't really fit in anywhere," he concludes. "We don't know who our people are. We don't belong."

A Free Country

The old gray mare of exile ain't what it used to be.

Joseph Brodsky

The first thing one notices on entering the Mohawk Valley Resource Center for Refugees is the gauntlet of desks and chest-
high partitions that defines a narrow pathway down the center of
the room. At these desks sit the secretaries, counselors, and
translators who are the agency's front line. They are the machine
through which refugees are "processed." Immediately to the right
and left of the main entrance lie the offices of the director, deputy
director and financial manager. These offices hold the windows
that used to light the big room behind them. Other windowless
offices and classrooms have been knocked together at the back
of the building.

Working in the sepulchral gloom of the agency's main floor
are a host of Italian-Americans (Utica's original refugee population), a Czech sewing teacher, a couple of Russian translators,
and a handful of Vietnamese. Typical of the latter is Loi Hoang,
a boat refugee in his early twenties. Loi finished high school in
Nanuet, New York, and went on to study radiology at the local
community college. He dreamed of becoming a science or math
teacher, but was hired instead as a medical translator at the refugee center. The job involves a lot of driving to hospital emergency
rooms, which is where refugees get their medical care.

"I had forgotten how to speak Vietnamese when I came to
work here," Loi says. "My sentences were upside down. Friends
taught me how to talk again, but my Vietnamese is impolite. I've
lost all the nuances."

Sitting at the desk next to Loi is another young medical
translator named Thom. Born into a family of fishermen living

near Vung Tau, the old French colonial resort on the South China Sea, Thom was eleven when his parents put him in a boat with his three sisters and a brother. After six nights at sea they reached Singapore. The police came on board, gave them food, and pushed them back to sea. After three more nights of sailing they reached Indonesia. Following a year's internment on Galang Island, the five children went to live with a foster family in Herkimer, New York. Thom finished high school in Albany and then got a junior college degree in auto mechanics. He, too, has forgotten his native language. "I write to my parents in English, and my sister translates my letters into Vietnamese," he says.

⟨ Working near Loi and Thom are old hands like Hoa Truong, or "Big Mama" as she is known, a pillar in the Vietnamese Catholic community, and Mr. Tha, a former USAID employee with a degree from the University of Michigan in refrigeration and air-conditioning. Stationed next to them is Chi Truong, a former Army interpreter from III Corps who spent seven years on a bushwhacker team in the Mekong Delta. "It was a dangerous job," he says, "but we loved each other and helped each other."

Barraged by people wanting help filling out forms, securing jobs, getting medical care or schooling, the translators at the refugee center are the matchmakers introducing refugees to America. Across the street at the Florentine Pastry Shop the same function used to be fulfilled by the *padrone*, the patron. What he did for family reasons is now mandated by law; America's newest residents are entitled to this aid. But to refugees from Southeast Asia, the process still *feels* like family business. They imagine it entails what anthropologists call "debt service." In exchange for English classes or job referrals, they will owe their patrons food, contributions, and other gifts. This indebtedness, invisible to Westerners, is timeless for Asians, which helps explain why the low-level bureaucratic positions at the refugee center are such plum jobs.

·　·　·

The man who "tends shop" at the refugee center, standing by the front door every afternoon to say *do svidaniya*, goodbye, to the Russians and *chao tam biet* to the Vietnamese is Dick Sessler, the agency's deputy director. Sessler is a soft-spoken, sandy-haired man whose posture and hearing aid are the only hints of his former life. To avoid offending people, he describes himself as a retired "systems safety engineer." He is actually a twenty-two–year Air Force veteran who served as a radar navigator on B-52 bombing runs over Vietnam.

A twinkly little man with pale blue eyes, Sessler is still tough enough to break up the occasional fight. "We intentionally don't separate the Russians and Vietnamese," he says. "We want them to mingle. It's their first step in becoming Americans.

"Everybody in town loves the Russians," he adds. "The men are all rugged and know how to work with their hands. The women are quiet and demure. As soon as they can, they go out and buy a lot of household items. They fit right into the American dream. The Vietnamese aren't like this. You can tell in a heartbeat they're different."

Sessler can often be found putting out firestorms at the refugee center. One day Sharon Eghigian trots into his office to say that Duc, Quoc, and other Amerasians from the street-corner crowd are headed upstairs toward a classroom of Russians. "We're back to the 1920s," he says. "The mob is running loose."

The affair is still at the name-calling stage as Sessler hustles the Amerasians out of the building and tells them to clear off or he'll call the police. "This is a free country!" yells Duc. "We can stand on the sidewalk if we want."

"They don't really know what it is to live in a free country," says Sessler, returning to his office. "There's enough doubt in their minds that in five minutes they'll be gone."

He is right.

. . .

Finances at the refugee center are handled by an old friend of the director's named Alice Putnam, who occupies the third office with a window onto the street. This office is accessible only by walking to the rear of the building, jogging right at the snack machines, and then heading back out toward Bleecker Street. In other words, it is not really accessible at all. Putnam further protects her anonymity by keeping her door firmly shut.

She juggles contracts with Washington, New York State, Oneida County, the Lutherans, and the Utica City School Board, which pays the salaries of the agency's six English teachers. Complicating Putnam's job is the fact that everyone involved in resettling refugees in the Mohawk Valley has different fiscal years, deadlines, start-up dates, and performance criteria. "Considering the amount of paperwork they demand, you'd think we were importing farm laborers or marrying off refugees by the truckload," she says.

The State Department is the gatekeeper, deciding who fills the 125,000 refugee slots available each year. The dozen voluntary agencies contracted to resettle these refugees receive $655 per head, which is meant to cover their clients' first month in the United States. As refugees start getting food stamps and Medicaid, their caseloads shift to the Office of Refugee Resettlement in the Department of Health and Human Services. ORR funnels money to New York State, which in turn reimburses the local agencies that spend money on refugees.

How long refugees receive public assistance varies state by state, with California being the most generous. New York cuts benefits after four months, or sooner, if refugees try to go to college instead of getting a job. California, until its recent belt-tightening, offered three years of welfare and encouraged refugees to go to college for free. No wonder many of Utica's refugees head west as soon as possible.

California is the capital of the Vietnamese diaspora, which now numbers close to eight hundred thousand people in the United States alone. The commercial center of the community is

Orange County, with its Little Saigons and Vietnamese malls, but the cultural center is up north, around San Francisco Bay and the Silicon Valley. So numerous are the Vietnamese newspapers, publishing companies, radio stations, and TV channels that one can live here for years without speaking a word of English.

Medical matters at the refugee center are overseen by Lucille Gallo, another longtime friend of the director's. A gray-haired, grandmotherly woman, Gallo is the agency's former sewing teacher. Her desk at the back of the main floor allows her to keep an eye on the clientele, and a good part of Gallo's job consists of yelling at refugees who refuse to take their tuberculosis medicine. This is prescribed for the sixty percent of incoming refugees who test positive for TB. "The Russians throw away their pills," she says. "The Vietnamese save them up for suicides." The Russians also refuse to get chest X-rays. They are afraid of the radiation.

The bulk of Utica's Pentecostal refugees are White Russians from Minsk and other towns bordering the Ukraine. Heavily irradiated during the Chernobyl meltdown in 1986, these people now display a remarkably high incidence of brain tumors and thyroid cancers.

Other family friends of Executive Director Battisti work as secretaries and counselors at the refugee agency, and so, too, does her father, who holds the title of job developer. A former combat soldier in Korea who served in the Seventh Cavalry, Battisti's father suffers from post-traumatic stress syndrome or shell shock, as it used to be called. He has flashbacks and vomits at the smell of Asian food. He sits in his office at the refugee center chain-smoking and reading the newspaper.

The agency also employs two hardworking Cambodians, who are the last of what was once a large Cambodian refugee population in Utica. Samedy Sok does double duty as a job developer and youth counselor, while his uncle-in-law, Synath Sous Buth, fills Battisti's old job as resettlement director. Both men are survivors of Cambodia's "killing fields," the utopian ground zero that eliminated most of their family members and a million other Cambodians.

Synath, a gentle, quiet man with a touch of sadness about him, has the unenviable job of dealing with Utica's slum landlords. He fills their unused housing stock with refugees. They return the favor by skimping on basic amenities like heat and electricity, which he has to go begging for in the middle of the night. Thanks to Synath's efforts, five hundred refugees a year are settled into apartments furnished with couches, stoves, kitchen utensils, beds, TV sets.

"I know what it is to be a refugee," he says. "There is a lot of pain. It takes time to heal. Maybe it never heals."

The next crisis at the refugee center is a rash of attempted suicides. "Khai is in big trouble," I hear on the street. I had met Khai in Sharon Eghigian's class, where he was known for "acting out." Being illiterate, he had no idea what to do with himself in a classroom, other than break furniture and harass girls. Khai is an Afro-Amerasian, short and tough, with a skinhead haircut and a big scar in the middle of his forehead. When not overcome by fits of rage, he is a great joker with a beatific smile.

Khai got in trouble one day for teasing girls and was sent outside to sweep the sidewalk. Back in class, he started teasing them again. Sam was called to talk to him. "Why are you doing this?" Sam asked in Cambodian, which Khai speaks better than English or Vietnamese.

"So I can get back to work," he said. Eventually Sam dropped the idea of sending Khai to school and hired him as maintenance man at the refugee center.

His files from the PRPC describe Khai as "emotionally retarded and subnormal in intelligence. It is impossible for him to understand concepts."

"I don't believe it," says Sam, who has adopted Khai as one
of his special cases. "How can you speak three languages and be
retarded?" Khai suffers headaches so violent they make his nose
bleed. He was sent to the hospital for tests. The results were
negative.

Khai was born deep in the Mekong Delta on the Cambodian
border. His Khmer mother bore two black Amerasians by different fathers and three Vietnamese children by a man who later
spent ten years in jail for trying to escape the country. Khai's
records say he is seventeen. "He is really twenty," says Sam, who
keeps the true records in his head.

Khai worked herding water buffalo until the age of fourteen,
when he got a job as a rice porter on the Mekong River. Three
years later he was captain of his own boat—one of the large sampans used for shipping rice from the Delta to the South China
Sea. One day he sailed downstream to the ocean and then up the
coast to Saigon, where he walked into the offices of the Orderly
Departure Program and demanded to go to America.

The first sign of domestic trouble came shortly after Khai
and his family reached Utica in 1990. He smashed his family's
apartment, leaving all the windows, mirrors, plates, and even the
TV picture tube in shards. He had asked his mother to cash her
welfare check and buy him a gold necklace. She refused, saying
she needed the money for rent and food. This ticked him into
a rage.

It looks like the act of a madman, but the more scenes like
this I witness, and the more I learn about what provokes them, the
more my sympathies swing toward the Amerasians. Six people—
maybe related to him, maybe not, including a mother whom he
hadn't seen for years—rode to America on Khai's back. He engi-
neered the escape that cost his stepfather ten years in jail. Money
had changed hands to get this family "papered over," and for all
I knew, payment on this debt was still owing to Khai.

Sam was called to the wrecked apartment, where he stayed
until midnight keeping mother and son apart. He rented the fam-

ily another apartment. He paid the landlord for damages. Khai was ordered into psychiatric consuling. After his court hearing, he apologized to his mother and Sam. "I got in with the wrong crowd," he said. "I promise to do better."

The next I hear of Khai, he is in St. Elizabeth Hospital after ingesting 120 tablets of INH—isonicotinic acid hydrapide—a tuberculosis medication. He is in a coma. The doctors give him a fifty-fifty chance of surviving, and if he does survive, his liver and brain are likely to be destroyed.

Khai's is the first of what becomes a wave of suicide attempts. In the usual pattern, the boys stab themselves in the chest or slit their wrists. The girls overdose on INH. Among the attempted suicides are three girls, Diep, Ha, and Kieu, who all try to kill themselves the same week in what becomes known as the "Pastor A. affair." While his father recruited Vietnamese converts to his evangelical church, the pastor's son busied himself deflowering the young female members of the flock.

Diep's mother was a farm girl until she started working in the Army mess hall at Long Binh. In 1970 she bore twin daughters to mess sergeant "Ken"—no one remembers the rest of his name. Ken already had a wife and two children in the United States, and after he and the Army had left Vietnam, his Asian family went back to growing rice.

After the usual bribes and years of waiting, the twins, their mother, and five other relatives reached Utica in 1990. Pastor A.'s son started driving the family to church. "He said he loved my sister, and she loved him back," says Diep's twin. "She wanted to marry an American. Then he went away and made her sad." Diep took fifty INH tablets and was admitted to the hospital unconscious.

The second young woman involved with Pastor A.'s son is Ha, a black Amerasian enrolled at Mohawk Valley Community

College. Ha also works swing shift at CONMED, a local manufacturer of throwaway surgical supplies. She ingests a hundred pills. She is unconscious for two days. When she finally opens her eyes, her heart is pumping so fast, all she can do is cry.

The third new arrival reporting to the hospital that week, because of her involvement with the pastor's son, is Kieu, a beautiful, dark-haired young woman who looks like a fine work of porcelain. Kieu is one of the many Amerasians in Utica diagnosed as subnormal in intelligence. She lives not with her mother—as her immigration forms claim—but with her aunt and the woman's husband and two children. "My parents are not fair," she says. "I am the only Amerasian in my family, and no one respects me." In Vietnamese culture, lack of respect is a good reason to kill yourself.

Born in Saigon in 1969, Kieu's earliest memories are of working in the market selling chickens and pigs. She never went to school. After her mother disappeared in 1975, she began living with her aunt. "My aunt was sweet to me before we got to America," Kieu says. "But now we fight all the time. She was just using me to get here."

The week of the attempted suicides, 133 new refugees arrive in Utica. "We're treating numbers instead of individuals," Battisti admits. "We'll never have enough staff. It's just the nature of the business." I do notice one small change at the refugee center. Battisti stops posting flight numbers and other advance information on the bulletin board. "Too many people are looking for converts," she says.

Three weeks after her first attempted suicide, Diep drops to the floor unconscious in Pastor A.'s church and spends another two weeks in the hospital recovering from INH poisoning. Pastor A. is summoned to the refugee center for a meeting with the director.

"He had the nerve to tell me we weren't offering enough social support and outreach services," says Battisti. " 'That's not it,' I told him. 'Our biggest problem is your son, who can't keep his pants zipped.' " Soon after this meeting, Pastor A. is called to God in Georgia. His son goes with him.

Khai survives his suicide attempt. On regaining consciousness, he is sent to the Mohawk Valley Psychiatric Center. He had tried to kill himself once before in the Philippines by cutting his throat, and his doctors think he is trying to kill himself again when he refuses to eat. Sam is called in. He discovers the problem is hospital food. He brings Khai a rice cooker and after that he eats like a horse. Khai is soon out of the hospital and back at work sweeping floors at the refugee center. He shows no signs of liver or brain damage. When I next see him, he flashes me his brilliant grin and says, "Everything's going fine."

The professional literature on Amerasians highlights the large number with burn marks, scars, and other self-inflicted wounds. Amerasians suffer from poor self-image and an intense sense of loss, say the psychologists. They deny problems or avoid them. They are impulsive, needy, clinging. They distrust people, so working with them is difficult. Amerasians act out their psychological hurt with physical wounds. Self-mutilation is the visible sign of their despair.

The National Institute of Mental Health has asked Meme English, a psychotherapist in Amherst, Massachusetts, to study depression, suicide, and long-term adjustment among Amerasians in the United States. On one of her visits to Utica, which she hopes to use as a research site, English and I meet for drinks at the Radisson Hotel. English first got involved with Amerasians when she was called to a hospital in 1984 to look at a young woman who had been admitted to the psychiatric unit. The attending psychiatrist told her the woman didn't fit any of his diagnostic categories. Seventeen Amerasians had just been resettled in Amherst, half of them black, one of whom was the patient in question. English teaches developmental psychology, and she is interested in how identity develops among non-Western cultures. "Who does this woman think she is?" she wondered.

"I hypothesized she was trying to deny her blackness. In an extremely race-conscious culture, which Vietnam is, if you want to be accepted as Asian, you have to pretend you're anything but black."

This turned out to be true. The black Amerasians in Amherst engaged in lots of make-believe about who their fathers were. One kid insisted he was Hawaiian. Another said his father was an American Indian.

English also got interested in the idea of Amerasians coming "home" to their "fatherland." What would happen when their pariah status followed them to America? "Amerasians remind us of an embarrassing war, so the kids themselves are an embarrassment," she says. "Most are in crisis. They suffer from flight trauma. Half the Amerasians I've seen display signs of neurological disorders, either from abuse or malnourishment. There is something unsettling about the way Amerasians look. Don't you find them peculiar?" she asks.

When I mention the Pastor A. affair, English surprises me by agreeing with his criticism of Rose Marie Battisti. English points out that the refugee center staff includes not a single psychologist, social worker, or mental health specialist.

"Rose Marie is into denying mental health problems," she says. "If she admitted that Amerasians have problems with cultural identity or difficulty adjusting to life in America, she might look at her own Asian children and get scared. That's why problems in Utica are swept under the rug as fast as possible."

I choose not to repeat this remark to Rose Marie Battisti, but she vehemently defends herself against similar charges. "I don't have a guilty conscience keeping me awake at night. Sure, I worry that we're not doing enough. We could use more outreach workers in the community and more counselors. But we don't have the money for them. Do we close down because we can't do as much as we could?"

As the crises mount around her, Battisti becomes increasingly edgy. But the local paper continues to run only good news out of the refugee center—stories about Amerasians getting high school diplomas and jobs at CONMED and other local companies. None of the suicide attempts is reported. None of the gunfights or arrests. Except for the increasing frequency of Asian names in the police blotter, no one suspects the problems facing Utica's refugee population.

Now when I walk into the former furniture store on Bleecker Street, it feels like a Potemkin village. Behind a stage set of grateful Amerasians studying "survival" English lies a more perilous world, with an alarming gap between appearance and reality. Just as the Utica program is gaining national prominence as the country's most successful Amerasian resettlement agency, its clientele is beginning to self-destruct.

Becoming American

Everyone is quick to blame the alien.

Aeschylus

One of the buildings attesting to Utica's former glory is the New York State Lunatic Asylum, which was opened in 1843 as America's first modern hospital for the insane. The 290-acre site, located between the brewery and the old Dunlop tire factory, is now called the Mohawk Valley Psychiatric Center. The original neoclassical asylum once housed over two thousand patients. The building is a national historic landmark, with Doric columns and a frieze that rival those of the Parthenon, but the gray limestone monument is now in ruins.

Next to this once noble edifice, with bars over its smashed-out windows, are the modern buildings put up for the facility's current residents. There is also a home for unwed mothers, a detox center, and a former nurses' residence called the Dixhurst Building. A three-story red-brick structure unoccupied for fifteen years, the Dixhurst is in the process of being refurbished for Utica's newest refugees when I first visit it in the summer of 1990. This is the future site of Welcome Home House.

The premise is simple. Seventy-five Amerasians at a time will spend three months in Utica adjusting to life in America, before being resettled in other mid-sized cities. The program is budgeted for eight hundred thousand dollars, with sixty percent of the money coming from the State Department. The experiment is more costly than warehousing refugees in the Philippines, but the argument that acculturation to American life is best done in America, and heavy political pressure from refugee resettlement agencies and contrite veterans' groups, forced the State Department to greenlight the project. The program is scheduled to end after fifteen months, because everyone assumes that by then there will be no more Amerasians left in Vietnam.

On that muggy summer day, the kind that turns upstate New York into a mass of hyperactive greenery, I drove onto the grounds of the psychiatric center. The lawns are shaded by sycamores and willows, and where there used to be madmen and -women shouting out the windows, there is only the sound of wind moving through the trees and a car backfiring—or maybe it's a gunshot—somewhere on the west side of town. Inside Welcome Home House, Anh Dung is running a work crew of a half-dozen Amerasians, recruited from the refugee center across town, who have volunteered to fix up the building. It is filled with dust and peeling paint. "We feel like we're making a home for our own people," he says. "We want them to be part of one big family when they get here."

I pick up a paintbrush and join them in slapping a coat of government gray on the basement walls. There are no ladders. We stand on overturned milk crates. There are no rollers. We make do with one-inch finishing brushes. The ceiling is laced with asbestos-covered pipes so it has to be painted by hand anyway. Everyone soldiers on without complaint, acting as if they *prefer* to paint ceilings with one-inch brushes. The fumes are thick, the tape deck loud with Vietnamese rock and roll.

We are relieved when John Sisley, or Father John, as the Vietnamese call him, announces a lunch break outside on the lawn. Barefoot and shirtless, we file out of the basement to confront a plastic sheet covered with take-out hamburgers and sodas. The Amerasians squat around the sheet. No one touches the food. "How much did this cost?" asks Anh Dung.

"Twenty-five dollars," says Father John.

"Give us *twenty* dollars tomorrow," says Anh Dung, "and we'll cook our own lunch: stir-fried steak and peppers, served with ice water. Vietnamese food is much better for you."

A Presbyterian minister whom the Vietnamese mistake for a Catholic priest, Father John is a hefty man with a white beard and red nose. He is locally renowned for impersonating Santa Claus and Harry Truman. Sisley is in charge of coaxing donations for Welcome Home House out of the neighboring community, and judging from the list of donors, he is doing a great job. A church ladies' auxiliary is sewing nine dozen curtains. The Masons have promised two hundred mattresses. Sears is donating fifty gallons of paint. Corpsmen from Griffiss Air Force Base will install the fire doors, and work crews from the local prisons will help with the painting.

"Assuming there aren't any more POWs in Vietnam," says Sisley, "we're finally bringing home the last victims of the war." He asks if I have heard the soundtrack to *Miss Saigon*, the musical about Amerasians that has just opened in London. He took a copy into Rose Marie's office and played it on his portable tape deck. They both started crying.

"I didn't think anything in this business could make me cry again," said Rose Marie. "I thought I'd seen it all."

"You think life shat on you?" Sisley asks rhetorically. "Hey, buddy, compared to being an Amerasian, your life is a piece of cake."

After lunch I sit under a maple tree talking to the Amerasians. Anh Dung's former fiancée, Le Ha, translates for me. A feisty young woman who speaks good English, Le Ha hits people over the head with a rolled-up newspaper when she thinks their answers are incomplete or untrue. Some of my questions she finds silly. "Is life better in the United States or in Vietnam?" for example. But when we later talk about her own life, and she is on the verge of tears thinking about growing up in Vietnam, she admits, "The answer is not so simple."

To man his work crew, Anh Dung has enlisted all the street punks, including Quoc with the tricolored hair, Khai and Duc, who is thinking of graduating from auto theft to home invasions. Facing Le Ha, they look like the Lost Boys sitting in front of

Wendy. A few months ago they were tending water buffaloes in a rice paddy, and now they are making new lives in America. The past is receding, the future is unknown, and the present is a mysterious amalgam of things that *look* familiar—trees, stars, streets—but are actually different trees, different stars and streets than anything they have ever seen before. No wonder, even with Le Ha's prompting, the answers to my questions are hard to elicit.

Among the street-corner crowd is Van, a squirrelly twenty-one-year-old covered with tattoos and burn marks on his arms and legs. Even without his front teeth, he has a sweet smile. His mother is Cambodian, his father Hispanic, he thinks. Van came to the United States a year and a half ago with his grandmother and younger sister. Tattooed on his chest is a picture of his wife, who is still in Vietnam with their two-year-old child. Le Ha translates the words written above the picture, "Always Remember Me." Tattooed on Van's right shoulder are more words: "Sad Hard Life."

"I want to join the U.S. Army, go back to Vietnam and kill all the Vietcong," he says.

The next person to face the rolled-up newspaper is "Big" Loc, a strapping twenty-one-year-old with brilliant green eyes and red hair. Loc transported six people to the United States as his fake family, before he was kicked out of the house. "I was mad at my family," he says, explaining why his left arm is scarred with a cross of cigarette burns.

"He will always be mad at his family," says Le Ha. "He gets depressed. He drinks. He is a good boy, but he gets into too many fights." She orders Loc to lift up his trousers and show us the ugly red holes where he was recently shot in the leg with four bullets.

So the stories go, one hard-luck tale after another, until Le Ha and I are left alone on the lawn. In the course of the afternoon she has been rolling her baton tighter and tighter, using it to coax out of people the truth about their ages, fake families, arrest records, aspirations. "Vietnamese people never tell you the truth," she says. "They don't want you to know too much about them."

Le Ha's plucked eyebrows have been replaced by two black slashes that when drawn together give her the look of an operatic warlord about to destroy the world. She is a short woman with a throaty voice and beautiful smile. She smokes too much. She has hazel eyes, a freckled face, and jet black hair, which she wears swept over her forehead to hide the scar where her mother hit her with a chair. She suffers from headaches and mercurial mood swings. She is a devout Buddhist, the most spiritual of the Amerasians in Utica. At times she also seems programmed for failure. With the first sign of success, she will drop out of school, quit a job, leave a boyfriend.

Le Ha's grandmother, who came from a wealthy family near Da Nang, was the first of her husband's eight wives. When he died, she converted her house in Phan Thiet into a temple and became a nun at the age of thirty-three. Only two of her eleven children survived the war. Her ninth child, Tuyet, ran away from home to work in a bar at the Vinh Long Air Force Base. Here Tuyet met a lieutenant named Wolfe who bought her a house and married her in both civil and Buddhist ceremonies. Their daughter, Le Ha, was born in 1966. Tuyet and Wolfe lived together for a year, until he returned to the States, where he already had a wife and two children.

Would she like to meet her father? "No," she says. "He has another family in America. What's he going to do with two families? I'm used to living without a father. Sometimes I forget babies have both mothers and fathers. I want to have a child, but I don't want to have a husband. I want to live alone, and if I have a chance, I'll become a nun. That's what I want for my future."

When her American husband left Vietnam, Tuyet moved to Saigon and began waitressing at the Dong Khanh restaurant in Cholon. The owner of the restaurant, who had no children of her own, fell in love with Tuyet's freckled daughter. She sent her to school in a chauffeur-driven car. Le Ha's mother rode beside her, but because she wore a restaurant uniform, people thought she was her maid. When Le Ha and her mother later started selling cigarettes on the street corner, the vendors remembered them. "Oh, you were once very rich!" they exclaimed. "And you still have the same maid!"

Le Ha dropped out of school in 1975, but continued studying literature with her Chinese stepfather, who was a welder in Cholon. From her grandmother, the nun in Phan Thiet, she learned how to lead worshippers in reciting the Buddhist sacred texts, and from her aunt, who owned a pharmacy, she learned how to cure people with traditional roots and herbs. Many of the Amerasian suicide attempts in Utica, especially the INH overdoses, are treated by Le Ha with herbal emetics.

"A lot more Amerasians try to kill themselves than anyone knows about at the refugee center," she says. "People call me in the middle of the night saying, 'I'm going to die.' Their mothers won't let them go to the hospital. So I rush over and purge them with a mixture of lemon juice and Vietnamese green beans, which makes you throw up real fast.

"They don't really want to die. They do it so everyone will see their love. The Vietnamese are very serious about love," she says. "We kill ourselves for lack of love. In Asia, we stab ourselves or jump in the river. Here we take drugs; it's part of our becoming American."

In 1978, as the Chinese were being flushed out of Cholon, Le Ha and her parents were moved to a *vung kinh te moi*, a New Economic Zone. "They gave us a house with a mud floor and walls made of coconut leaves. We had to become rice farmers, although we had never planted rice before, and we almost starved to death waiting for the first harvest."

Four years later the family moved back to Saigon. Since their house had been confiscated, they slept on mats in the open air and survived by selling cigarettes in front of the Palace movie theater. Le Ha speaks matter-of-factly about the beatings she received from her mother. "They were meant to teach me to be a good person," she says. A fight between her mother and stepfather over one of these beatings broke up their marriage.

"People treated Amerasians like slaves or animals, as if they had no heart or soul or feelings. 'You make my family look bad,' said my aunt in Phan Thiet when I went to visit her. She beat me with a bamboo stick or the tail of a ray fish, which left welts on my skin that stung and later became infected. Sometimes she hit me so hard the stick broke in her hands. I never said a word or cried. 'When you're finished, let me know,' I told her. My head was harder than bamboo."

Le Ha's life with her mother was not much better. One beating left a splinter lodged in her skull. Le Ha hides the yellow welt on her forehead under a fringe of hair. As a result of these beatings, she suffers from dizzy spells and fits of rage in which she smashes everything around her. When she finishes, she "wakes up" and says, "Oh, no! What have I done now?" Sometimes she finds herself walking in the snowy streets of Utica without a coat. She has no idea where she is or how she got there.

"Amerasians all have the same stories," she says. "We remind people of the things they want to forget—the war, the bombs, the killing and suffering. We carry bad memories. Here in America, we remind people of the soldiers who went to Asia and never came back. Le Ha means 'river of tears.' My life is too much like my name."

After spending twelve long months at the refugee camp on the Bataan Peninsula, Le Ha and her mother reached Utica in 1985. Her first dream about her new life in America was dashed when she was told she was too old to go to high school. She worked for a year at the Juilliard cloth factory in New York Mills. Then she joined her mother at the Meyda Stained Glass Corporation, where they stayed for a couple of years, until her mother's eyesight began to fail. "We worked long hours soldering stained-glass lamps, but the fumes from the solder eventually make you go blind."

While her mother sewed suit collars at Joseph and Feiss during the day and tended plants at Baker Greenhouses in the evening, Le Ha took jobs working back-to-back shifts at McDonald's, Burger King, Hemstrought's Bakeries, CONMED, Mele Manufacturing, Joseph and Feiss, and the Dunlop tire factory, now called Utica Converters, which manufactures tire cord.

"I've had every job an Amerasian in Utica can get," she says. "I never slept more than five hours a night, until 1990, when I injured my back working the night shift at Utica Converters and went on disability."

Le Ha by then had saved ten thousand dollars, which she gave to her mother to buy a house. They share this house with Anh Dung, his mother, and Le Ha's new stepfather, a former ARVN soldier, who has another wife and three children in Vietnam.

Le Ha met Anh Dung in 1985 when he tutored her in English at the refugee center. Two years later they were engaged to be married. They lived together for two more years and then broke off their engagement. "Nobody is good enough for me to love," she says, smiling. She tells me their relationship is over. They are nothing more than friends. But one still senses, from the murderous knit to her eyebrows, how jealous she can be.

As the sun goes down behind the maple trees shading the asylum's lawns, I ask Le Ha what she remembers about Vietnam.

"When I think about the street where I grew up, where I worked, and where I had a hard time, it makes me want to cry. I miss the food, the market, how warm and beautiful it was. I lived there seventeen years. I miss my country. I love my country. But they have been very stupid to me."

Anh Dung sits in the living room of the house he and his mother share with Le Ha's family. The room is packed with two sofas, a coffee table, TV, stereo, tropical fish tank, and shelves loaded with Hong Kong videos dubbed into Vietnamese, which Anh

Dung rents to his neighbors. The remaining wall space holds two framed photos.

They show a Vietnamese woman with a Jackie Kennedy beehive hairdo and a dapper man with closely cropped hair and a pencil-thin mustache. The woman's eyebrows have been plucked and shaped. She wears a white off-the-shoulder dress, a jade ring, and a watch with a gold band. He wears a suit and snappy tie with a zigzag pattern. She leans to her left. He leans to his right. In these hand-tinted photos, shot in a Vung Tau studio in 1966, the peach-colored wash makes the man look like a Vietnamese Negro.

From under the coffee table Anh Dung pulls a photo album holding other pictures from Vietnam. One shows him as a two-month-old baby in his mother's arms. The most remarkable thing about him is his size. He says he came out of the womb two months late and weighed twelve pounds at birth. By the time this photo was taken, he must have weighed fifteen pounds.

Other photos in the album show a young woman, Anh Dung's cousin, swimming in the ocean off Vung Tau, friends of his mother's posing on the beach, his uncle's house in Bien Hoa. Then the scene switches to Saigon, where his mother is working as housekeeper for Ong Diec, "the Deaf Man." A photo dated New Year's Day 1975 shows the gray-haired American pilot dining with two women in the My Canh floating restaurant on the Saigon River. The table is loaded with food. A silver bucket holds a bottle of champagne. *Having a good time with Ly and Hon,* reads the caption on the back.

Hon—her real name is Bang—is Anh Dung's mother. Her face in the photo is heavier, more careworn than it was ten years earlier in Vung Tau. Ly is the "love connection" Hon procured for her American employer. The young, winsome Ly is dressed in a yellow *ao dai*. She wears a bright smile on her face. The pot-bellied pilot, his arm around her neck, is also smiling broadly for the camera.

The last of Anh Dung's Vietnamese photos shows the wedding of a half-brother, who is six years older. The bride wears alternately a white Western dress and a traditional red Vietnamese gown. The groom's relatives—minus Anh Dung and his mother, who by then were already in the United States—stand at her side. The bride's parents stand at his side. This is a sign of acceptance into each other's families. The photos are shot in front of two ceremonial arches. Written on the arch at the groom's house are the words, "We accept you." The bride's arch says, "I will follow."

I ask Le Ha, who is sitting at the dining-room table studying for her high school equivalency exam, if she has any photos of her own from Vietnam. She shows me a picture of her grandmother, a small woman with a shaved head, who is wearing the yellow robes of a Buddhist nun. Le Ha stands beside her. The nun is seated in a well-appointed room with tile floors, a TV set, a stereo, and pictures on the walls. Her down-turned mouth shows not a hint of forgiveness. "All day long all she had for me was a frown," says Le Ha.

Nuns are not allowed to wear shoes in the temple, which explains why Le Ha's grandmother is barefoot. Nor are they allowed to touch money. Le Ha's grandmother ate one meal a day and spent the rest of her time studying the Buddhist sacred texts. Le Ha helped with the temple rituals. She read the *Kinh Dieu-Phap Lien-Hoa*, the Buddhist Bible, out loud for an hour, four times a day.

When I ask her to recite some lines, Le Ha picks up a well-thumbed copy of the book and begins reading. I stare at the family altar, placed on a plywood shelf on the wall. The altar holds a goddess rising out of a lotus bloom, three jade Buddhas, a fresh pomegranate, an incense burner, three electric candles, a canopy of blinking Christmas lights, and a handful of rice in memory of some newly dead family member. Le Ha sings the Buddhist text like a chant. Suddenly she stops reading and blushes. "This is a religious experience for me," she says. "It makes me peaceful and calm. It is the only time I am no longer sad."

.   .   .

There is a knock on the door. In walks Charlie Brown with a long face and some photos of his own. "Look at these," he says, throwing an envelope full of snapshots on the table. "This is proof that Thi Le Ha was betraying me with another man. Ever since they got here, I sensed my family was bullshitting me. I couldn't explain at the time, but now I can."

Shot at the Bataan camp, the photos show Charlie's fiancée standing beside an Amerasian boy. A teenager like her, slender and handsome, the boy is dressed in a white shirt and dark trousers. A cute couple, I think to myself. How much happier they look than the May-December couple I have seen in photos of Thi Le Ha and Charlie.

"When they came to Utica I asked her mother, 'Is Thi Le Ha in love with someone else? Is there anyone she wants to be with apart from me?' " says Charlie. " 'No,' her mother said. 'She wants to be with you. In two or three years, when she is older, she will be your wife.' Then this letter came, and I opened it. When I saw these photos of her with someone else, it broke my heart. Her mother is standing beside them. She knew all about it. She must have approved. In the letter, the boy says he wants to help the family move to Pennsylvania.

"Why didn't they tell me?" asks Charlie. "All these months I'm preparing for them to come. I do all the paperwork to sponsor them to Utica. I get them clothes, an apartment, all sorts of nice things. I stop seeing my friends, just to work and bring home money. Now I have no friends and no girlfriend either. This was my first time in love, and she stole my heart."

Frowning down at the table, Anh Dung fingers the photos and then tries to cheer up his friend by referring to his own love troubles.

"Our two Has are both heartbreakers," he says. "But you're lucky. It took five years for my heart to get broken. Yours got broken a lot faster."

The Father Search

Exile is life.

Victor Hugo

Exile is death.

—Ovid

Operation Homecoming supposedly returned the last American soldiers from Vietnam. The Amerasian Homecoming Act airlifted their children to the United States. With all this talk of *homecoming*, one would expect to find a program for reuniting fathers and children, and another program for helping them talk to each other after two decades apart. Neither program exists. Professionals in the refugee business publish papers and hold seminars on what they call the "father search." But by the time the psychologists and other experts have finished "clarifying" the subject, one is supposed to understand why Amerasians should be *prevented* from searching for their fathers. "We are dealing not only with a father search, but also an identity search," warns a Lutheran document. Like most papers on the subject, it affirms the "paramount importance of privacy and confidentiality." In other words, the interests of the fathers are more important than those of their children.

A Veterans Administration document on family reunification states, "The veteran's wishes regarding the establishment of contact are controlling." All precautions should be "taken to protect the veteran from unwanted and embarrassing disclosures."

The National Personnel Records Center in St. Louis, which stores information on former military personnel, keeps its files closed to the children of soldiers. When denying requests for information, the NPRC cites the "Department of Defense Privacy Program," which stipulates that no information be released without written permission from the man involved. This oath of silence is why no more than a couple of hundred Amerasians, out

of the twenty-five thousand airlifted to the States, have found
their fathers.

Shirley McGlade, director of the British organization War
Babes, sued the U.S. Department of Defense in 1990, in an effort
to overturn its oath of silence. McGlade is the illegitimate offspring of a British mother and American soldier stationed in En-
gland during the Second World War. Similar liaisons produced
250,000 babies during the war, half of them illegitimate.
"They're overpaid, oversexed, and over here," complained the
British about the one and a half million Yanks then occupying
their island. Signs posted in villages near military bases warned,
"Please drive carefully. That child might be yours."

It was U.S. government policy to break off these Anglo-
American relationships with payment of one hundred pounds to
the pregnant woman, who had to sign an agreement promising not
to search for the father of her child. He was then transferred to
another post. McGlade and three hundred other War Babes had
spent years searching for their fathers. The St. Louis federal ar-
chives acknowledged that they had these men's addresses, but
refused to release them.

War Babes finally took its case to the U.S. District Court for
the District of Columbia. Their supporting documents included
affidavits from eight American fathers who said their reunions
with their British children were among the happiest moments in
their lives. Lawyers for the Pentagon countered by arguing that
"Fatherhood of an illegitimate child during youth is at worst embarrassing and at a minimum highly personal. Contact by any individual, particularly a long-lost illegitimate child, is clearly
intrusive, whether welcome or not."

Ruling in favor of War Babes and "similarly situated individuals," the court recognized that soldiers' children have three
interests more compelling than their fathers' right to privacy.
They are entitled to know their genetic origins and medical history; they might be legatees of inheritances; and they have a psychological need to establish their identity. The court ordered the

Department of Defense to open its files to McGlade and her colleagues, and it specifically extended these rights to other children looking for their fathers, including Amerasians.

I drive down to St. Mary's Street in Utica looking for John Yankevich, a car salesman at Mohawk Motors, Pham, the woman he married nineteen years after he left her pregnant in Vietnam, and Manh, or John Yankevich, Jr., their son. The older Yankevich, wearing a Hawaiian shirt with shorts and bare feet, is a handsome, strong-featured man with a graying mustache and a quiet, unassuming way of talking.

He tells me he is no longer working at Mohawk Motors. "You're supposed to sell twelve cars a month, but I never managed more than nine." Pham, a slender, dark-haired woman, who is barefoot like her husband, serves us ginger ale. At Yankevich's insistence, she sits in the room, but refuses to come closer than a seat in the corner near the kitchen.

Yankevich and his wife are now working the day shift at Mele Manufacturing. Located in one of the city's old knitting mills, the company makes jewelry boxes and book bindings. "It's minimum wage, but Pham is happy speaking Vietnamese with her friends all day," he says. Before moving to Utica, Yankevich worked in California as a concrete finisher, where he made good money. "I put financial aspects aside when I married Pham," he says, smiling.

John Yankevich was born in the northern New Jersey town of Franklin in 1947. He was a poor student. "I was super skinny, which made me pugnacious and violent." His father worked as a clerk and his mother was a secretary at the military arsenal in Dover, New Jersey. He was an only child.

After high school, Yankevich enrolled in Jacksonville University in Florida, where he met lots of vets back from Vietnam. "I had no politics," he says. "I was selfish and wanted to do something and it seemed there was a lot going on over there." He quit school in 1968 and enlisted in the Army. He scored high on the entrance tests so they sent him into military intelligence.

Yankevich became a special agent for Army intelligence stationed in Reading, Pennsylvania. He investigated other people for security clearances. He fingered an agent who falsified records and was commended. He volunteered to go to Vietnam in place of another agent whose wife was pregnant. "They sent me to counseling. They thought I had a problem. I told them I wanted to go because it would better my rank, but I really wanted to go because I thought it would be an adventure. I told them I hated Communists and wanted to fight them, but really I was only concerned for myself."

Another agent in Reading got caught falsifying records, and the entire office was shipped to Vietnam in 1970. Yankevich was sent to Vung Tau to train as an agent in the Phoenix Program. "We fed intelligence up through the channels to CIA assassination squads, who were supposed to 'neutralize' three thousand VC a month. Without any language training, I was supposed to identify reliable Vietnamese informants. I'm sure we made mistakes and killed some innocent people. But that kind of thing went on all the time."

Yankevich was transferred to military intelligence in the 101st Airborne Division at Camp Campbell in Phu Bai, south of Hue. "It was late in the war, and all the countryside around Hue was a free-fire zone. We weren't allowed in the cities or villages. There was no fraternization with the local people. I wasn't exposed to them that much in Vietnam, so I know very little about the Vietnamese."

Yankevich's contacts with local people came mainly through evaluating information from enemy soldiers who had surrendered under a special "open arms" amnesty. "I liked them," he says. "I was impressed by how these people believed in what they were doing. Accused of being dirty and underhanded, they were actually intelligent, earnest, professional people.

"As I developed a political consciousness, I had second

thoughts about whose side I was on. I also began questioning whose side I was on in the U.S. military. There was a war between the officers and enlisted men. I was supposed to be on the officers' side, but instead I felt sorry for the soldiers."

One day Yankevich looked out his office door to see a pretty Vietnamese girl hopping from pallet to pallet through the muddy street. He continued watching as she washed her feet under a spigot. On learning that the girl worked next door as a seamstress in the tailor shop, Yankevich remembered that he needed to sew his name tag on his dress uniform. Soon he and the girl were smiling and waving to each other on their way to work.

Pham lived with her parents in Hue. She rode the bus or hired a cyclo to Phu Bai, except when Yankevich, worried about enemy action in the area, drove her home. She appreciated the rides, but didn't think they were necessary. "VC no sweat," she'd say. She was eighteen. He was twenty-three. They fell in love.

"I was a troubled person," says Yankevich, assuming all the blame for what he did in the middle of an impossible war. "Pham became pregnant the first time we made love. I had told her I would never get married or take her to the United States. She said, 'Fine.' But she couldn't believe I wouldn't marry her when she got pregnant. She thought she'd sprung a trap on me. But I didn't want a woman forcing me to do things. I was strong of mind and weak of character."

Yankevich shipped out of Vietnam in April 1971. His son was born the following month. As a going-away present, he left Pham four towels and two hundred dollars in cash. "She was a woman of extraordinary character. I failed to see that," he says, on the verge of tears. "Everyone in camp thought I should marry her. I was hated for not marrying her. The only thing I can say in my defense is that I never lied to her."

He gave her his father's address in New Jersey. She gave him a lock of hair and her picture. He tried to give her a Buddha he wore around his neck on a gold chain, but she hated the sight of it, because it wasn't Christian. She wouldn't even take the chain. "Before I got married for the first time," he says, again on the verge of tears, "my wife found Pham's hair and picture and destroyed them."

We sit in silence as he holds his hands over his face. "I missed this girl so much when I got back to America. I assumed it would go away, but it didn't. I just couldn't get her out of my mind." His commanding officer in Phu Bai wrote to tell him he was the father of a son. The news made him even more depressed.

"She was American," Yankevich says of the woman he married on returning to the United States, "but my father said she looked Asian. All during that marriage I thought of Pham continuously. I sent her fifty dollars before my wedding. I didn't want a child, but my wife did. The boy died of crib death. After that I made her take birth control pills. She left me in Florida in 1975."

Yankevich did construction jobs. He started working the shrimp boats off Louisiana and Texas and then moved into the Gulf of Mexico oil fields. "I was very antisocial, antigovernment, antireligion. I was a heavy drinker, a very unhappy person. A lot of the guys with me on the rigs were vets. We were all in the same shape." Three-month tours on the oil boats off Freeport, Texas, alternated with nonstop barroom binges.

The only contact he had with normal society came from watching TV in rented motel rooms, if he was sober enough to watch. Whenever news about Vietnam came on, he would turn the channel or leave the room. He can't even remember the make and model of cars he owned after 1975. He lost touch with the world and didn't check back in for another ten years.

After blowing most of a $3,500 paycheck in the bars, Yankevich caught a bus to Santa Barbara, California. After a night in the rescue mission, he moved into a skid row apartment on his fortieth birthday. "I was old and skinny," he says. "Every day I thought about finding Pham and my son. This is what I wanted more than anything else in the world."

Down at the rescue mission Yankevich had learned he

could make good money fishing for pollack in Alaska. He shipped out on a factory trawler plying the Aleutians. Here he met a lot of nineteen-and twenty-year-old Vietnamese boys. One of the kids referred to himself as Amerasian. Yankevich had never heard the word *Amerasian* before. Until then, he assumed that everyone born in Vietnam was Vietnamese. The boy said his name was Cang. Pham had told Yankevich that if she had a son she would name him Cang. The boy was eighteen, just the right age. He said his mother came from Hue. Yankevich couldn't stop thinking about his family.

He met more Amerasians in Seattle, where he worked in the siremi industry, making fake crab legs out of pollack. When it got too cold to fish, he moved back to Santa Barbara in the fall of 1989. After Thanksgiving dinner with a couple of fishing buddies, he drove his Suburban truck out to the ocean. "I loved to watch the sun set over the water. There was one place in particular I went—a meditational, inspirational point with pine trees on it. I was looking out over the ocean, when all of a sudden a voice came into my head: 'Pham and your son are in America.' I shook my head and said to myself, 'Take it easy, old man. You're having a flashback.' "

He was driving home, wrestling with himself over this vision, which he had just decided to dismiss, when he was knocked unconscious in a car crash. After two operations and a lot of physical therapy, he ended up with a metal screw in a separated shoulder. When he got around to phoning his father that Christmas, he was told, "There's a letter here from a man in Utica, New York. He says he's seen Pham and your son. Pham wants to know if you're still carrying a lock of her hair."

The letter was from William Fitzpatrick, Pham's landlord. Fitzpatrick was in love with her and wanted to marry her, but her son objected and punched out the windows in Fitzpatrick's house. Fitzpatrick thought he could get the boy to change his mind if he could prove his father was already married.

Yankevich phoned Fitzpatrick in Utica, who confirmed the news that Pham was in America. Yankevich started babbling, "Tell her I still love her."

"Tell her yourself," said Fitzpatrick. "Here's her phone number."

Yankevich called Pham. "Hello, this is John."

"John?" she said.

"John Yankevich. The father of your son." He heard a huge sigh on the other end of the line.

"Are you married?" she asked.

"No," he said. "I have no wife or children." She sighed again.

"We wrote each other and exchanged photos. After a brush with death and a revelation, I was ready for this moment. It made my life whole again. It changed my outlook on the Supreme Being and the meaning of life, one hundred percent."

Yankevich bought an old pickup truck, waved goodbye to the Pacific Ocean, and headed east. Outside Cheyenne, Wyoming, he broke an axle and rolled off the road. The truck was totalled. He unloaded his concrete and plastering tools, a duffel bag of clothing, and a guitar he had bought for his son. He left behind all his winter clothes and books and caught a bus to Utica. He arrived on the evening of May 18, 1990, the day before his son's nineteenth birthday.

"Pham opened the door and hugged me. She looked exactly the same as when I'd left her. I held her in my arms and kissed her, realizing what a treasure she is. All the neighbors came out of their apartments to meet me. Beyond the crowd of people, I saw someone walk into the kitchen and sit down. I stared at him. The thought struck me, 'He looks exactly like my father.' I stood there staring, until Pham pushed me toward the kitchen. I went over and shook his hand. Then I handed my son his guitar and said, 'Happy birthday.'"

.   .   .

For all her outward deference, Pham is a tough survivor. In 1975, she and her son fled to Da Nang and then farther south to Cam Ranh Bay and Lam Son. Here she earned enough money sewing hats to send her son to school. He studied kung fu and learned to play American folk songs on the guitar. They applied to leave Vietnam in 1986 and reached America four years later.

"It's easy for me to get depressed or angry about all those wasted years," says Yankevich. "Maybe it was better for our son to grow up in Asian society, which is more successful than ours at building strong personal character. But I can't say those intervening years were beneficial to me. I have no savings from that period or any useful skills. I'm a Vietnam vet who hasn't escaped the pitfalls we're noted for," he concludes, with a wry grin, "but I've survived them and gained some knowledge in the process."

Yankevich tells me he recently saw a TV show about homeless vets living on the streets or sleeping in their cars. "The pictures stared back at me with my own face when I was living apart from society," he says. "Americans still can't admit we lost the war. The Vietnam vets take the blame for it, and they blame themselves. But whatever we suffered is nothing compared to what our kids went through. I feel an obligation to help the Amerasians here in town, particularly the orphans. I didn't think our government would ever do anything so morally correct as bring these children to the United States. But now that they're here, somebody has to do something for them."

John Yankevich and Pham were married in the Church of Our Lady of Lourdes in August 1990. His nineteen-year-old son, Manh, was the best man. William Fitzpatrick gave away the bride. A local limousine company donated a car and champagne. Mohawk Motors presented the newlyweds with a truckload of furniture. Much of the thousand-strong Vietnamese community in Utica turned out for the wedding. "Love shall triumph, though lovers be parted," trumpeted a four-column, page-one article in the Utica newspaper. The accompanying photo shows a smiling Yankevich, his arms around his wife and son. Pham barely comes up to his chest. Manh stares gravely out at the world from under the same bushy eyebrows as his father.

Before agreeing to marry him, Pham wanted him to straighten up his appearance, and become a Catholic. She also wanted to test him. He had not touched alcohol for three years but she made him drink a six-pack of beer to see if he became violent.

"When it comes to bossing you around," Yankevich says, "Jewish mothers can't hold a candle to the Asian women I've known. Pham had to wait twenty years, but she finally got everything she wanted."

Manh—John Yankevich, Jr.—walks into the apartment with two Amerasian friends. He is a slender duplicate of his father, with darker hair and golden skin. Manh has an ulcer. He has been in lots of fights. He was thrown out of high school for being disruptive and suspended from a job at Mele Manufacturing. "They don't use half-measures when they think violence is necessary," says Yankevich about his son and the other Amerasians in Utica. "They have an 'on-off' switch when it comes to violence."

I ask Manh what he likes best about being in America. "My father showed me how to drive and bought me a car," he says. "We spend a lot of time fishing for catfish and sunfish in the Mohawk River."

"What do you want to do here?"

"Become a police officer, specializing in intelligence. I want to catch bad people and help good people."

"The first time I saw him I misunderstood him," he says of meeting his father. "I was angry. When I was born I didn't see him. My mother was working hard to take care of me. I didn't know why he left me. But now we get along well."

"What do you remember about life in Vietnam?" I ask.

"Because I was Amerasian and my father wasn't there, I got extra love from my family. My grandmother gave me money for school. I wore my father's collar pin—the brass US of Army intel-

ligence agents—every day. I got in lots of fights. At sixteen I had
to register for the military. They told me I couldn't write down my
father's name, but I refused to change it."

Pham glides across the floor and returns from the bedroom
with her *so gia-dinh cong-giao*, the little cloth-covered book that
every Vietnamese Catholic carries as a family record and internal
passport. At the end of a long list of Vietnamese names come
John J. Yankevich and his son—new branches grafted onto an
old family tree.

"It was my mother's idea to go to America," says Manh. "I
didn't want to come here. I am Vietnamese. But America was a
surprise for me. I like the people, going to school, working."

I provoke a family debate by asking Pham whether she
thinks her son is Vietnamese or American.

"He is American," she says.

"No, he isn't," says her husband. "He is Vietnamese. The
only American food he likes is Jell-O."

"He hates American food, but he has American blood," she
says. "Even in Vietnam, he thought he was American."

"He has Vietnamese table manners," says Yankevich. "A
big slab of meat on his plate grosses him out. He doesn't like
loud behavior or boisterous physical gestures. I think he thinks
of himself as Vietnamese."

"This country belongs to him," says Pham, speaking quietly, but with utter conviction. "His father was 101st Airborne.
He goes where he wants and does what he wants."

The Yankevich men allow her to have the last word. To
change the subject, I ask Pham why she never remarried. "My
mother didn't want me to marry a Vietnamese. He would hate my
son. She beat me with a stick one day for going to a coffee shop with
a Vietnamese man. My mother is very happy I am married to John."

Manh's two Amerasian friends have been sitting quietly on the
sofa listening to our conversation. Ngoc Minh is a reed-thin young

man who makes circuit boards for a company called Trenton Terminals. "Missy" Ngoc—so-called to distinguish her from the other Ngoc in the room—is a slender young woman with white skin and dark hair who works double shifts at Baker Greenhouses and Mele Manufacturing.

Both of them know their fathers and have spoken to them, but these contacts did not have the same happy result as Manh's. Minh produces a photo of his father. It shows a young man, the same age as the boy sitting in front of me. He is smartly dressed in his Army uniform. "Happy New Year, Merry Christmas," it says on the front of the card. On the back is written a name and address in Michigan.

"Mr. Yankevich got his phone number and called my father a few months ago," says Minh. "When he found out who was calling, there was a long silence. Then he said, 'I can't help you,' and hung up. Manh tried calling my father once more, but he yelled at him, 'Don't ever call me again!' "

There is so much weight on his shoulders as he tells this story that Minh's storklike body looks ready to collapse onto the floor. This handsome boy who wears his dark brown hair parted in the middle—exactly like his Spec 4 father—was born in 1968. He grew up living in a Saigon balloon factory, where he earned two hundred *dong*, about five cents, a day. "All I want to do is see my father one time," he says.

Missy Ngoc tells me her mother and father were married in a Catholic ceremony. They lived together for three years on the military base in Bien Hoa, where her mother was a cashier. After the war, she and her mother moved to a small town on the Cambodian border, where they worked as rice farmers, like everyone else in the village.

John Yankevich tried phoning her father at an old number in a midwestern town. He reached the man's daughter, who said she hadn't seen her father in six or seven years. The last she knew, he was working the shrimp boats in the Gulf of Mexico.

"I am not going to get mad at him," says Missy Ngoc. "I just want to see my father's face. I'd like to live with him if he wants me to, but if he doesn't, I'll just go away after seeing him."

Missy Ngoc and Minh know lots of stories about Amerasians who have called their fathers and met denial or rejection on the other end of the line. These children have pictures of their fathers, addresses, documents, love letters. Minh's roommate, for example, carries around with him the divorce papers his mother received one day in Saigon. He pulls them out from time to time to check the name of his father, which before receiving the papers he had never known.

Love Trouble

When you're stabbed in the back you fall like this, and if you're stabbed in the front you fall like this, but if you stab yourself you fall differently. Like this.

Jean Rhys

At the inaugural meeting of the Amerasian Club, Nguyen Anh Dung, a.k.a. Clarence Taylor III, is elected president of the one-hundred-member organization. Charlie Brown, former leader of the Amerasians, receives no votes for elected office. The voting is followed by a spirited debate on whether to serve Coke or Pepsi at club meetings.

Motions are passed to print stationery, organize an Amerasian soccer tournament, and hold a Halloween party at the refugee center, where the club will meet until it can find its own space. Unfortunately, this never happens, as the next meeting will be the club's last.

At six o'clock, when the Halloween party is supposed to begin, the refugee center is empty. At half past six, Anh Dung, wearing a pale green Elvis suit, arrives with a truckful of stereo gear, strobe lights, and mirror balls, which he unloads into the big ground-floor classroom. At seven o'clock the first Amerasians arrive. They nod hello to Rose Marie Battisti, who stands at the door with a worried look on her face.

The boys are dressed in black. They wear slipper shoes, pajama pants, and wide-sleeved shirts. The girls wear off-the-shoulder party dresses with lots of ruffles. Truong Thi Minh Ha, a new girl in town, wears skintight leggings in a leopard-skin pattern. Everyone jokes about her being Anh Dung's latest girlfriend, while his old girlfriend, Le Ha, who is dressed in a gold pants suit, sits scowling in the corner.

Girls dance with girls, boys with boys. The lead dancer rests her fingers delicately in her partner's outstretched palm. People do swings and dips, like the great ballroom performers of the fifties. Thang, the former male taxi dancer, spins around the room nonstop. The music is a mixture of American rock and *nhac vang*, "golden music," which includes all the love songs banned in socialist Vietnam.

There is a momentary chill in the air as Duc, Quoc, and other street-corner toughs shove their way into the building. Rose Marie locks the front door, which is made of glass, and pushes a file cabinet against it. Duc is dressed in a black lounge suit decorated with silver belt buckles. He grabs Minh Ha, the girl in leopard-skin leggings, and glides over the floor in a two-step. One sees why the Vietnamese win all the dance contests in town. Other boys and girls pair off. In the windowless classroom, the temperature begins to rise.

I hear a commotion at the front door and look back to watch it fall off its hinges. Holding the door in his hands is a tall man with a black pompadour. He sets the door aside and pushes his way into the room. He is wearing what looks like a frock coat and white ruffled shirt. Beside him is a scowling woman with black rings around her eyes. Sanh Chi Do, Utica's resident gangster, and his wife have arrived. She checks out the crowd as her husband starts dancing with Thang.

Rose Marie locks her daughters in her office and calls the Utica police. She also phones Kevin Mahoney, chairman of the refugee center's board of directors. "Sanh Chi Do carries a gun and claims to have killed a police officer in Boston," she says. "He ran the Saigon pool hall until he walked out the door with his partner's ten thousand dollars.

"He tried the same thing again a couple of weeks ago. He stole the pot from a poker game he wasn't playing, but this time, "Big" Loc almost stabbed him to death. Too bad he didn't finish the job. He extorts money out of Amerasians and Vietnamese in the community. I'm the only person in town who stands up to him. He's threatened to kill me, injure my children, smash my car. I don't know if he's all there mentally. I've seen his wife in the hospital with her face beaten to a pulp."

Mahoney arrives. A tough-looking guy with close-cropped hair, he works at the psychiatric center and looks like he knows how to box. The police show up and start flashing their lights. The party is over.

Later that night, Sanh Chi Do corners Rose Marie in the parking lot and threatens to rape her. She and her daughters spend the night at Mahoney's. Sanh Chi Do is arrested in the early hours of the morning. The police turn his apartment upside down. They throw him in jail and threaten to have him deported as an undesirable alien. When he makes bail, the court issues a restraining order keeping him off Bleecker Street.

"If they catch him bothering Rose Marie in Little Falls, he'll get a taste of small-town justice," says Dick Sessler. "They'll take him out to a prayer meeting, the kind where you bow down and kiss the ground. Later you see stars."

No word of the Halloween affair appears in the local newspaper, save for a couple of lines in the police blotter, where it is reported that "Che Do Sanh Hong, no age available," arrested for "third-degree criminal trespass," has pleaded innocent.

I now start reading the police blotter more carefully, noticing the Vietnamese names that begin to appear with increasing frequency. I see people arrested for criminal trespass, assault, and petty larceny. Nothing big, yet. But the Vietnamese and Amerasians are starting to establish their turf.

Charlie Brown paces behind his girlfriend. Thi Le Ha sits glumly at the table, fingering a bill she just received in the mail for $557—the cost of her airplane ticket to America. Their lunch of stir-fried beef and vegetables sits uneaten. Charlie and Thi Le Ha's mother are fighting over where the teenaged girl should go to school. Charlie wants her to go to the local community college.

Her mother wants her to go to high school. Apart from the merits of the case, this is also a struggle over who is going to head the family in America—Charlie, the worldly Amerasian, or Thi Le Ha's mother, the tough survivor, who managed during the war to get her family rescued by helicopter from a village where everyone else was killed.

When I mention the recent case of two Vietnamese refugees who lost their food stamps when they enrolled in college, Charlie explodes. "Rose Marie doesn't care about Amerasians!" he yells. "She's just using us to build her political fortunes. She lures us here under false pretenses, telling us we can go to school. But then when we try to go, she kills us."

Charlie has other problems beside love. He told his boss at work about being forced into becoming a Vietnamese spy in the United States, and his boss phoned the FBI. An agent named George Frick stopped by to see Charlie. Then Frick started making appointments for Charlie to meet him in his office after work. After two weeks of interrogation, lasting until the early hours of the morning, Charlie is being squeezed into a sting operation. Tomorrow he is supposed to present the FBI with a letter addressed to his handlers in Vietnam. "They want to set a trap, and I'm the bait," he says.

I ask why he's agreed to write the letter. "They gave me a telephone. They promised to pay my college tuition and buy me a car. They told me my country needs me to catch spies. It's patriotic."

What can Charlie spy on? The manufacture of paper-towel holders in upstate New York? Is it worth two weeks of FBI interrogations to guard this information? It seems a colossal joke. But the joke, I am afraid, is going to be on Charlie. The morning newspaper reports the assassination of two Viet Kieu journalists in Washington, D.C. I tell Charlie I smell a rat. Mr. FBI is looking to promote himself as an international spy catcher. But Charlie is too strung out by now to take any outside advice.

"I think I'll get some hand grenades and blow up everyone

around me," he babbles. "I'll run away to Texas, where that ass-hole FBI man will never find me." But as I look into Charlie's bloodshot eyes, I suddenly realize why the game appeals to him and why I expect he'll go through with it. Spy catching puts him back in touch with the kind of people he grew up with. "My FBI agent is like a fox," he assures me, and I know this is a character trait much admired by Charlie.

"I brought Charlie over here with the idea of hiring him as a counselor at Welcome Home House," says Rose Marie Battisti, when I stop by to get her side of the story. "But the other kids in town blew him off. He's not the 'leader of the Amerasians' he was when I met him in Saigon, and now I'm concerned for his safety."

Rose Marie had had breakfast that morning with Charlie's FBI contact. She and Frick have been friends for years. "I questioned him on what possible use Charlie could be to the Vietnamese government. We haven't had a case like this before. Not even the Russian mafia in New York City has made its way up to Utica."

"I'm in business to catch spies," Frick told her. "The Vietnamese are bumblers and amateurs. The FBI has been catching them by the dozens. He won't get rich on it, but Charlie will get paid for his work."

"George looked dismayed when I told him everybody in town knew Charlie's story," says Rose Marie. "He couldn't have spread it farther if he'd rented a billboard. I think Charlie is clinically depressed. He's unstable. His accounts aren't always reliable. He keeps telling me he's moving away, and I haven't done anything to discourage him."

The girl in leopard-skin leggings who danced nonstop at the Amerasian Halloween party is rumored to be Charlie Brown's new girlfriend. She is also reported to be Anh Dung's new girlfriend.

In fact, she is so talented and beautiful, she becomes *everyone*'s girlfriend. Loi, the refugee center translator, drives her home after class. Anh Dung stops by in the afternoon to take her shopping. Charlie Brown comes around in the evening to eat supper with her. Endowed with bold green eyes and fair hair, a high school diploma, and fluent English, Truong Thi Minh Ha belies all the myths about wandering homeless Amerasians.

Born in Da Nang in 1969, Minh Ha is the daughter of William Catherine, an Air Force pilot who was killed in the war when she was two years old. Or so she was told. This could be a lie, like almost everything else she was told about her life when she was growing up. Pham, for example, the woman she thought was her mother and who accompanied her to the United States, is actually her mother's sister. Pham is the second wife of Truong Ngoc Thom, a military mechanic who was once wealthy enough to have five wives, but who has not worked since 1975.

Because Minh Ha's real mother was planning to marry a Communist official, she gave her Amerasian daughter to her sister, who had no children of her own. At the same time, she changed Minh Ha's birth date and listed Truong Ngoc Thom's *first* wife as the girl's mother. "She was afraid I would grow up and find her; so she changed everything, and now I have *three* mothers!" says Minh Ha, laughing.

After seeing a notice in front of the police station announcing a special program for helping Amerasians go to America, Minh Ha and her aunt—whom she thought at the time was her mother—applied to come to the United States in 1982. They never imagined they would have to wait eight years. "My stepfather paid a lot of money and gold to the police to get me here," says Minh Ha. "He kept selling his houses. We moved into smaller and smaller houses as the years went by."

Finally there were eight people living under one roof, and Minh Ha was the only one with a job. As an Amerasian, she was paid less for her work than a Vietnamese. She sewed buttonholes in the morning. She carried fruit to the market at midday and swept a coffee shop in the afternoon. At night she sang in a rock band entertaining Russian tourists at the Pacific Hotel. "I learned my English from The Carpenters, singing 'Yesterday Once More' and 'Close to You.' I felt these songs were written for me. They choked me up with emotion."

Minh Ha was visiting one of her aunts in Da Nang when she noticed a new girl who had been brought into the house as a maid. She was a country girl who had never been to school. She was illiterate and barefoot, but she looked exactly like Minh Ha, who knew immediately that the girl was her younger sister.

Visiting the house again a few weeks later, Minh Ha met the girl's mother, who soon confessed that she was also Minh Ha's mother. She broke down crying. She said she was sorry for what she had done and apologized. Later, she gave Minh Ha a picture of her father, a large man with blue eyes and a beard. She had been a secretary for the Americans. He was a pilot, with a family in the United States, but they lived together in Chu Lai and Da Nang, until he died.

"She was wearing rags," Minh Ha remembers of this first meeting with her mother, who was then a poor farmer in a village an hour and a half from Da Nang. "She wasn't pretty. I always thought the women who got the Americans were beautiful. I pitied her. After that I began saving money and sending it to her."

Minh Ha asked her mother and sister to go to America with her, but they said it was too late, and there was no way to prove their relationship. "A few days before I left, my mother came to my stepfather's house. I hadn't told anyone I had met her, so I pretended not to know her. She had come to see me. I saw the emotion in her face, but she couldn't talk to me without crying. She covered her eyes and ran away from the door."

Minh Ha and her aunt rode the bus to Saigon for their ODP interview and then waited over a year for their flight out of Vietnam. They lived in Saigon with a distant relative, a woman with three Eurasian children in France. "Every time she needed something, she'd send a letter to France, and in two or three months, back would come a refrigerator or a motorcycle."

Minh Ha helped cook for the family and studied English at home. On her way to Mass, she passed the Amerasians who were living in the park behind the cathedral, but she didn't talk to them. "They looked like bag people. I was afraid of them."

As soon as she stepped on the airplane to the Philippines, Minh Ha herself became a homeless Amerasian. Up in the clouds, she felt like an angel over the earth, but when she landed, it was like going from heaven to hell. She and her aunt were taken to the transit center in Manila. It reeked of gasoline. The dirty water made them sick. "The camp was full of boat people, and all we got to eat was a ball of rice with *com heo*, pig slops. They threw the food on our plates like we were dogs."

The following day the Amerasians were bussed to the Philippine Refugee Processing Center. Minh Ha fainted from hunger. She sold her rings and a necklace for food. Friends in the United States sent her money, but the police opened the letters and stole it. Six months passed before she and her aunt ate another full meal.

The few photos Minh Ha possesses from her life in Vietnam show her swimming at China Beach or attending a family wedding. None of the women at the wedding is wearing an *ao dai*. "We were too poor to wear *ao dai*s," she says. There is also a picture of her stepfather, a strapping man in a South Vietnamese army uniform. He is leaning against a Ford truck loaded with oil drums.

Pictures from the Philippines show Minh Ha singing "Yesterday Once More" to win the Miss Talent award in the PRPC beauty pageant. More recent photos show her performing traditional Vietnamese dances at Utica's Cornhill Senior Center. On a stage draped with the old flag of the Republic of Vietnam, she is finally wearing an *ao dai*.

.   .   .

I meet Minh Ha's stepfather and one of her three mothers on my
first visit to Vietnam in the spring of 1991. Before its recent opening to the West, Vietnam was a rice-based culture of exquisite
politesse over which had been laid a gray net of state surveil-
lance. In Minh Ha's hometown of Da Nang, I am shadowed by not
one but two security agents, who are described as my tour guide
and translator. I have to pay for their services, although the tour
guide is worthless, and the translator has the bad habit of answer-
ing my questions before asking them. On one of the few occasions
when I am able to give my handlers the slip, I set out to find Minh
Ha's family.

I tell the pair there is no need to rise from their comfortable
chairs in the hotel lobby, as I am merely walking across the street
to the camera store. But once there, I keep on going. I race around
the corner and jump in a cyclo. I hand the driver a letter with
Truong Ngoc Thom's address and lean back to hide my face
under the rickshaw's canvas hood. We cycle for twenty minutes
through a crush of bicycles and pedestrians before ditching our
cumbersome three-wheeled cart on the sidewalk. Then we hustle
on foot down one of the city's narrow alleyways. Coming from the
houses pressed around us are the sounds of gongs and people
chanting evening prayers. I look through the open doors to see
faces lit by the yellow light of oil lamps. Many people wear the
white headbands and robes of Vietnamese in mourning.

We branch from the main alley into a suballey and pick up
a crowd of followers who look like minnows schooling in the wake
of a great white whale. I am probably the first American they have
seen since the war, and even then, this maze of streets in Da
Nang's old Chinatown was probably out of bounds. The cyclo man
stops at a little vine-covered house with an iron grille over the
porch and shouts inside. An elderly woman comes out to unlock
the grille. I remove my shoes and enter a narrow, lamplit room to

present a letter from their daughter in America to Truong Ngoc Thom, Minh Ha's stepfather, and Nguyen Thi Tuyet, who is legally her mother on the altered birth certificate.

Thom is a large man with a tender face. He seizes my hand and holds it, as if it were a lifeline thrown across the sea. "We miss Minh Ha very much," he says, slowly assembling the sentence out of what he remembers of English.

They show me pictures of Minh Ha as a girl in Da Nang. Tuyet writes her a letter, which is handed to me unsealed. A hubbub rises from the crowd pressed against the grille. My cyclo man shouts inside, "Have to leave. Police come." Thom clears a path for us down the alley. Out on the street, he again holds my hand for a long goodbye that I know he wishes would never end.

Charlie Brown announces to everyone at the refugee center that he is moving to Hawaii. There are tears in his eyes as he says goodbye to Dick, Rose Marie, Samedy, and even Stania, the sewing teacher. Charlie holds in his hand an airplane ticket sent to him by his friend, Al Webb, a former sergeant in the Twenty-Fifth Infantry Division, the Big Red One. Webb owns a farm on Maui. He has promised Charlie a house, a job, even money for school.

Charlie pulls a picture of his benefactor out of his pocket. It shows a tall, balding man in blue jeans and T-shirt standing in front of a pile of toothbrushes, cotton blankets, shoes, sleeping mats, tin pots, soap powder, and aspirin. "He came to Amerasian Park and gave us a thousand dollars' worth of supplies," says Charlie. "It was a gift from the Vietnam vets of Maui."

Charlie asks me to drive him to Minh Ha's house. As he slumps in the seat next to me, I glance over at his sallow cheeks and black hair brushed low on his forehead. Charlie has a clown's face, always moving. He can laugh and cry at the same time. But today his face is closed down, frozen with fatigue. Charlie wears tennis shoes, white Levi's, and a powder blue sweater. The ropey clouds in the sky look like wet wool. The temperature is near freezing. It begins to snow. It is a good day to move to Hawaii.

Charlie drums his fingers on the dashboard. They are the long, thin fingers of an artist, nicotine-stained but steady, and I realize I am going to miss having Charlie grab my notebook to draw me maps of Vietnam and prison floor plans. He also writes out Vietnamese words, often looking them up in the dictionary to verify their spelling. "I am very careful with words," he says. "French, Vietnamese, Russian, English—I always check to get them right."

I downshift through the stop signs planted at the end of every block. Charlie's neighborhood looks shabbier than it did during the warm days of summer. Its weedy lots are strewn with the rubble of buildings that have been torched and cleared away. Some burned-out houses are boarded up. Others are still being lived in. Most of the buildings, Charlie's included, have FOR SALE signs nailed to them. This part of Utica looks like flotsam left on the beach after the tide went out; the people living here are hermit crabs occupying the shell of a once-living creature.

Charlie tells me he was awake most of the night. George Frick drove him to a motel in the Adirondacks where he and two other FBI agents wired Charlie for a lie-detector test. "I passed everything. No problem," he says.

"Have you sent the letter to Vietnam?"

"Yes," he says. Then he changes the subject. "There are no Vietnamese on Maui, which is a good thing. I hate the Vietnamese. If I had a gun, I'd shoot them all."

Is he still planning to work for the FBI? "They told me they were notifying the Hawaiian office. I told them to leave me alone.

"I don't want to run away, but I must go," he says. "I have love trouble. I won't kill myself over it. I only tried to kill myself once or twice before, in prison. I'm not crazy. If I don't have this girl, I can get another." I wonder which of his two girlfriends—Thi Le Ha or Minh Ha—he is talking about.

After stopping at Charlie's house to pick up some things he

wants to give her before he leaves town, we find Minh Ha outside her apartment, gamboling in the snow. "Have you ever seen snow before?" she yells to Charlie. "I'm an old-timer," he says. "I've seen plenty of snow."

We go upstairs and listen to music. Minh Ha has three records she plays on a tiny machine. "They are the best three," says Charlie—Santana's "Moonflower," The Carpenters' "Close to You," and The Eagles' "Hotel California," which is Charlie's favorite. Minh Ha's favorite is "Close to You."

Charlie grimaces as the love song comes on. "You know what marriage is?" he asks. "It's like two prisoners locked in the same cell." He stands up and starts shadowboxing.

Anh Dung knocks on the door. Minh Ha puts on her coat and gets ready to go shopping. Charlie hands her a going-away present: six tins of USDA honey and an Olympic typewriter. Minh Ha's mother invites him to dinner. Since Charlie refuses to eat rice, she has stocked her cabinets with what looks like a month's supply of noodles. "Charlie, you're just an old beggar, going door-to-door for food," says Minh Ha, laughing.

By morning, Charlie will have flown off to his new fire base in the Hawaiian countryside. Our wandering homeless Amerasian is on the road again.

The Bell Curve

All you need is a dollar and a dream.

The New York State Lottery

Thursday morning at eight-thirty, a dozen Amerasians and young Russians crowd into Samedy Sok's windowless office for something called Job Club. Two fluorescent tubes under the pressed-tin ceiling cast a green glare over a room filled with secondhand furniture and a bouquet of plastic flowers. Sam stands at the white board explaining a diagram labelled "Getting Started in Life."

The diagram shows a car chugging over a bell-shaped curve, which represents the refugee life cycle. Refugees step on the gas for the first two years, investing a lot of time and money in getting resettled. By the fifth year, after a long haul up the slope of American acculturation, refugees crest at the top of the curve, and by the end of their tenth year in America, they have coasted through school, marriage, and their first mortgage.

"When you come to Utica you are worried," says Sam. "How do you feel right now?" he asks a black Amerasian.

"I worry about my future," he says.

"Why?" Sam asks.

"Because it's cold. Because we have nothing, and we have to work."

"Some of you are pretty smart," he says, "but you won't get anywhere in America without speaking the language. Your job right now is to study English. You don't know it, but this is a good job. Later you can go to work."

Sam translates his comments into Russian for the benefit of two Byelorussians in blue jeans and a girl in red pumps. He then switches back through Vietnamese to English. "What happens if you sneak around here and don't learn English?" he asks. "You waste your time, and time is very expensive. The guy who sneaks around isn't going to get up the hill. Gravity will pull him down. He'll fall back and die."

Immigrants to Utica have been getting this advice since Italians began arriving here in the 1800s. The advice used to come from uncles and aunts. Now it comes from a case worker at the refugee center. A Cambodian Buddhist speaking Russian to a roomful of Amerasians and Pentecostals is explaining the Protestant work ethic.

Sam turns back to his diagram. "When you first get to America, you give your car a lot of gas to make it go uphill, but you feel like you're driving a station wagon towing a trailer. Look at me. It took me ten years to get up the hill. What is my trailer? My wife and child, my wife's school, and my school. I still have to finish college. I'm about here," he says, pointing to the apex of the curve.

Sam studies his diagram and decides to amend it. He doubles the numbers written on the timeline, thereby giving refugees ten years to struggle uphill and get established in America, rather than five. "I don't want you to fool around for ten years and end up with nothing," he warns his audience.

"Have you heard what happened to Thao, the Amerasian kid who used to run with Duc and Quoc?" he asks. "Last week he was sitting here in class. Then he went out and got drunk. He fought a policeman and resisted arrest. He's been here four months and now he's in jail." Sam draws a stick-figure diagram of Thao crying behind bars. "This guy hasn't even started up the hill," he says. Sam gives another example. "Yesterday an Amerasian kid came to see me. He said he wanted to take six months off from his job at CONMED, because it was too cold there. For half my life, I've been cold. I look out the window and say, 'Oh, no, not snow again.' But no matter how cold you are, you still have to go to work and study English."

Not sharing this climatic problem, the Russians in the room

have started talking among themselves. "It's hard to get the right mix," Sam confesses after class. "The Russians and Amerasians are the same age, but they're not the same kids."

Sam's mother, a French teacher who named her children Lundy, Mardy and Samedy, depending on what day of the week they were born, is now dead, and so, too, are three of her six children. They were killed by the Khmer Rouge when they came to power in 1975. Sam and his father, an electrical engineer, were sent to labor in the countryside, where Sam spent three months chained to a tree and six months in a Khmer Rouge prison. He was fed swamp grass and fish bones dropped through the floor of the guard house under which he lived. He and his father escaped to Thailand in 1978. Sam was fifteen. "We walked for a week over a trail of bones and skulls. The stench was horrible. Every morning in the shower I still smell that stench. It reminds me what it is to be a refugee."

Sam worked for a year as a paramedic in Thailand's Khao I Dang refugee camp. Khao I Dang at the time was the largest Cambodian city in the world. One out of every ten residents was missing a limb or was otherwise maimed. "I was covered with blood up to my armpits," says Sam. "I went so many days without sleep I felt as if I could drop on the ground and die. I tell the Amerasians who come to see me, 'I know you faced discrimination and a hard life in Vietnam. But at least you didn't get caught in the middle of a war.'"

Sam worked for another year as a refugee interviewer in Bangkok and then spent six months at the Philippine Refugee Processing Center before finally reaching the United States. He finished high school in Philadelphia and most of a pre-law degree before moving to Utica to marry a Cambodian woman. Her uncle, Synath, housing director at the refugee center, got Sam a job on Bleecker Street, where he started having flashbacks to his own refugee experience. "I have nightmares worrying about these kids. I worry most on the weekends. What harm can they do themselves in the next forty-eight hours?

"I take my stress home and fight with my wife about it. Sometimes I feel really sad. My wife looks at me and says, 'Why did you make that face again?' and I tell her some problem I've been thinking about for days. We Asians live in the past," he says. "We walk around with our ghosts. It's like the photos Charlie Brown carries around in his pocket. They'll be there until the day he dies."

Outside Sam's office the sewing teacher—the former Miss Czechoslovakia, or was it Miss Hungary?—is pinning miniature stockings on people's chests. Synath looks quizzically at his red stocking. He fingers it like a freshly opened wound. "What does this mean?" he asks, unfamiliar with this symbol of Christmas.

Synath is a polite man, but today his smile looks awry. He explains that he and other Buddhists in Utica are trying to raise money to restore a Cambodian temple destroyed during the war. "We could only find three hundred dollars. It's not enough, but it's the best we could do. There just aren't many of us here," he sighs.

Rose Marie Battisti and her boyfriend join the Christmas party. Her bobbed blond hair is set off nicely by a black cocktail dress. He cuts a more casual figure in a Syracuse Orangemen sweatshirt. The merriment is interrupted by Sam running in to report that someone has scratched the paint on his car. Earlier, I had seen the two likely suspects, Duc and Quoc, drifting around the edges of the party. One of them had knocked over a can of soda and refused to clean it up. "I don't get any respect from them," Sam complains. Along with what was done to his car, the week's damage includes a couple of slashed tires on the refugee center van. "This isn't part of everyday life in Utica," says Sam. "It's getting us all worried."

Recently the Utica police arrested Duc for fighting on Bleecker Street, but he lied to the judge about his age, saying he was seventeen, and got off as a youth offender. Next came a drunken scrap with Sam that had to be broken up by Dick Sessler. Sam then got Duc a job at Mele Manufacturing, which lasted three days, until he disappeared to Boston. Ditto for Quoc, with one additional problem. Quoc, who grew up in Saigon living under a bridge, was recreating similar conditions in Utica, until the health department raided his apartment and threatened to close it down.

"One day I opened Duc's school bag and found seven car stereos," says Sam. He was picking them up like nuts off a tree. They go to the apartments of new refugees and steal things. Once they even stole a public assistance check and cashed it. Everybody says these kids are bad people. I tell them not to listen to this 'Asian talk.' I keep grabbing them back, trying to prevent them from getting lost, but one of these days somebody is going to get in serious trouble."

Another glum face at the party belongs to the Reverend John Sisley, the naturally ebullient impersonator of Harry Truman and Santa Claus. "Today's my last day on the job," he says. "I've called in all my chips. There's nothing more I can do for Rose Marie, so she's showing me the door."

Sisley says Welcome Home House is ready to open, but the State Department is delaying the project. "They hate Rose Marie's guts. She's made some nasty remarks about their operation in the Philippines, and now they're trying to put a spoke in her wheel. But she'll wear them down in the end."

Sisley marvels at the volunteer labor that went into getting the old nurses' residence refurbished. "Even the city building inspectors pitched in to get the place up to code. They were so helpful I got suspicious. They returned a dozen times, doing a lot of the wiring themselves. When the job was done, they said, 'We were there.' They meant Vietnam. They were real quiet about it, but I knew that's why they were doing it."

. . .

Even Dick Sessler looks a bit preoccupied. Along with the usual mix of Pentecostals and Vietnamese reeducation camp prisoners, he is awaiting the arrival of four handicapped Amerasians, for whom he has to rent an apartment and find a full-time nurse. Why is Utica resettling them? "Rose Marie and children are like peanut butter and jelly," he says. "She saw them in Vietnam and had to save them."

Sessler is also expecting a shipment of Libyans newly expelled from Kenya. "They're being brought here under the premise that an enemy of Muammar Quaddafi must be a friend of ours. We need a flow of thirty-three refugees a month to keep our resettlement contract. You have to be diversified in this business. If wing nuts aren't selling, you move into U bolts."

Sessler mentions that Sanh Chi Do is fighting the charges brought against him by Rose Marie Battisti, and he is demanding a jury trial. "If he gets it," says Sessler, "we'll nail him to the wall with a jury of twelve Italian grandmothers."

There is another grim party goer involved in the Sanh Chi Do case. "The guy needed a translator, so I helped him out," says Anh Dung. "He was entitled to a fair hearing. I do this for a lot of Vietnamese who don't speak English. But Rose Marie saw me in the courtroom and flipped. She acted like I was betraying her."

Anh Dung has his own reasons for being angry at Battisti. Only two of the twenty-three people hired for the staff at Welcome Home House are Amerasian, and both have well-placed Vietnamese relatives working at the refugee center. "She can hire a Vietnamese kid trained as an auto mechanic, but she can't hire an Amerasian? This is a *big* program, and there's lots of money going into resettling Amerasians in Utica, but none of it's coming our way.

"Whenever Rose wants to look good, she calls me up to go to a meeting or speak before some congressional hearing," he says. "But otherwise she ignores me. She's read a lot of books.

She's worked with Amerasians for seven years. But she doesn't know Amerasians. She doesn't know anything."

The party is interrupted by the arrival of two Amerasians dressed in shiny leather coats. The taller of the two boys wears a pigtail down his back. "Are you still driving that fancy Chevy?" Sam jokingly asks the boy with the pigtail.

"No," he replies. "I have a new Toyota Supra." Sam and the boys shoot the breeze and then start talking specific cases. "How's Tam? How's Ngoc? You be a good brother to my boy," Sam admonishes them.

The Amerasians tell Sam they are looking for girls to take back to Boston. "Who's going with you?" he asks. "They're good girls," he tells them. "I want them back here in a week, no trouble." The boys shake his hand goodbye and stalk out of the refugee center. Everybody stares after them as they go.

"These guys are big-time gang leaders in Boston," Sam explains. "Gang members are calling me all the time. They like me because I'm a fair man. If you keep your mouth shut, you can leave a gang and start a new life. So I never write these boys off. They have hearts, and if you ask them, they're willing to help you.

"I feel sorry for this generation," he adds. "They think life is supposed to be easy when they come to America. But it isn't easy when you're washing dishes at minimum wage and you can't speak the language. So you get an offer, and it looks good. These gang leaders are professional people. They know how to talk, just like me. Charlie Brown was a leader. You take care of your boys and girls. You feed them, counsel them. You're their father, their brother. I could run a gang, but instead I try to turn things from bad to good."

Sam is called a job placement counselor and works for a public agency, but he is really a labor contractor—not the kind who dumps wetbacks over the border, but the kind who guarantees after-placement job satisfaction, which means a lot of hand-holding and counseling of confused refugees. A boy called him one day from Smith's Laundry to say, "I can't work, Sam. The boss is always watching me."

"I went down and talked to the manager," Sam says. "I explained to her she was frightening people by looking at them. In our part of the world, only the Communists stand around watching you."

After the party, Sam and I are driving down Bleecker Street through the old Italian, now Puerto Rican and Vietnamese, part of town. We pass the former Savage Arms factory, which employed eight thousand people during the First World War and later served as the Univac computer factory. This massive red-brick hulk is now decaying into the floodplain east of Utica. Beyond the factory, we come on a green metal shed so nondescript that I have never noticed it before. This is Joseph and Feiss, the local manufacturer of Hugo Boss suits, whose labels imply they are made in Paris.

Utica thrived in its heyday between the Civil War and World War I by manufacturing textiles, copper pots, silverware, guns, and other metal products—all nineteenth-century industries that took a nosedive in the twentieth. The city had already peaked by 1910, but its collapse was delayed by a depression, in which no one flourished, and two world wars, in which everyone flourished. So it was not until 1945 that people noticed Utica was dying, and even then, its death throes were sometimes mistaken for revival.

General Electric moved into town in 1944, establishing a radio tube works and then a receiver works that briefly made Utica the radio capital of the world. "From loom to boom" was the term used by local boosters to describe the city's transformation from a textile-based economy to a cold war–based economy manufacturing airplane engines, military radar, and other appliances for the area's largest employer, Griffiss Air Force Base. But

Griffiss is closing, and the boom has given way to Utica's senior years in which the city survives as the back office for banks and insurance companies based in Manhattan. Utica also stockpiles New York City's criminals. The Mohawk Valley's four major prisons are now the region's largest employer.

We walk into the reception room at Joseph and Feiss and lean through a glass window to chat with the secretaries—three Italian "girls," who say they have to check with the boss before a stranger can visit the cutting room. Frank Vito comes out of his office and gives Sam a big hello. He invites us to sit down for a chat. A short, balding gentleman from Calabria, Vito is wearing a handsome suit and tie, both made on the premises. He says the company used to be staffed entirely by Italians, mainly from southwestern Italy, but now more than half the 360 employees are Asian refugees. "They're hard-working, industrious people," he says. "They don't give us any problems."

I ask if he could make Hugo Boss suits in Utica without refugees. "No, we couldn't," he says.

Given permission to tour the factory, Sam and I walk into a room the size of a football field. Large Calabrian women carry stacks of suiting to their workstations. Beside them Amerasian girls run sewing machines and Vietnamese women work the heavier equipment used for attaching sleeves. Then we come on a cluster of Cambodian men laboring as suit pressers. Only one local element is missing from this racial stew. There is not a black face in sight. This will be true at other factories we visit during the day, where Asians fresh off the airplane have leapfrogged over African-Americans to crack the local hiring barrier. "If you hire an Asian for eight hours a day, she works eight hours a day," explains Vito. Actually, she works sixteen hours a day, because for many of the people on the floor, this is only one of the two jobs they hold.

Heading back into the city, we come to the old textile mill that served as GE's radio factory. A huge building, the length of a city block, it still sports a General Electric neon sign on the roof, but space in the building is now sublet to various start-up companies in electronics. They are like beans in the pocket of a giant, but these companies are good news from Sam's perspective. The GE radar factory in Utica, later owned by Martin Marietta, but now closed, used to pay high-scale union wages, but it hired no refugees. They are considered security risks for military work. Only when the GEs and Martin Mariettas in town go belly-up and the wages drop below five dollars an hour can refugees get their foot in the door.

One of the subleasers rattling around GE's old radio works is Trenton Terminals Incorporated, which occupies a work space with eighteen-foot wood-plank ceilings and solid brick walls. TTI makes computers—everything from motherboards to industrial printing presses. Why are they making computers in Utica, instead of Asia? TTI fills in production gaps with small runs and takes advantage of sudden changes in technology. It gets its computers on the market faster than Asia, but who does the work? Asians.

The floor boss introduces me to the two Amerasians he calls "my best employees." One of them is Ngoc Minh, the reed-thin boy I met at John Yankevich's. These Amerasians are TTI's "master builders." They assemble everything from printed-circuit boards to computerized TV systems—one of which was rushed to Kuwait for the Gulf War.

The boss tells us that during a recent slowdown he fired employees with more seniority in order to keep his Amerasians. "They're great workers, fast, accurate. I couldn't wish for anything better. But they've got to learn English," he says in a voice loud enough for both of them to hear. Why's that? "Because they're afraid to call me on the phone and talk to me," he says.

Next stop is Empire Recycling, the old scrap handler down by the railroad tracks that has become big business in the age of mandated recycling. When he sees us drive into the parking lot, the boss, dressed in a blue suit, comes tearing out of his office.

"Sam," he yells. "You gotta get your ass in gear and straighten out that Tran kid. He's missed eleven days this year. One more day, and he's outta here." Sam apologizes and says he'll talk to Tran.

"Tran has had jobs all over town. But every time I get him hired, he gets fired," says Sam. "He goes out drinking on Friday night and calls in sick on Monday. He gets his girlfriends pregnant, and now he has two children. At the birth of each child, I worry about him and get him a job."

Empire has ten refugees on the payroll, most of them Amerasians. The work, salvaging engines and scrap metal, is familiar to anyone from the third world. You don't need to speak English, and there is plenty of overtime. We watch one man slice through a car radiator with a buzz saw. Then his partner attacks it with a torch. Another Amerasian is shoveling aluminum cans into a crusher. Next to the crusher is a secured area for recycling government documents. Through a window in the locked door I see a room filled with Amerasians bundling bales of shredded census forms.

In west Utica—the Polish side of town—Mele Manufacturing occupies a former knitting mill with arched windows as grand as those in a Gothic cathedral. We enter a gloomy space in which the shadowy figures of women can be seen hovering around a conveyor belt covered with boxes. Shoved off in the corners are heaps of equipment left over from the days when this building hummed with knitting machines. Up on the third floor we find another line of women assembling jewelry boxes. Among them is Pham, John Yankevich's wife. She is quick. She says she makes a lot of extra money by coming in over quota. For the first time today, we see African-Americans working alongside the Asians. Pham tells me the black woman standing next to her is even faster than she is. Back on the ground floor, we find John die-stamping book binders. He works alone. His machine is broken, and he's tinkering inside it with a pair of pliers. He says Pham usually works nearby, on the box line. "We get a big thrill out of waving to each other during the day," he says.

Down the block in another hulking brick structure is Utica Converters, which weaves the nylon in multi-ply tires. The process is not unlike the knitting mill for which the building was constructed. The air inside is thick with the smell of oil and plastics. A sign warns us not to enter the shop floor without ear protection. Every few seconds the building shakes with the sound of metal walloping metal. We enter a room full of machines wrapped in what look like oily spiderwebs. The heat and noise are intense. All the workers in sight are Amerasian.

We end the day with a cup of coffee at Dan-Dee Donuts on Mohawk Street. Sam tells me he passed his citizenship test last week. "The judge was really tough. He quizzed me on everything from Columbus to Quayle. They say a regular American couldn't pass that test."

Sam's wife is studying nursing at the local community college. "When she finishes her degree, our dream is to go back to Cambodia and help our people. We'll give up our house and all the fancy things we have. My transportation will be a bicycle, which is OK with me. I don't need possessions to make me happy."

One hundred and twenty-nine people are enrolled in Sam's youth program at the refugee center. "I treat them like my brothers and sisters," he says. "But one day I woke up and said to myself, 'Why am I doing all this work for Amerasians and Russians when my own people need me?' That's when I realized I had to go back to Cambodia.

Sam has applied for jobs with the church-related voluntary agencies working in Asia, but they are prejudiced against hiring Cambodians, and other potential employers disqualify him for being Buddhist. "It's not easy getting home," he muses. "It's like being a refugee in reverse."

Tet

Myself I know that exiles feed on hope.

Aeschylus

The biggest event in the Vietnamese refugee calendar is the celebration of Tet, the Chinese Lunar New Year, which usually falls
sometime in February. Le Ha spends two sleepless nights preparing for the party by making yellow paper flowers with red sequin
eyes, which she ties onto willow branches. The flowers are meant
to remind people of the *mai* blossoms that are the symbol of Tet
and bloom everywhere in Vietnam at this time of year.

Anh Dung comes home from school to report that he has
passed his air traffic controller's exam with the second-highest
score in his class. Le Ha calls him "big brother"—the first time
I have heard her use this traditional form of Vietnamese address—and wishes him a happy New Year. Anh Dung gives her
a box of candied lotus seeds and a red envelope holding five dollars of "good luck" money.

Their house has to be tidied and new clothing bought for the
New Year. Once Tet begins, the house cannot be cleaned, in case
one sweeps out the gods of the hearth and good fortune. "You
should also repay your debts," says Anh Dung. "You want to start
the year off right. But people in Utica are too poor to pay their
debts."

While Le Ha makes paper flowers, Anh Dung begins taping
music for the big party on Saturday night. Mostly he will play
nhac vang, golden music, which is banned in Vietnam. "Golden
music is capitalist music," he says. "It's about love, privacy,
selfishness—all sorts of antinationalist sentiments." He plays me an
example, Kieu Nga singing "Da Vu Xuan," "Spring Dance." The
music is lambada world beat overlaid with Asian strings.

The New Year is coming
We'll celebrate like we used to

"She means before the Communists took over," he explains.

When you come back from the foreign land
Don't forget who you are and
All the good times we had

"This is *nhac Viet Nam hai ngoai*," he says, "Vietnamese music from 'the foreign land,' which means America. You don't want to hear this music if you have family in Vietnam. It makes you too sad."

After "Spring Dance," Anh Dung cuts to rap music. "The kids want to hear Vanilla Ice," he says. "For them, Kieu Nga is like country music. It's not cool."

The Tet party is held in the basement of the First Presbyterian Church on Genesee Street—John Sisley's pulpit. Three hundred people sit at folding tables or run around the room handing each other envelopes of "lucky money." Minh Ha, dressed in a yellow *ao dai*, exchanges envelopes with Loi, her translator friend, while the girl next to her exclaims over Minh Ha's mounting pile of red envelopes.

The party begins with everyone singing the old South Vietnamese national anthem and a minute of silence "to honor the memory of all Vietnamese and American vets who gave their lives to preserve freedom." After singing "God Bless America," the sixteen elected officials of the Vietnamese Association file on stage, which is decorated with Le Ha's yellow blossoms. Under the flowers lies a pile of gift-wrapped presents that will be raffled off at the end of the evening. The only Amerasian among the Vietnamese Association officials is Anh Dung, who is "vice chairman in charge of teens." Dressed in high-top sneakers, blue jeans, and

a black-and-white-checked cardigan, Anh Dung is also serving
tonight as master of ceremonies, light technician, and audio
engineer.

He introduces Le Ha's stepfather, president of the Vietnamese Association, who gives a speech about the organization's
goals. "The first thing we have to do is establish the soccer team
in Utica," he says. I wonder if the vice chairman in charge of
teens is also the president's speech writer.

Minh Ha and other girls in *ao dai*s come on stage to sing
traditional folk songs. Two comedians demonstrate how a blind
man and a deaf man arrange their marriages. Then come sad
songs about refugee life in America, one of them about a girl in
Orange County who sings to her boyfriend in Vietnam: "The sunshine in California is not the same as the sunshine in Saigon."

The evening lightens up again when the door prizes are raffled off. The gift-wrapped boxes disclose a variety of toasters, coffee makers, and radios. Then a fistfight breaks out between an
Amerasian and a Vietnamese. "Please take your seats, ladies and
gentlemen," says Anh Dung. "There's nothing to get alarmed
about." After the fight, families with young children leave the
church, while everyone else settles down for a long night of
gambling.

Soon after Tet, Utica witnesses its first home invasion. Five Vietnamese hoodlums from the Born-to-Kill gang in New York raid
a gambling party—described by the newspaper as a "birthday"
party—at the Six Nations housing project. The BTKs carry side-
arms and an Uzi submachine gun with thirty shots in the clip.
They tie everyone's hands and mouths with duct tape and collect
about thirty thousand dollars in money and gold. In New York
City, where the police are thought to be a gang almost as potent
as the BTK, criminal acts like this go unreported. But things are
different in Utica. The young Laotian college student whose
"birthday" is raided calls the police, who catch the gang driving

around town looking for more action. Translators from the refugee center are rushed down to the courthouse, where these BTKs are headed straight to jail.

It is another bad day for tough guys in Utica when Sanh Chi Do throws in the towel and pleads guilty to harassing Rose Marie Battisti. The judge gives him a stern lecture about Asian criminals not being welcome in Utica and sentences him to wear an electronic bracelet for sixty days of house arrest.

At about the same time, Khai finds himself back in the hospital. He had caught the flu and was feeling so poorly that he "coined" himself. According to the Chinese medical practice of *cao gio*, toxins can be released from the body by scratching the skin. A coin is used to rub the chest or neck. This raises large red welts, which should disappear in a few days. Khai must have coined himself rather vigorously, as he began frothing at the mouth and had to be rushed to the emergency room. "Who beat you so badly?" asked the doctor, writing him up as an assault victim.

Early in the New Year Anh Dung and his mother move into a new house across from the funeral parlor on Mohawk Street. "The house was a mess before we moved in," he says. "Now that we've fixed it up, the landlord loves us. 'Hey, you're always working,' he yells to my mom when he sees her. 'You've cleaned up the neighborhood!' "

When not shuttling back and forth to the coast, either Atlantic or Pacific, the Amerasians in Utica tend to switch addresses every few months. These moves are often motivated by family fights. In this case, Le Ha's stepfather is named as the culprit. "He's mixed up," says Anh Dung. "Sometimes he runs hot, sometimes cold. Since he's become head of the Vietnamese Association, all he and Le Ha do is argue." She herself has moved into an apartment of her own on Albany Street.

Over a lunch of artichoke tea and rice cake soup spiced with black pepper and cilantro, Anh Dung tells me he has given up the idea of becoming an air traffic controller. "They eat aspirin for breakfast," he says. "I don't want to kill myself young." Instead, he is pushing ahead on his degree in electrical engineering.

Anh Dung's mother, Bang, tidies her already spotless kitchen while we eat our soup in the living room. Summoned by her son, she sits facing me on a three-legged stool and apologizes for speaking *tieng boi* English, the language of "boys" or servants. Behind her on the wall hang the glamorous matching photos of herself and her American husband, whose last name she has forgotten.

"I used to speak good English," she says. "But when I got to America the language sounded like barking dogs."

Her first memory of arriving in Utica was being cold. It was spring, 1983. She wore a winter coat all the time, even in the house. "I was crying a lot. It was totally strange to me. People tried to comfort me. 'Soon you will forget Vietnam.' But it is not true. Even if I am in America fifty years, I will always remember Vietnam."

This former rice farmer from Bien Hoa worked at Baker Greenhouses for seven months until she was laid off. She worked at the Sunnyside Motel as a maid. Then she got a job at CON-MED, standing all day on an assembly line making heart pacers and blood-pressure gauges. Next she moved to Boston, hoping it would be less isolated than Utica. She worked double shifts in factories making microwave ovens and ricotta cheese.

"I went to the temple to pray on special occasions. The monk told me how to practice my religion in a foreign land. 'Keep to yourself and do all the things a Buddhist should do. Maintain your altar at home and pray on the days when your ancestors have died. They are still with the family, even this far from home.' On the day of my operation for cancer of the ovaries, Buddha came to me and said I would get better if I prayed."

No longer able to work, Bang started collecting Social Security benefits of four hundred dollars a month. "It's enough money for an Asian person, but not for an American." After her operation, she returned to Utica to be with her son. "I missed my family, and he is the only family I have."

I ask Anh Dung why he looks so glum. He tells me Minh Ha and her aunt are moving to Atlanta to live with a girlfriend who washes dishes at the airport. He has done everything to keep her in Utica, even securing bank loans for her to go to college. "She doesn't know the American system. If you don't want to be a hamburger flipper, you have to get an education. Utica is the third safest city in the United States. Atlanta is the least safe." My friend is obviously lovesick.

I say goodbye to Bang, who is polishing a countertop on which sits a five-gallon container of soy sauce and an equally large box of sheetrock joint compound. "Minh Ha, Le Ha," she says. "One Ha is tall. One Ha is fat. I can't keep them straight!"

I drive down Mohawk Street to Lumière for a *café sua*, a glass of filtered coffee sweetened with condensed milk. This coffee shop next to the refugee center has become my favorite haunt for catching up on Amerasian news, which arrives here faster than if CNN were covering it live. The café functions as a kind of shadow refugee center. I walk in the door and the owner asks, "You want to see Le Ha? You want to see Sam?" and within minutes, the person in question materializes from next door or wherever they happen to be. Lumiére is also where I am taking instruction in *co tuong*, Chinese chess.

I sit down to watch two tables of men at play. They fill the room with the cracking slaps of red and black wooden discs crowning each other. Le Ha comes in and says, "Don't look at me. My face is horrible. I was napping. I can't sleep at night." She is studying for her high school equivalency exam, which keeps getting postponed, but which she needs to pass if she wants to enroll at the local community college. "Do you think social services is a good career for me?" she asks. I tell her she's a natural.

Over coffee we discuss Anh Dung's broken heart. "He comes crying to me every time he has a falling out with Minh Ha, but when things are going fine, he ignores me," says Le Ha. Anh Dung and Minh Ha are engaged, she says, but I am not certain whether this report comes from a credible witness or a jealous ex-lover.

Duc glides into the café. He doesn't walk. He prowls. His hair is slicked into a black pompadour with a rat's tail in back. He gives me the radiant smile of a long-lost friend, which quickly disappears into a frown. "I'm in trouble," he says, accepting my offer to buy him a coffee. "Just when I start to go straight, I get in trouble again."

Sam got him a job as a dishwasher at Grimaldi's. The boss was mean. Duc quit. Sam got him two more jobs. Duc quit these. He got into a fight a couple of weeks ago and was cut to the bone. He couldn't go to the hospital for fear the police would nab him. Le Ha took him in and nursed him back to health.

Duc, son of "John," an Army man, maybe from Puerto Rico, was born in Saigon in 1970. He was brought up by his grand-mother, until one day his mother arrived to reclaim him for an ODP interview. "She was made up like a tiger. She scared me to death," he says. They reached the United States in 1989. "It was too cold, but it was good to be in America, the land of freedom. I made American friends. I went to school."

"You like to go to school, heh?" Le Ha ribs him.

After a month of English classes at the refugee center, Duc was sent to tenth grade. "It was too hard for me," he says. "I couldn't understand anything." This was followed by six months in the county jail for auto theft and another stint for "fighting an American who called me *chink* on the street."

"I'm looking for a job," he says. "I can't get hired because I've been in jail." I ask him why he left his last job at Mele Manufacturing.

"Because he's lazy," says Le Ha. Duc looks sheepishly at the floor.

"I want to go back to school and study," he says.

"The only thing you study is movies," says Le Ha, who reports that Duc sleeps until two in the afternoon and then stays up all night watching kung fu operas and Hong Kong war movies dubbed into Vietnamese.

"I have no money in my pocket. Nowhere to go. All I can do is get in trouble," he says, finally telling the truth.

The next person dropping by the coffee shop is Thang, who says he wants to be called "she" and has changed his name to "Lite." Thang affects a bushy hair style, gold chains, lacquered nails and a diamond in one ear. He smiles nervously over his buck teeth as we decipher the words on his yellow T-shirt, "I got naked in Daytona Beach."

"If I lived in Vietnam, my life would be better than here," he complains. "I was a dancer at the Rex. I bought makeup and lipstick from Viet Kieu and sold them on the *cho den*, the black market. I was a good seller. I had money and everything."

Thang's mother and sister live in Dallas. His mother is an astrologer, his sister a secretary. Thang recently flew to Texas, thinking he would move there. "It was too hot and too scary," he says, explaining why he changed his mind. "The Vietnamese in Dallas are rich, but they don't want to form a community. All they think about is making money. Utica has more feeling."

"America is not what I thought it would be," he complains. "I thought no one worked in America, and they still had lots of money. But now I see that most people work all the time, and they are still poor. I thought I'd have American friends. But the only Americans I talk to are the people I dance with at gay bars. I thought I was Vietnamese. The Vietnamese think I'm American. The Americans don't know what to make of me. I'm beginning to forget who I am."

Tagging along behind Duc and Thang is Quoc, who is wearing a Bart Simpson flattop and a lot of gold jewelry. There are tears in his eyes and a look of dead-end misery on his face as he tells us about going to high school this morning and trying to get back into his eleventh-grade class. He quit school when he was seventeen, and now that he is eighteen, he is too old to enroll.

He asks me to help him learn English. Being illiterate in the language of the world around him is beginning to get to him. He is looking for another kind of power than that offered by the tough-guy swagger of Sanh Chi Do. The power to make a doctor's appointment, buy a car, rent an apartment—none of which a refugee in Utica can do without English. Belatedly and with a lot of trepidation, Quoc is asking me to help him become American. Or maybe he is just making small talk.

I settle the bar bill and excuse myself to join Nhung, the stocky Amerasian girl with close-cropped black hair who is my chess teacher. Nhung spends her days in the café gossiping and playing *co tuong*. This is new, girls playing Chinese chess. It is part of refugee life.

She explains to me how there is a river in the middle of the board. Opposing armies face each other across this river. There are no women in Chinese chess. The position of the queen is filled by one of the king's two viziers. The pieces move along lines on the board, rather than through spaces. At rest, they occupy corners, rather than sitting inside squares.

The pieces on the board consist of kings, viziers, horses, castles, and cannons, which I call "jumpers," because they hide behind other pieces and can only kill opponents by leapfrogging over their shields. The kings, like the cannons, are never allowed to face each other directly. Other players must always stand between them. These mediated moves remind me of the days I spend trying to understand Amerasian life in America. The opponent—reality—can only be approached indirectly, and out from behind harmless observations sometimes jump the most striking truths. I never completely master the rules of the game, but I think it worthwhile spending a lot of time trying.

.   .   .

"After two months this is the first letter I am sending you because my situation is very bad," Charlie Brown writes in a New Year's letter from Hawaii.

> The man I came to live with did not keep his promises. He forced me to work every day in the rain and sun that burned me. He is a vet who sometimes becomes dangerous. He has two sons, but both ran away from the farm.
>
> Four weeks after I came I let him know I didn't want to live there anymore. I repaid the money he sent me for my plane ticket. He was in a rage. He took me down to the city and threw me in the Maui shelter.
>
> I lived in this shelter for three weeks until I got a job at seven dollars an hour doing heavy lumber handling. Then I met a Japanese who brought me to Lahaina. Now I am living here in a small room with nothing. Five days ago I got into an accident. Now my face is broke. I cannot go anywhere or eat. I don't know what will happen to me next. Thomas, how come people keep trying to hurt me, when I never wanted to hurt anybody? I stop now, my eye can't open well. I have to get back on the bed.
>
> —C. B. Phuong

Anh Dung and Minh Ha report that they, too, have heard from Charlie. "He called to say he bought airplane tickets for me and my mom to go to Hawaii," says Minh Ha. "But then he got mad at me and never mailed them. Before he left town, Charlie gave me a copy of Camus's *The Stranger*. After reading it, I think *he*'s the stranger."

.   .   .

"I hope you and your family will have a nice and good life in New Year," begins Charlie's New Year's letter to Samedy Sok. "I know you'll be surprised I moved to a new place already." Charlie goes on to describe how the man he originally went to live with in Hawaii is "mentally handicapped."

"He forced me to work all the time on the farm, with no time off. He forgot all the talk of my going to college. Many times at the end of the day he became violent with his wife and me. All the Hawaiians and Vietnam veterans here grow marijuana around their farms. The police use helicopters to destroy it. It is a nice place, but too dangerous for me. . . .

"Now I am living in Lahaina, a really nice town beside the beaches. It is much better than Utica with snow and Vietnamese people! I am painting great pictures of landscapes and seascapes and selling them to tourists. I kill my time spending money in the bars and walking around town with women. Oh, boy, the girls here are international beauties. Sam, you better get here, man. This is a very special paradise. There are many girls for free waiting for you. Give me a call and let me know when you want to come, and I will have ready for you a Japanese girl or Chinese girl and a very good bed."

Other reports on Charlie's activities are equally contradictory. According to the sleepy-headed prostitute I met near Vung Tau, Charlie, when she lived with him in Amerasian Park, arranged to sell her services to men and kept the money. He ran similar scams in the Philippines, except that here he added a large dose of self-invention.

"He was involved up to his ears in drug rings and prostitution," says Mark Bishop, who runs the refugee camp's assistant teachers' program, which trains qualified refugees as tutors. "He spied on Amerasians for the Communists and then played the other side when he got over here. He extorted money from refugees, saying he could speed up their processing. He went off on fantasy trips. We heard lots of spy stories concocted to get our attention."

Charlie told Bishop and other administrators he wanted to write a report on gangs in the camp. He said a gang was chasing him and his life was in danger. He was put in a safe house next to the police station. "They were probably out to get him because he had ripped them off," says Bishop. "By the time we got wise to him, and Charlie was referred to counseling, there was a long list of complaints against him."

Early in the new year, Sam gets a phone call from Charlie. He says he has just returned from a forty-five-day trip to Vietnam. The FBI sent him. He had contacts with Japanese businessmen and voluntary agencies. His boss is a deputy assistant in the White House. The first three digits of Charlie's new phone number are *F-B-I*.

"Charlie is like a bird out of the nest," says Sam. "He is just going to keep on flying. Charlie is like me," he adds. "I thought I was going to write my life story when I came to America. I bought a hardbound book with a beautiful brown cover. I chose brown on purpose, not black. This was a ray of light beginning to dawn, the first sign of hope. But if you go into my office and open up this book, all the pages are blank."

Miss Butterfly

I wish to assure you very definitely that I have never
pursued my own death.

Wole Soyinka

On July 17, 1991, the first group of seventy-four Amerasians as-signed to Welcome Home House flies into the Syracuse airport. No Vietnamese get off the first scheduled flight. But on a later arrival, a black Amerasian comes ditty-bopping off the plane wearing a 1930s fedora. "It looks like we're getting a load of class clowns," says Dick Sessler. Both the temperature and humidity hover in the nineties.

An Amerasian girl walks off the plane crying. A reporter from one of the local TV stations covering the event describes these as "tears of joy." I learn later that the girl is crying because she was forced to leave her husband behind in Vietnam.

Two Amerasians wearing winter coats careen into the termi-nal like drunks. "They still feel like they're flying," jokes a trans-lator from the refugee center. Actually, after a week in the Manila transit center, which they left hungry and dehydrated, they are ready to pass out from hyposthenia.

Thom the auto mechanic gives a little speech of welcome to the fourteen Amerasians who stand in front of him clutching their chest X-rays. Then Rose Marie Battisti says a few words. "Her Vietnamese is funny," whispers Minh Ha.

The TV cameramen kill their lights. The refugee center staffers head for the airport restaurant. The Amerasians wander downstairs to retrieve their luggage. Then they squat on the curb to wait for another load of refugees arriving on the night flight from Seattle.

A girl, who later learns she is pregnant, throws up on the pavement. She apologizes and says she is sick from drinking bad water in the Philippines. "They couldn't stomach the food on the airplane," explains Minh Ha. "They are hungry and thirsty, but no one has brought anything for them to eat."

The Amerasians are a battered-looking lot, with numerous cut marks and other signs of physical abuse. They pose a few timid questions to Minh Ha. "Is it hot or cold in America? Who will be our mother? Can we find our fathers? How will we eat?" They say they are sad about leaving their families behind in Vietnam. Most have lied about being orphans in order to get out of the country sooner. They also thought they would get more money if they came alone.

The Seattle flight arrives two hours late with a load of refugees wearing name tags on their chests. This group looks more battered than the first, with the exception of an Amerasian boy and his mother, who is dressed in a smart-looking *ao dai*. It is nearly midnight by the time all seventy-four arrivees and their family members are gathered in the basement of Welcome Home House. A nurse from the Oneida County Health Department gives everyone a quick medical exam and a bottle of Kwell for lice. People are served bowls of chicken noodle soup and bread, which they eat ravenously.

Processing continues the next day with more medical exams and blood tests. A woman from social services registers the Amerasians for Medicaid, cash assistance, and food stamps. Many are incapable of signing their names, even with an X. Their average length of schooling is three years. On the other hand, the Vietnamese relatives accompanying them are quite literate. One Amerasian woman, for example, is married to a medical doctor.

Hot dogs, which no one eats, are served for lunch. Rose Marie Battisti instructs residents not to leave the grounds. She tells them they have to wait for their green cards before they are free to walk outside. The building has no public telephone. There are no pencils, paper, stamps. Everyone is desperate to contact their relatives and friends in the United States. "I feel like I'm in jail," says an Amerasian boy. "I know America is out there, but I can't see it."

On the same night these Amerasians reach Utica, the recently opened *Miss Saigon* is playing to a packed house on Broadway. With record advance ticket sales of thirty-four million dollars, *Miss Saigon* will be one of the longest running, most lucrative musicals in Broadway history. This story of an ill-fated romance between an Asian woman and her American lover is an updated version of Puccini's *Madama Butterfly*, which is itself a retelling of Pierre Loti's *Madame Chrysanthème*.

By the time the story is recast by two French authors and produced on Broadway, the scene has shifted from Japan to Vietnam, and Puccini's hero, the hard-hearted Lieutenant Pinkerton, has been transformed into Chris, a peach-faced GI driver at the American Embassy. Just before the fall of Saigon, Chris falls in love with an "almost" virgin prostitute. Their one-night liaison produces an Amerasian baby. Three years after the war's end, Chris and his American wife fly to Bangkok to recover the boy. Chris's Vietnamese lover conveniently kills herself, and Junior flies off to America with Dad.

"We improved the plot," says Claude-Michel Schönberg, who wrote the "bamboo rock" music to *Miss Saigon*. "Chris is not a bastard deceiving a Vietnamese girl. He is really in love. He wants to take the girl with him, but the war proves stronger than he is. We were very specific not to introduce a terrible capitalist American fighting the good people of Vietnam. Nobody can say we are either pro-or anti-American."

Richard Maltby, who wrote the lyrics to *Miss Saigon*, offers a less romantic interpretation. "Vietnam was the dark mirror image of the American Dream," he says. "We went over to sell our American values and ended up with every horrible corruption of them imaginable—beginning with the English language: 'winning their hearts and minds' meant napalming the village."

Other than the dead girlfriend and spaghetti-western ending, another telling irony in the "improved" version is the part
played by John, the go-between who fixes Chris up for his night
of love. After the war, John becomes director of an agency that
specializes in caring for orphaned Amerasians. He even shows
the audience a short movie on the *bui doi,* dust of life. But the
cute toddlers in his film look nothing like the scruffy Amerasians
disembarking in Utica. On Broadway, pity has turned to kitsch,
and the house is full.

The final head count of Amerasians settled into Welcome Home
House is thirty-one men and forty-three women between the ages
of eighteen and fifty-five. Mixed in with the orphans are eleven
married couples and a few small families. A fifth of the group is
illiterate in Vietnamese. Everyone is a "free case," meaning they
have no relatives sponsoring them. They are also "Lutheran
cases."

"They come out of our regular quota," says Rose Marie Battisti. "I don't want other volags claiming Utica is stealing their
share of Amerasians."

Touring the premises, we find a half-dozen Amerasians
watching MTV in the basement dining room. The chef scurries
over to complain to Battisti. "You can't cook Vietnamese food on
this," he says, pointing to an old electric range. "It's useless, even
for boiling water." The day's menu, written on a chalk board, is
noodle soup for breakfast, soup with pork for lunch, and cabbage
soup for dinner.

Back upstairs, we find a dozen girls doing hand stitching
and sewing on old Singer machines. Next door is a class of boys
soldering circuit boards. "These are called DIP switches—*D*ual
*I*nline *P*ackages," intones the instructor, reading from his
manual.

Apart from English as a second language, the curriculum
consists of hotel housekeeping, janitorial training, kitchen assis-

tant training, soldering, sewing, and meat packing. A board member's wife will teach cake baking. Other volunteers are teaching makeup, haircutting, and baby care. Field trips are planned to the local zoo and to Rose Marie's house in Little Falls.

The bedrooms on the second and third floors are outfitted with wooden bunk beds, old metal desks, and secretaries' swivel chairs. The attic is overflowing with donated clothes. Standing in a halo of dust motes, Battisti explains how she conceived the idea for Welcome Home House during her first trip to Asia in 1989, when she and a group of American veterans spent a week in Vietnam and four days at the Philippine Refugee Processing Center.

"Traditionally, the vets are really conservative," she says. "They're still fighting the war they lost." But in this case, they were so "outraged" by what they saw at the Refugee Processing Center that they came up with twenty-five thousand dollars in seed money and helped Battisti bully her way into meetings at the State Department, which runs the camp. Two and a half years later Amerasians were flying straight to Utica.

She has summoned four "orphans" to her office for an interview. "It doesn't matter to us," she says, when I ask if they are really orphans. "There is no way we can send anyone back to Vietnam."

One Amerasian turns out not to be Amerasian at all. He is a plump Chinese man married to an Amerasian. Another boy, who *is* Amerasian, answers our questions by rote. "I was so happy to arrive in America," he says. "Everything is fine here."

An Amerasian girl with a bruised cheek says how nice it is to have food to eat every day. Then one of the boys admits that he really does have a mother in Vietnam, along with a stepfather and several half-brothers and sisters. The fourth Amerasian in the room, a beautiful young woman named Lisa, or Ly Sa, as she spells it, is in such obvious distress that her voice disappears into her chest and she cringes in front of us, as if expecting a blow. Abandoned at birth, she supported herself working as a maid in Vung Tau.

"Ah, the beach. Fun!" exclaims Rose Marie, remembering her own good times in Vung Tau. The girl gives her a blank stare.

"I feel alone in America and sad," she says.

Anh Dung is watching a video of Chuck Norris in *Braddock: Missing in Action III*. In this rematch against the Commies, martial artist Norris reinvades Vietnam to wipe out their army and rescue his Amerasian son. "I'm sorry. I'm no longer beautiful for you," apologizes Norris's former girlfriend at their reunion. She then dies. Now absent of any potentially good Vietnamese, the movie unleashes a fearsome display of firepower. Norris and his son shoot their way to the border, where their yellow adversary announces the Final Solution to Vietnam's Amerasian problem: "We will burn them up!"

This and other American films about Amerasians are based on the equation that Amerasians are synonymous with POWs. Rescuing Amerasians, though, proves slightly less cathartic than rescuing prisoners of war. This explains why sons were substituted for fathers—the subject of the first two *Missing in Action* movies—only after the POW premise had begun to wear thin. Released in 1987, *MIA III* announces in its last frame, *Fifteen thousand Amerasians are still trapped in Vietnam*.

"It's a great movie, isn't it?" asks Anh Dung, who seems to relish exploding Communists.

Later that evening, he and I drive over to Welcome Home House. He wants to meet the new Amerasians and scout out potential soccer players. We find the residents hanging around outside on the lawn after dinner, amusing themselves with a couple of soccer balls and a badminton set. Anh Dung strikes up a conversation with a skinny Amerasian in flip-flops.

"Why haven't you come to visit us?" the boy asks. "Did you get lost or something?"

"I'm not allowed to visit, because I don't work here," Anh Dung explains. "So how's life treating you?"

"We feel like prisoners. During breaks in our classes we go look at the crazy people in the asylum next door. So far that's all I've seen of America."

"Why can't you walk around?"

"Because we don't have our *giay to chung minh*, our police identity papers. They told us we'd be arrested if we went anywhere without them."

"It sounds just like Vietnam," says Anh Dung. "You guys seem to have swapped one prison for another."

Seeing the crowd of Amerasians gathered in the parking lot, the housing director, a blubbery giant who doubles as the project's bouncer, barks out an order for us to leave the grounds.

"This is public property," says Anh Dung. "I'm allowed to be here."

"Time's up! Everybody inside!" yells the counselor. The Amerasians file into the building.

"I'm not going near this place again until I'm invited," says Anh Dung, bitterly. "I don't want Rose Marie stabbing me in the back if anything goes wrong."

We stop by Minh Ha's house to say goodbye. She and her mother are catching the bus to Atlanta in the morning. The apartment is bare. The beds are stripped. While Anh Dung is upstairs talking to her mother, Minh Ha and I sit on the front stoop.

She is blooming here in America, with good color to her even-featured face and a shine to her long, reddish brown hair. She got into college and secured a bank loan, but has decided instead to move south. "My mom has arthritis. She can't stand the cold weather. There is also too much gossip in this town. People talk about you behind your back."

Will she miss any of her friends, like Anh Dung? "He can come visit me in Atlanta if he wants," she says, with the cool resolve of a woman who expects to have men falling in love with her all her life. "I don't want him to feel like he's caught between two women, Le Ha and me. Anh Dung is a man, but he has a heart like a woman."

Anh Dung joins us on the stoop and says that he, too, is moving away. He is going to enlist in the Air Force. "Minh Ha's going to send me the money to get my pilot's license," he jokes. "Forty-five dollars an hour."

"I like pilots," she says. "They fly free up in the sky. My father was a pilot."

I ask Anh Dung if he thinks he is the right kind of guy for the military. "I have permission from my godparents and my mother," he says.

"How do you feel about killing people?"

"That's what I promised to do when I became a U.S. citizen—defend my country. There's something in me from my father calling me into the military. It's something I have to get through. If I take a regular job and settle down now, I'll regret it for the rest of my life."

I ask him how military life jibes with being a Buddhist. "I'll be an officer," he says. "I'll be sending soldiers to kill people. I won't be killing them myself. There's no one I wouldn't kill, so long as I was defending my country—with one exception. I won't kill Vietnamese. I'd kill the VC, but not the Vietnamese. All the other enemies of my country, nuke 'em!"

Anh Dung and I laugh at his Dr. Strangelove imitation.

"*Nuke 'em.* What does this mean?" asks Minh Ha.

"She thinks I'm saying *nuoc mam*," he explains. The Vietnamese word for "fish sauce" sounds similar to Anh Dung's prescription for world peace. The three of us laugh at the joke until tears come to our eyes.

We stop only on hearing one of the B-52s from the neighboring Air Force base thunder overheard. We stare up at the big gray plane hosing the sky with exhaust. As its shadow moves over us, I wonder if Utica feels to the Vietnamese who have resettled here like a free-fire zone, with bombs about to rain on friends and foe alike.

Vietnamerica

What exile from his country ever escaped from himself?

Horace

By the fall of 1992, a year after it opened, Welcome Home House is in shambles. The residential director and most of the staff have either been fired or quit. The Amerasian project is awash in scandal, and by the end of the year it will cease to exist. Opinion is divided on why the program ended. Rose Marie Battisti calls it a success whose money ran out. Almost everyone else calls it a failure whose time to prove itself ran out.

Welcome Home House was supposed to be the lucky break Amerasians had been waiting years to get. It would offer them fast-track immersion into American culture and a real welcome "home." But by the time it died, the program had failed to meet its stated goals. The 375 Amerasians and their family members who passed through Utica were not better prepared for life in America. They tested worse than refugees from the Philippine Refugee Processing Center in linguistic ability. They were exposed to similar levels of domestic violence and sexual coercion. They suffered the same degree of anxiety and depression. They had the same physical ailments, the same feelings of being alien creatures dropped on the back side of the moon. The program's sole accomplishment lay in shaving three months off the time it took Amerasians to get dumped in America's inner cities.

Ron Blassingame, who worked for six years at the Philippine Refugee Processing Center before leaving to complete a doctorate at Boston University, was Welcome Home House's first residential director. Blassingame claims that Amerasians were customarily routed through the Philippines because the camp served a police function. Fake families, criminals, and con artists got shaken out of the system. Bad elements got detained offshore, sometimes for years. But even Blassingame was surprised by the amount of fraud and sheer chicanery that arrived with the first load of Amerasians who flew into Utica in July 1991.

"We weren't prepared for the number of phony relationships or mental health problems, and no one in the State Department had tipped us off on what to expect," he says. "Half the people who walked through the door claiming to be married weren't really married. We didn't have enough translators to handle these problems. We were short on books, paper, pencils. I had more educational supplies in the Philippines than I did in Utica."

Blassingame is a soft-spoken African-American who carefully chooses his words. But I can tell from the way he is speaking that he feels aggrieved. "It came as a big surprise to Rose Marie when she learned you have to report spouse abuse in residential facilities. It's common practice for a guy in Vietnam to beat up his wife, but when this happens in America, and she ends up in the hospital, you have to file a police report. We found more and more issues like this, which Rose Marie started circumventing. Her preferred mode of operating is to sweep bad news under the carpet."

Patronage and nepotism appeared to be common at Welcome Home House. One employee secured a job for his son-in-law as a bilingual counselor, although he spoke little English and had to be supplied with a translator of his own. "There's a Tagalog word that describes how Rose Marie operates in the refugee business," says Blassingame, who is married to a Filipina and speaks the language. "It's *utang na loob*, which is the Asian concept of 'indebtedness for life.' Rose Marie has perfected the art of surrounding herself with people who feel as if they owe her everything for their survival.

"With few exceptions, the staff perpetrated all the negative aspects of Asian culture," he says. "In Asia, you are supposed to defer to an older male. When he asks you to do a favor for him, you do it. This includes sexual favors."

The first official word that something was wrong with the Amerasian program came in a report written for the New York State Bureau of Refugee Affairs in October 1991, three months after the program opened. The report was so damning that New York State considered closing the facility. Evaluators said the staff was unprepared for dealing with parasites, tuberculosis, tooth decay, and other diseases related to malnourishment. The program was shorthanded in health translators, nurses, drivers, and other personnel.

Only two of the seventy-four residents in the first group were high school graduates. The majority had never got beyond sixth grade, and twenty percent were functionally illiterate. "Staff was surprised to find that the English comprehension level of most of these refugees was at the beginning of the entry level," said the report. Rose Marie Battisti had claimed that the program, after 120 hours of English instruction, would produce a gain of twenty-five points on the BEST standardized language test. The average gain was only fifteen points, and on the New York State Placement Test the results were even worse.

Of the educational "curricula" offered at Welcome Home House—sewing, soldering, janitorial training, hotel housekeeping, kitchen assistance, and meat packing—all were seriously flawed. Meat packing was dropped for lack of insurance. Janitorial training was contracted to a local maintenance firm, which essentially used refugees as unpaid laborers. The hotel housekeeping curriculum provided another two dozen free workers to the city's downtown hotels. Instead of learning English, Amerasian girls spent their mornings making beds. Rather than this narrow "skill-specific preparation," concluded the report, Amerasians would be better served by "preparation for work in America, in a general sense."

The report also criticized the program's attempts at cultural orientation, which "tended to be piecemeal." Apart from carefully guarded visits to local factories and shopping malls, residents were segregated from the local community. "Greater use of students and community volunteers would prove warranted," said the report.

The program was also censured for its "very modest effort to provide individual counseling." This procedure was borrowed from the Mohawk Valley Resource Center for Refugees, which never employed psychological counselors, even when dealing with attempted suicides. "Client counseling services were rarely documented, even if provided," said the report. In fact, the entire program suffered from "spotty documentation" and "little client-specific recording."

The evaluators went on to criticize "the lack of education and training of some of the key staff for their respective func-tions." The building itself was "found to be insufficiently clean, not properly secure, and posing unacceptable health and safety risks for its residents." The evaluators concluded by saying, "The agency and project leadership had not been involved in directing a *residential* program before, and may have underestimated the sheer complexity of the endeavor."

Ron Blassingame was fired soon after the state report ap-peared. "I was the fall guy," he says. "Somebody had to cover Rose Marie's ass."

The original proposal soliciting funds for Welcome Home House was written by Sharon Eghigian, former English teacher at the refugee center. Eghigian had been education director and head teacher at Welcome Home House, until she quit in disgust. She currently works in a Utica elementary school, where I find her teaching English to tow-headed Russians with names like Sascha and Alexis. Sitting in the classroom during her lunch break, I ask her how she likes her new job.

"I read 'Cinderella' to these kids and they say, 'No one lives happily ever after. We don't believe it.' 'Oh, children, really it's true,' I feel like telling them. It's a terrible thing when second graders can't believe in happiness."

Eghigian gives an involuntary shudder before talking about her experience at Welcome Home House. "Rose Marie didn't want to confront things like fraud and fake families. She thought she could close her eyes and wish them away. The rest of us were left to deal with the phony marriages and guys beating the hell out of their wives.

"What really got to me was being told I couldn't buy notebooks for my English classes. 'It's not in the budget,' Rose Marie said. But I *know* it was in the budget. I *wrote* the budget."

One day Rose Marie told Eghigian her job title was being eliminated. "We don't need an education director anymore," she announced. This meant Eghigian was being demoted. "I'm cautious and cynical, but I'm still idealistic," she says. "I kept hoping things would get better, and I was heartbroken when I had to leave."

Eghigian says I should see William McGowan. McGowan was the second residential director at Welcome Home House, before he, too, quit in disgust. McGowan is a former Marine and deputy sheriff. He is also a former business partner and personal friend of Battisti's.

McGowan and I arrange to meet for lunch the following week at an Italian restaurant outside Utica. But within hours of my calling him, he begins flooding my desk with express mailings of notebooks, letters, computer discs, and other documents. These are carefully indexed and annotated, with pull tabs and cross-references and wide streaks of yellow Hi-Liter splashed over the more incriminating passages.

McGowan is a Marine Corps–trim, gray-haired man with a pink face and spectacles. He spent a dozen years in Asia, two of them in Vietnam, working as a military translator. He has an undergraduate degree in Asian studies, and most of a master's degree in international studies. "I was in human intelligence collection," he says of his twenty-two years in the military. "This gave me hands-on experience dealing with refugees from Vietnam.

"A lot of Vietnam vets have PTSD, post-traumatic stress disorder," he adds. "I have the PTS, but not the D."

McGowan begins recounting the surprises that hit him on becoming residential director of Welcome Home House. "Half the people who presented themselves as married couples turned out to be fraudulent cases. Most of these 'marriages' split up within a day or two of arriving in America. Bob Capriles, Rose Marie's boyfriend, handled the divorces. This was the first thing we did when people arrived in Utica. We arranged the divorces."

McGowan's original argument with Battisti came over the abortion issue. "I went to Catholic schools all my early life, and I don't approach the subject lightly," he says. "But you can't deprive people of their rights." He describes phoning Battisti on behalf of a girl who had been impregnated by her fake husband and wanted an abortion. "A wall went up on the other end of the line. There was complete silence, and then she hung up the phone."

Battisti tried to handle the problem by having everyone sign a contract when they arrived in Utica. "I agree not to create any new dependents while assigned to the Amerasian Residential Program," said the document, in Vietnamese. "Did this mean legitimately married couples couldn't have a baby?" asks McGowan.

He and Battisti tangled again over a rape case involving an Amerasian girl and two boys. McGowan never would have learned of the incident if the boys hadn't been stupid enough to write a letter saying they would slash the girl's face if she opened her mouth. "Bob Capriles came over and called Toronto, where one of the boys had a half-brother. Capriles leaned on the guy, saying, 'Take these two Amerasians, or we're going to prosecute.'"

They threw the boys in a van and drove to Canada. With McGowan were Capriles, a Vietnamese translator, and a local police officer. They crossed the border around midnight and dropped the boys at a donut shop on the Queen Elizabeth Highway. In the early hours of the morning, just as he was returning home, McGowan got a call from the Canadian federal police. They said the two Amerasians were being deported. In spite of Capriles's presence, the half-brother had changed his mind about sponsoring them to Canada.

McGowan called Battisti and asked what he should do with the boys. " 'Goddamn it,' she said. 'I don't care what you do with them. Do whatever you want,' and then she hung up the phone."

McGowan picked up the boys at the border and decided to send them to California. He emptied all the money he could out of an automatic teller machine and bought them tickets to Los Angeles. "We know they arrived all right," says McGowan, with a grin on his face. "Lutheran Immigration and Refugee Services in New York got a phone call from Mary Nguyen at the refugee center in Garden Grove. 'What kind of resettlement program are you running up there in Utica?' she asked. 'Why are you dumping your Amerasians in our mall?' This was the first LIRS had heard of the problem."

Without telling Battisti, and working on his own time, McGowan began researching Amerasian psychology. He tested residents with the Hopkins System Checklist, also known as the Harvard trauma questionnaire. Developed at Johns Hopkins University in the 1950s for studying the effects of psychotropic drugs, the questionnaire was later adapted by Harvard psychiatrists to measure anxiety and depression among Indochinese refugees. People are asked to respond to statements such as "I am suddenly scared for no reason" or "I have feelings of being trapped or caught." "The test was surprisingly accurate," says McGowan. "A quarter of the group scored high enough to indicate psychiatric problems, and eighty percent of these people did in fact have problems."

McGowan discovered another surprising fact. "We gave the test twice. We still don't know why, but people scored higher—

in other words, they were *more* depressed and anxious—at the end of the program than they were at the beginning."

Another agency scandal involved the residents' health. Amerasians are supposed to be screened for tuberculosis before arriving in the United States, but there is a big market in Asia for fake X-rays. So when they arrived in Utica, carrying their perfect X-rays, half the Amerasians were actually TB-positive. "We began finding active cases of the disease, including the new drug-resistant strains," says McGowan. "This wasn't supposed to happen, and everyone was very careful about keeping the story covered up."

"We never had money for the educational part of the program." says McGowan. "Our requests were always stonewalled. So we ended up using the activities fund, about two thousand dollars per cycle, to buy books. Our only educational material came out of leftover activities money."

"Basically, we ran an assembly line," he says. "Bring 'em in, process 'em, place 'em. We taught Amerasians 'survival' English and sent them on their way."

I ask him why the program closed in the fall of 1992, when Amerasians were still being resettled in the United States in large numbers. "Rose Marie says the money ran out, but I think it really had more to do with her private business dealings in Vietnam."

McGowan and Bob Capriles had worked together in the courts, where Capriles represented Amerasian clients and McGowan handled cases for the sheriff's department. "I tried to be an advocate for these kids," he says. "There wasn't a whole lot of justice coming their way."

When Capriles became Battisti's boyfriend, the three of them started doing business together. McGowan had founded a company called Pacific Consulting, later known as PAC-CON. He wanted to develop plastics recycling businesses in Korea, Thailand, and elsewhere in Southeast Asia—except Vietnam. Mindful that it was still considered an enemy country, McGowan decided Vietnam was one market he would avoid. PAC-CON's official papers of incorporation, filed in February 1992, list the company's shareholders as Battisti, Capriles, and McGowan, who also served as president.

"Once Battisti and Capriles bought positions on the company board, they began looking exclusively at business deals in Vietnam, against my will," McGowan says. He describes how Capriles and Battisti's trip to Vietnam—the one where I drank a toast to their marital happiness—had been partly financed by a Dallas-based manufacturer of wireless fax machines. The company was counting on Battisti's government contacts to open up the Vietnamese market.

In August 1992, ten weeks before Welcome Home House was scheduled to close, McGowan resigned as residential director. He also resigned as president of PAC-CON and sold his shares in the company to Capriles and Battisti.

"Why did I go to work for the Amerasian program in the first place?" he asks. "Maybe it was a way to deal with the past—the human tragedy of an ugly war we lost. Maybe I was trying to make a victory out of defeat, or right some wrongs. I felt the program was noble. It was an opportunity to do something good for a small segment of humanity. But in the end, the vision was lost. We forgot why we were doing this work."

Not long after Welcome Home House closed down, Le Ha moved back into her mother's house on Morris Street. The house has changed from the days when Le Ha's old boyfriend, Anh Dung, lived there. Gone is the fish tank and half the furniture. Also gone is Anh Dung's lending library of Hong Kong videos. The shelves are now filled with pickled vegetables and canned goods. Le Ha still has Chinese opera singer eyebrows, but there is a big change in her life—a baby daughter named Gia Tuong, which in Vietnamese means "strong family."

The second floor of Le Ha's house has been turned into a

crash pad for Amerasians, including former residents of Welcome Home House. Among them are Hoang and his Amerasian girlfriend, Lieu. Lieu is a slender, brown-haired young woman in floral pajamas. Hoang is a scrappy young man with a chip on his shoulder. He wants a new life in California and a new girlfriend. Instead, he is stuck in Utica with a new baby and a job at CONMED that pays $4.50 an hour.

"It was just like living in prison," he says of Welcome Home House. "It would have been better if we'd gone to the Philippines."

Another Amerasian, Thanh, is visiting from Syracuse. He is a handsome, soft-spoken young man who wears blue chinos and a gold pinkie ring. Thanh is one of the rare Amerasians who finished high school in Vietnam.

"My parents were very good to me," he says. "They worked hard to send me to school."

"Why didn't they come with you to America?" Le Ha asks.

"They failed the interview. ODP didn't believe they were my parents, so I had to come to America by myself."

"I liked it there," he says of his experience at Welcome Home House. "They took care of me. I learned English. The food was good. There were some bad people in the building who wanted to fight and make trouble, but I listened to the good ones."

It was after he left Utica that things got difficult. He was one of five boys sent to Riverdale, outside Washington, D.C. They got ten dollars a week from public assistance. Forty-five days after they arrived they got food stamps. But by then they were so hungry they had started begging at the local churches. The Baptists fed them if they prayed with them on Sunday. The boys had to walk an hour each way to get to school for English classes. They had no jobs. No rent money.

Thanh moved back to New York to live with a former counselor from Welcome Home House, who got him a job sewing armholes at the Learbury suit factory. "I'm glad I'm here," he says, "but I miss Vietnam."

His description of what happened to the Amerasians from the Utica program is not an isolated story. Nor are the people who went through Welcome Home House any different from the other Amerasians in the United States. They include the same hard-luck cases, mixed-up kids, and brave souls.

Also living upstairs at Le Ha's is Thang, the Saigon taxi dancer, who is sporting a new bleach blond afro. "My name is 'Alison' now," he says. "I'm working at Baker Greenhouses earning $5.30 an hour. My boss loves me. He says nobody makes the flowers grow better."

Le Ha orders the three young men—Hoang, Thanh, and Thang—to sit next to each other on the couch. Tapping each one on the head, she sums up their dreams and aspirations. "Hoang wants to rob a bank, Thanh wants to go to college, and Thang wants to become a show girl on Broadway."

Many of the Amerasians who once lived in Utica have moved to Boston or drifted out to California to hang around the malls in Garden Grove. Duc is in jail for shooting a cop. Khai is also in jail, although everyone thinks he got a bum rap. He was caught in bed with his sister-in-law. To cover up the scandal, the girl's mother cried rape. Khai was sentenced to seven years in prison.

"I took the hard times and carried on in school," Le Ha says of herself. She has another year of course work before finishing a degree in human services. Her baby's father lives in Tucson, where he met Le Ha when she went to visit friends. He moved to Utica briefly, but then headed west again, probably for good. Thang, who has a crush on Le Ha's boyfriend, describes him as "half-Chinese, half-Vietnamese. He looks like a model."

"He's a sweet guy and a good cook," says Le Ha. "But he has seven girlfriends in Tucson. I had an awful time when he left Utica, but everything is over now."

As a single mother, she gets welfare payments of $200 a month for rent, $209 in cash, and $187 in food stamps. "The money is good," she says, "but I want to go to work."

.   .   .

The Mohawk Valley Resource Center for Refugees has moved into the former convent next to St. Francis De Sales Church in Cornhill. Instead of a cavernous hall reminiscent of Ellis Island, everyone now works in little cubicles, each with its own bathroom. Rose Marie Battisti occupies what must have been the nuns' old living room. When Welcome Home House closed, she toyed with the idea of turning the building into a residence for homeless Amerasians. But she dropped that concept and decided instead to take a leave of absence from the refugee center. Hired by an adoption agency, she would open its first office in Vietnam. "They want me to look into expanding into China and other parts of Asia," she says.

Dick Sessler is beaming about his promotion to acting executive director of the refugee center. He was the third of the ill-fated residential directors at Welcome Home House, the one who closed down the operation. Synath in the housing office, the Vietnamese translators, the ladies from Little Falls, and Battisti's father are all seated at the same desks they used to occupy on Bleecker Street. The only person missing is Samedy Sok, who has returned to Cambodia to help his people. He has been hired by the United Nations to aid Khmer refugees repatriating from Thailand.

"I'm getting divorced from the United Nations," says Kyle Hörst in a phone call from Bangkok. His boss, who never shared Kyle's zeal for detail, had given him a choice between getting promoted to Bangladesh or quitting. He quit. Various American companies, needing political help moving back into Vietnam, have been courting him for a job. "It's obscene how much money they're offering, but I can't do it," he says. "Everyone else, on the other hand, is selling out as fast as they can. We're back to the 1960s around here. Vietnam is being flooded with Americans who have bought the dream: 'Only we know how to save this country!' "

Kyle's travels through Vietnam have taken him to forty-seven of the country's fifty-three provinces, and everywhere on his missions into the interior he finds Amerasians. He even discovered one living in the mountains with the Rhadé Montagnards, which is as far away from civilization as one can get. He also knows lots of Amerasians who failed their ODP interviews. "I see them working in the countryside as day laborers, vendors, beggars. So much for America helping its own."

Kyle is taking a job as country director for a big international volag. Based in Hanoi, he will have a staff of seventy, including fifteen expatriates, and a multimillion-dollar budget. He speculates for a moment on whether he could use some of this money to help the Amerasians remaining in Vietnam, but then decides against it. "Neither the Viets nor the Americans would like it," he says. "The fact of the matter is, there aren't supposed to be any Amerasians in Vietnam."

Troubled by thoughts of Huynh Thi Huong and her family living on the streets of Saigon, I appeal her case to the Orderly Departure Program. I write letters and send photographs and other documents to ODP headquarters in Bangkok. My correspondence goes unanswered. I ask various senators and congressmen to write on my behalf. Back come cables from ODP stating, "Insufficient credible evidence was submitted at the time of the interview to establish that Huynh Thi Huong is the child of an American citizen."

I write more letters to Bangkok. Send more photos and documents. Then I receive a phone call from a State Department official who identifies himself as the new desk officer in charge of the Orderly Departure Program. He begins by discussing the

ODP "fraud rate," by which he means the number of fake families who have bought their way out of Vietnam. "There are even some fake Amerasians who have made it to America," he informs me. "What we really need are experts on skull formation. But when you start examining people's teeth, this is Mengele territory.

"The State Department will soon have on line a DNA test for establishing American paternity," he says. "We're developing it with the American Association of Blood Banks. It's seventy percent accurate."

In spite of his claims, there is no blood test for establishing American paternity, nor is one ever capable of being devised. And in genetic testing, a success rate of seventy percent is no success at all.

As a special favor, the official offers to look into Huynh Thi Huong's case when he flies to Asia on his maiden voyage to Vietnam. A few weeks later he calls me to say her file is closed. The officer who interviewed her is positive she is not Amerasian. She will not get a rehearing. "There really is no appeals process per se," he acknowledges.

In January 1994 I receive a letter from Huynh Thi Huong. "Father," it begins in Vietnamese:

> "Me and my husband and two kids are in great difficulty. We are living *lang thang*, wandering homeless from here to there. When I get a chance to work, I serve as a hireling. Sometimes I have to open my palm to beg for food to eat.
>
> "We have no house. It rains. It is hot. It is very hard living the life of a wandering Amerasian. We often go to bed hungry. Many times I think I wish to die, but I lack even a hook on which to hang myself.
>
> "We have no blood relatives to help us. Seeing as you are the one who saved me from death before, can you open your heart again?"

I contact a friend in Saigon and ask him to give Huynh Thi Huong fifty dollars. This is not a solution to her problem.

Bill Fleming, former ODP director who is now a State Department official at the American Embassy in Hanoi, finally intercedes on Huynh Thi Huong's behalf. Looking at her picture, it takes him a second to agree with me that her face is the only document she needs for legal entry to the United States. He opens the back-channel contacts required to get her interviewed again by ODP.

Huynh Thi Huong and her family finally reach San Jose, California, in July, 1995. Among the last Amerasians to claim their rights under the Amerasian Homecoming Act, Huong's "homecoming" consists of three months' instruction in English and a Silicon Valley job making computer chips.

Remembering my promise to Phuong Thao, the Amerasian film star, I start looking for her father. The National Personnel Records Center in St. Louis, Missouri, sends me a copy of her mother's employment record. It verifies that Nguyen Thi Hoa worked for the U.S. government as a clerk typist and interpreter from 1965 to 1972. The reason she left her job: "Position abolished." I track down one of Hoa's former bosses, Vincent Kauffmann, who had written his address—"Virginia Beach"—on the back of a photograph. Kauffmann now works as a building contractor outside Atlanta. When I phone him, he says he remembers Hoa, who worked as a secretary in his office when he was district senior adviser in III Corps, based in Duc Hoa. "She had a wide smile and a friendly, engaging manner. I may even have a picture of her."

Kauffmann has no recollection, though, of Phuong Thao's father, James Brown Yoder. "During my five years in Vietnam, I had all sorts of mobile advisory teams coming and going. So if I can't remember a name, it doesn't mean the person wasn't there."

I am about to hang up when Kauffmann clears his throat and says he would like to ask me a question. "How is it out there in Vietnam? How are the people doing who used to work for us? I've been haunted by the thought of what became of them after the war. It looked like a fate worse than death. We were the losers, but these loyal people, and their children, suffered for it."

Because his "presumptive daughter" lives in Vietnam, the Red Cross office in Washington refuses to initiate a father search for James Yoder. They tell me to contact the Red Cross office in Hanoi. The State Department has no information on James Yoder. Nor do the Department of Veterans Affairs, the U.S. Agency for International Development, or the Vet Centers of Roanoke, Richmond and Norfolk, Virginia.

I place an advertisement in the Locator section of the *Veteran* newspaper. A reader sends me a computer printout listing phone numbers across the United States for seventy-five James Yoders. None of them is the man I am looking for. The most likely place to get his address proves the least helpful. I secure a power of attorney, I invoke the Freedom of Information Act, I cite the War Babes case, but dozens of written requests to the National Personnel Records Center produce nothing more than form-letter rejections saying, "The Department of Defense Privacy Program, 32 CFR 286a.41(d), considers the release of rosters (lists) or compilations of names and home addresses, or single addresses of current or former service members, to be a clearly unwarranted invasion of personal privacy, and is prohibited. We are sorry, therefore, that we are unable to furnish the information requested."

I crack the case only after enlisting the aid of Samantha Wright of Brooks, Kentucky, whose hobby is uniting Amerasians with their fathers. She has scored a hundred matches, all appreciated, she claims.

When pictures of Phuong Thao and her mother reach him

in the mail, James Yoder is so shaken he spills his coffee over the morning paper. "I've been married twenty-five years. I don't want to destroy what I have here," he says in his deep Virginia drawl. He explains to me in a phone call how "there is no room for extra wives" in his family.

"She does favor me in many ways," he admits. Apparently the women in his household have been holding Phuong Thao's picture up to his face and exclaiming over the resemblance.

Yoder's service record in Vietnam, his commanding officers, and dates—all the facts but one—check out. His middle name is Marvin, not Brown, which is one reason I had trouble finding him. "I'm still in a state of shock," he murmurs, before putting his wife, Ilene, on the line.

"I was sure he had a child over there," she booms in a cheery voice. "I can't wait to meet the girl."

"Phuong Thao is a pretty young woman," Yoder acknowledges. "She looks just like Hoa, her mother." Yoder spent seven years in Vietnam and Thailand in military intelligence. He tutored Hoa in English for a few months while they worked together in Duc Hoa. But he claims they made love only once, during a chance encounter in Saigon, before Yoder caught a plane for home leave. They never saw each other again.

He returned to serve another term in Vietnam without knowing Hoa had given birth to his daughter. Yoder is the adoptive father of his wife's four offspring from an earlier marriage, but Phuong Thao is his only blood child. A few days after getting the news, he mails a letter and photo to Phuong Thao.

"I am not denying fatherhood, it is just that it takes time for my mind to digest this information," he writes. "You will have to admit that this is quite a shock to learn you may have another daughter that you did not know existed."

"Do you speak or write English?" he asks. "What are your hobbies? Are you married? What is your favorite color? Do you like flowers, animals?"

He goes on to talk about himself, how his black hair has

turned gray, and most of it has fallen out. Retired from the Army, he works as a prison guard outside Richmond. "I farm a small piece of land as a hobby and like to raise vegetables, flowers, and small animals (dogs, cats, chickens, and ducks). My hobbies are fishing and watching sports on television."

"Give my regards to your mother," he writes, wishing Phuong Thao and Hoa a happy Tet. "I have wondered many times over the years about the fate of my friends in Vietnam after the event of 1975. I do not believe any American can truly comprehend the degree of suffering the Vietnamese people have endured over the past fifty years."

Anh Dung, or Clarence Taylor III, sits in his Mohawk Street living room as his mother serves up steaming bowls of shrimp soup. The TV set and stereo are missing from a recent home invasion. Bang was tied up with duct tape, while everything of value was cleaned out of the house.

"I know the Amerasians who did it," he says. "Duc was their scout. But I can't prove it, so the police aren't going to help."

Except for this setback, things are going well. Anh Dung received a six-thousand-dollar scholarship to finish his bachelor's degree in engineering. When he graduates, he might follow in his father's footsteps and become an Air Force radar technician. The Air Force recruiters are encouraging him to go into officer's training, but they also want him to lose twenty pounds. "They say it's bad for me living at home, eating my mother's cooking."

Instead of officer's training and losing twenty pounds, Anh Dung will probably accept a job at MCI. They want to hire him as a telecommunications specialist working out of their headquarters in White Plains. The job involves a lot of traveling to Texas and Florida, but they say they will pay for him to get his master's degree.

Waiting for another bowl of soup, I leaf through a photo

album on the coffee table. It is filled with pictures of a visit Anh Dung and Minh Ha made to Niagara Falls. This could be a honeymoon album, like Tay Thi's trip with her boyfriend to Dalat. The young lovers are standing beside the falls, buying cotton candy, crossing the bridge into Canada. Anh Dung tells me the visit did not go well, though, and Minh Ha flew home to Atlanta early. "Minh Ha is moving to Orange County for her singing career. I think she's making a mistake," he says. "She should go to school first, then do singing.

"All around me Amerasians are going to work, instead of going to school. That's what the refugee center wants. It fills their quotas. The Amerasians want it, too. Right away they can send money back to Vietnam. So they hustle down to CONMED, which is like going to the slaughterhouse. No matter how long they stay, they're never going to earn more than five or six dollars an hour.

"In the future, how many Anh Dungs are you going to find in Utica?" he asks. "None, because nobody will have gone to school. The Russians are doing better than the Vietnamese. Their kids are going to college. Ten years from now, we'll look back and see that all we did was work, work, work for minimum wage."

Anh Dung slumps in his chair. "We've lost contact with each other," he says of the Amerasians in Utica. "There's no sense of community. We've become Americanized. We stay in our houses and no longer reach out to each other."

Later in the afternoon, Charlie Brown's name comes up. I tell Anh Dung I still find all the stories I have heard about him hard to believe.

"You have to know something about Amerasians," he says. "The good people are not always good people. They are only good to the people they like."

He tells me that he, too, has heard a lot of stories about Charlie. Charlie is still in Hawaii. Charlie has moved to Texas. Charlie is back in Vietnam. "It doesn't matter where he is," he concludes. "Just like the rest of us, Charlie will always be a wandering homeless Amerasian."

Acknowledgments

During the ten years spent researching and writing this book, I accumulated debts of gratitude to a long list of people, including refugees throughout Asia and the United States and refugee officials from Geneva to Ho Chi Minh City. As many of these people would prefer not to see their names in print, I have decided to acknowledge no one and everyone. To all those who aided this project, and without whom it would not exist, I extend my heartfelt thanks.

Vietnamese names are written in reverse of those in the West. First comes the family, then one or more given names. The Vietnamese format tends to be switched after a refugee arrives in the United States. In this book, I have adopted whatever names, in whatever order, people prefer.

Another potential confusion is the change in spelling undergone by many Vietnamese words after 1975. Both spellings might appear here, depending on the date in question. For example, once it ceased to exist, the would-be country South Vietnam became south Vietnam.

For their research assistance I am indebted to Judy Abel, Sharon Britton, Julia Dickinson, Susan Juliano, Lynn Mayo, Catherine Miller, Kristin Strohmeyer, Louise Teachout, and Joan Wolek. I thank Blue Mountain Center and the New York Foundation for the Arts for literary fellowships. For logistical support, I appreciate the aid of Margaret Getz. For organizing my first trip to Vietnam, I thank Le Ly Hayslip. For stepping forward to serve as translators, I am grateful to Thuy Da Lam, Kieu-Nhi Le, Nguyen Anh Dung, Trinh Mong Nguyen, Samedy Sok, Van-Minh Tran, and Truong Le Ha.